RONALD REAGAN

Recent Titles in Greenwood Biographies

RONALD REAGAN

A Biography

J. David Woodard

GREENWOOD BIOGRAPHIES

 GREENWOOD

AN IMPRINT OF ABC-CLIO, LLC
Santa Barbara, California • Denver, Colorado • Oxford, England

Library of Congress Cataloging-in-Publication Data

Woodard, J. David.
　　Ronald Reagan : a biography / J. David Woodard.
　　　　　p. cm. — (Greenwood biographies)
　　Includes bibliographical references and index.
　　ISBN 978-0-313-39638-0 (hardcopy : alk. paper) —
ISBN 978-0-313-39639-7 (ebook)　1. Reagan, Ronald.
2. Presidents—United States—Biography.　I. Title.
　　E877.W66　2012
　　973.927092—dc23
　　[B]　　　2011034884

ISBN: 978-0-313-39638-0
EISBN: 978-0-313-39639-7

16　15　14　13　12　　　1　2　3　4　5

This book is also available on the World Wide Web as an eBook.
Visit www.abc-clio.com for details.

Greenwood
An Imprint of ABC-CLIO, LLC

ABC-CLIO, LLC
130 Cremona Drive, P.O. Box 1911
Santa Barbara, California 93116-1911

This book is printed on acid-free paper ∞

Manufactured in the United States of America

CONTENTS

PREFACE

A fact of American politicians in general, and of presidents in particular, is that they begin office with high expectations and approval ratings and then fade into public rebuke and disapproval.[1] That didn't happen to Ronald Reagan. He improved in popularity and won the largest landslide in recent political history in 1984. Thirty years later, he still inspires a kind of nostalgia rarely seen in American politics. When scholars look at survey data on individual confidence in government measures, with questions about "trust in government" and "care about what people like me think," they find an unprecedented rise when Reagan was in office.[2] Subsequent presidents were not the beneficiaries of his landslide mandates or historical circumstances, and it is only natural for them to envy his enduring popularity. He is rightly credited with restoring the American economy after a difficult crisis and with ending the Cold War without firing a shot. Yet it is important to remember that recognition for these accomplishments came later in life. At the time when he was in Washington, Ronald Reagan was a political oddity: a conservative ideological rose amid liberal thorns.

If Reagan was a hard president to dislike, he remains a harder one to know. He had a demeanor that inspired followers, but it also kept them at a distance. One biographer summarized the thoughts of all when he wrote, "Despite the decades he spent in the public eye, he remained a mystery to his friends and admirers."[3] The only person who knew him well was his wife, and while theirs was a show-business marriage, it became a love story for the ages. Knowing Ronald Reagan, and understanding something about his character, is essential to grasping the history of the United States at the end of the 20th century and into the 21st. During his presidency, the nation reversed a drift to the liberal welfare state begun 50 years earlier and defeated Soviet communism. After his presidency, the currents of social and political change flowed in a different course. No more significant tribute to him could be made than to say that subsequent politicians were "Reaganesque" in either their rhetoric or their posture.

His 1984 reelection victory was accomplished by emphasizing that it was "morning" in the country and that the nation's greatest days lay ahead. Reagan's personality, optimism, humor, and confidence reshaped the political landscape. Because his philosophy was conservative, he stamped an entire generation as disciples, with many not even understanding why they believed the way they did. The people who worked for him, who were loyal to him and made his legacy, were inexplicably struck by the man virtually none of them knew. One speechwriter, Peggy Noonan, may have captured their feelings best when she wrote, "He acts as if he's lucky to be with you."[4] That's a remarkable trait and one worth remembering. But it is Reagan's elusiveness that remains his most abiding characteristic. William F. Buckley thought the times and the man were the same when he wrote in his book, *The Reagan I Knew*, that the 1980s were a triumphant decade. "He told us that most of our civic problems were problems brought on or exacerbated by government. That of course is enduringly true."[5]

Ronald Reagan was the maker of the times of his presidency and the beneficiary of them as well. For this reason, knowledge of the inner workings of his character, and the broader issues of his life, is a way to understand what happened in the 1980s and how it influenced the world in which we now live. He was, in the words of his best biographer, "the ultimate American success story."[6] His parents were poor, his family scarred by alcoholism, yet he was able to attend a small church-affiliated college, secure employment as a sports announcer, and then become an actor, an almost undreamed-of possibility at that time or since. Reagan's simplicity, good looks, and disarming demeanor opened doors shut to less gifted people. No one was more enchanted with his story than the man himself; it is no wonder, then, that Ronald Reagan titled his autobiography *An American Life*. He saw his accomplishments as synonymous with the country he led, and as he told the Republican National Convention in 1984, "every promise, every opportunity, is still golden in this land."[7]

When trouble came, as it always does, Ronald Reagan relied on a simple faith and optimism that reflected his view of life more than the troubles at hand. He believed he had a calling on his life from God, and he wanted to fulfill that mission. When his marriage collapsed, he found a more devoted wife. When his movie career stalled, he moved on to television, which became a platform for his election to the California governor's office and, ultimately, to the presidency. He saw himself as a man of principle, and he refused to change when his mind was made up. Yet everyone who knew him found him to be the most winsome of personalities. In Ronald Reagan's world, it was always "Morning in America."

NOTES

1. Harold W. Stanley and Richard G. Niemi, *Vital Statistics in American Politics* (Washington, DC: Congressional Quarterly Press, 1988), p. 227.

2. Ibid., p. 131.

3. William E. Pemberton, *Exit with Honor* (New York: M. E. Sharpe, 1998), p. xiii.

4. Peggy Noonan, *What I Saw at the Revolution* (New York: Ivy Books, 1990), p. 67.

5. William F. Buckley, *The Reagan I Knew* (New York: Basic Books, 2008), p. 241.

6. Lou Cannon, *President Reagan: The Role of a Lifetime* (New York: Simon and Schuster, 1991), p. 32.

7. Ronald Reagan, "Acceptance Speech," Republican National Convention, August 23, 1984.

ACKNOWLEDGMENTS

I thank the Department of Political Science at Clemson University for their support in making this book possible. The resources of the Strom Thurmond Chair of Government were especially helpful in allowing for a rapid completion of the manuscript. Our departmental secretary, Angie Guido, tirelessly assisted in the electronic manipulation of the chapters and helped shape them into a manuscript.

Three research assistants, Kristin Archie, Alix Barrett, and Rachelle Korinko, were readily available to check details, read chapter drafts, and make suggestions. They often served as a sounding board for my ideas, and I appreciate their dedication to this project.

As always, my wife, Judy, was a source of encouragement and a willing partner in this endeavor. To her I owe much more than the thanks for this one book, but I acknowledge her for one more effort in this adventure. Any mistakes, errors, or prejudices of interpretation are mine alone.

J. David Woodard
Clemson University
Clemson, South Carolina
February 2011

TIMELINE: EVENTS IN THE LIFE OF RONALD REAGAN

February 6, 1911 Ronald Wilson Reagan is born in Tampico, Illinois, the son of Jack and Nelle Reagan.

1920 The family relocates to Dixon, Illinois, which becomes the hometown of Reagan's youth.

1928 Graduates from Dixon High School.

1932 Graduates from Eureka College.

1937 Moves to California to work for Warner Bros. as a B film actor.

1940 Marries Jane Wyman.

1941 Birth of Maureen Elizabeth Reagan.

1942 Enters active military service, assigned to the First Motion Picture Unit.

1945 Adoption of Michael Edward Reagan.

1947 Elected president of the Screen Actors Guild.

1948 Divorced from Jane Wyman.

1952 Marries Nancy Davis.

1952 Birth of Patricia Ann Reagan.

1954 Becomes the television host of *General Electric Theater*.

1958 Birth of Ronald Prescott Reagan.

1962	Switches his political party affiliation from Democrat to Republican.
October 27, 1964	Delivers a nationwide address titled "A Time for Choosing" in support of Republican Barry Goldwater for president.
1966	Elected governor of California.
1968	Unsuccessful campaign for the Republican nomination for U.S. president.
1970	Reelected governor of California.
1976	Unsuccessful campaign for the Republican nomination for U.S. president.
1980	Elected 40th president of the United States.
March 30, 1981	Unsuccessful assassination attempt by John Hinckley Jr.
1984	Reelected president of the United States with the most electoral votes of any candidate for the office.
1991	Dedication and opening of the Ronald Reagan Presidential Library.
1994	Diagnosed with Alzheimer's disease.
June 5, 2004	Death of Ronald Reagan.

Chapter 1

HEARTLAND

Jack Reagan arrived in Tampico, Illinois, on March 23, 1906, as senior salesman in charge of the clothing and shoe departments of H.C. Pitney's General Store on South Main Street. The Reagans had come to Illinois from Ireland before the Civil War, but both his parents died of tuberculosis, so an elderly aunt raised him as a proper Irish Catholic. He was 23 years old and had been married to Nelle Clyde Reagan, who was 11 days younger, for 16 months. Pitney's establishment was the largest general store for about 20 miles in either direction, and the job seemed a fit for the qualities Jack Reagan possessed in abundance: optimism, self-confidence and ambition. He was a talker, a storyteller, and had the Irish trait of blarney, meaning charm and flattery.

Tampico was similar to thousands of other towns spread across the American Midwest in the early 20th century. It had eight street lights, a busy downtown on weekends, churches, schools, a population under a thousand and farms in abundance. It was here that Ronald Wilson Reagan was born on February 6, 1911, at 4:16 A.M., after 24 hours of labor and a storm that dumped seven inches of snow on the town. Tampico's doctor was out on call, so the birth began with a midwife until the doctor finally arrived to complete the delivery. The labor was long and hard, and this would be Nelle's last child. The baby was born in a four poster bed in the front bedroom of a five room flat above the general store where his father worked. He weighed in at 10 pounds and had a penchant for crying, so much so that his father compared him to a "Dutchman." So was born the nickname "Dutch," which would follow him the rest of his life.[1]

A large part of Ronald Reagan's early life is explained by his father chasing rainbows in a desire to achieve financial independence by owning his own shoe store. Jack Reagan was a drinker and a dreamer who fancied himself as a premier salesman since he graduated from something known as the American School of Proctipedics. During World War I the father tried to sign up for the military, but was turned down. His younger son recalled, "He always protested his bad timing . . . too young for the Spanish-American—and too old for 'Over There.'"[2] To fulfill his father's dream, the family lived in a succession of small Illinois towns: Galesburg, Monmouth, and Tampico again until they finally settled in Dixon in 1920. The source of President Reagan's faith in America came from these childhood experiences. "Almost everybody knew one another," he wrote in his memoir *An American Life*, "and because they knew one another they tended to care about each other."[3]

Dixon, with a population of 10,000, was the largest city in Lee County. It was a metropolis by Midwestern standards, 10 times larger than Tampico, and located 90 miles from Chicago. The place was 92 percent white, with a 92 percent American-born population. The town had 2,500 farms, about half operated by owners and the other half operated by tenants.[4] Ronald Reagan put down his roots here from age ten, after moving seven times in the previous nine years. It was a family of four: Jack and Nelle, with Ronald's older brother Neil, nicknamed "Moon" by his father. In later years the president described people in his hometown as hardworking, united in a sense of purpose that enabled them to overcome adversity, take risks and build something for themselves and their children. All in all, it was what he said it was, "a Tom Sawyer and Huck Finn childhood."[5]

At least that was the ideal in Dixon, "City of Opportunity on the Hudson of the West," but it was not realized in the Reagan household. Neil remembered, better than his brother, the years of family itinerancy, living off soup for a week and sharing a cramped, wet bed with his brother.[6] Alcohol was Jack Reagan's cross, and the cause of his family's misery and misfortune. He went to Chicago on "buying trips," ostensibly for the store Jack and Mr. Pitney owned in town, but really for escape. "I was eleven years old the first time I came home to find my father flat on his back on the front porch and no one there to lend a hand but me."[7] The binges alienated the family from feeling very close to their father, and kept them from realizing any financial security. "My mother would pray constantly for him," Ronald Reagan recalled, "she just refused to give up, no matter how dark things looked."[8] On the eve of Prohibition, a cold January night in 1920, the members of the Christian Church in Dixon gathered to hold a midnight service of celebration.

Nelle, a small and pretty woman with auburn hair and blue eyes, found strength in her faith. She had accepted a Catholic wedding to Jack and a Catholic baptism for Neil, but in 1910 she was baptized on Easter Sunday into the Disciples of Christ denomination. She was not swayed by her husband's cynicism or failure; instead, she became a pillar in her local church. Her second son remembered that she "had the conviction everyone loved her because she loved them."[9] Her prayers, humility, and faith were the bedrock of the family, and a bridge over troubled water. Nelle's abiding faith had a dramatic influence on her second son. "Dutch was always Nelle's boy," said one biographer.[10] She assumed responsibility for the spiritual preparation of the children, told them to pray often for their father, and led them in devotionals. Nelle left it up to the children to make a decision for baptism, and Reagan made it at age 12. The Disciples of Christ denomination separated from liberal denominations, opposed slavery, supported temperance, and emphasized human responsibility before God. "Because a lot of Nelle's great sense of religious faith rubbed off on me," wrote her son, "I have always prayed a lot, in those days, I prayed for our country, for our family, and for Dixon."[11]

At his inauguration, Ronald Reagan used Nelle Reagan's Bible to take the oath of office, and he kept it on his desk when in the Oval Office. With his father often absent, whereabouts unknown, he developed a kind of protective barrier to insulate himself from being hurt. He was a quiet boy, rarely downcast, but he also learned to protect himself from other people. Later in life, Ronald Reagan liked to put a good face on the family's uncertain lifestyle. "Jack could have sold anything," he liked to say, and undoubtedly the son inherited a personal warmth and gift of storytelling from him.[12]

As he grew older, Ronald Reagan came to better understand what had driven his mother and father apart. Children of alcoholics sometimes escape into imaginary worlds of fantasy and role playing to help cope with an everyday world of disappointment and pain. Ronald's response, by all accounts, was to replace his father with imaginary heroic figures of his own making. Sometimes these were people he read about, and at other times they were people he saw. In his own hand, Reagan recalled, "sitting in the Family Theatre watching the marvelous flickering antics of Tom Mix and William S. Hart as they foiled robbers and villains and escorted the beautiful girls to safety, waving back from their horses as they cantered into the sunset."[13] This escape served Ronald "Dutch" Reagan well as a child, and it later helped in his radio and acting career. The day-to-day reality for the family, though, was disappointment and frequent unemployment.

Solace came in the imagined adventures and actual ones in Dixon. The Pitney and Reagan store was right downtown, and the family lived not far away, on South Hennepin Avenue, within walking distance of the old Red Brick School where Ronald went to class. The country was enjoying postwar prosperity, but the Reagan family seemed exempt. The two brothers, still called "Moon" and "Dutch" by everyone except their mother, had little in common except a love of sports. Even though the second son was two and a half years younger than his brother, he was just a year behind him academically. The town straddled the Rock River, which froze in the winter and became a skating rink, and served as a recreation area for swimming and canoeing in the summer.

"Hearty Midwesterner" is no exaggeration for anyone familiar with the cold and isolation of the northern Illinois region. The farms were spread out over miles of ridges that rolled endlessly over the plains. Coming to town in Dixon was a refuge, an island in the ocean of land. People were drawn to one another in that environment, and so was Ronald Reagan. "All of us have a place we go back to," wrote the president in his campaign biography, "Dixon is that place for me."[14]

Later, Reagan's scenario of his early life would be criticized for its narrowness and innocence. But young "Dutch" didn't feel that way as a child. "As I've grown older, perhaps there has always been a little of that small boy inside of me who found some reassurance in the applause and approval he first heard at nine or ten."[15] His was a life of rustlings in the trees and splashes in the Rock River, coal smoke, snow and frost, and winter storms when the wind howled around the house and tore through flimsy walls. He stayed inside and developed a lifelong habit of reading. He read *The Last of the Mohicans, The Count of Monte Cristo*, Horatio Alger books and a forgotten book about a Midwestern boy who marries a beautiful socialite and saves her from a life of desperation.[16]

Reagan's biographers endlessly pour over his childhood looking for clues that suggest his future. Peggy Noonan believes that in these years Reagan developed a natural talent for listening, speaking and seeing things as an artist.[17] As an adult, Reagan read to his children, which probably means he was read to as a child. His prose as an adult was smooth and simple, suggesting that he linked his imagination to his hand when he wrote.

His mother was a celebrity of sorts; she did dramatic readings, humorous passages from plays, speeches and books. Her motto was: "To higher, and nobler things my mind is bent," and she was the living embodiment of that slogan, loving poetry, the dramatic arts, and the Bible. Ronald Reagan would later say that Nelle was a kind of "frustrated actress, meaning that she envisioned a life on the stage prior to marrying Jack."[18] Subsequent biographers noted that the one thing Dutch inherited from her was, "a distinctive mellow voice, tinged with a hopeful cadence . . . that impressed people with the honesty of the words he spoke."[19] Dixon was an environment in which he flourished, with an equable personality, content in his situation.

When young Ronald was 13 or 14, Jack Reagan took the family on a Sunday afternoon drive. His mother left her eyeglasses in the back seat of the car and her second son put them on. In an instant Ronald Reagan discovered that he was extremely nearsighted. A whole world opened up when he was fitted with glasses, and could play baseball and football. Before this time, he had been somewhat withdrawn in school, and because he had trouble seeing he relied on a highly tuned oral ability to concentrate and remember what he heard. "Dutch's best sport by far was swimming, where agility helped and eyesight was less an issue."[20] Lowell Park was a 300-acre naturally forested reserve that bracketed the Rock River. At age 14, Ronald Reagan began a job as summer lifeguard there that he would retain through college. One of his contemporaries remembered him as, "the perfect specimen of an athlete, tall, willowy, muscular, brown, good-looking."[21]

As teenagers, the boys began calling their parents by their first names. It was a turning point of sorts in the process of growing up to discover a core of strength within you to address adults that way in life. Gossip was a powerful force in small towns, and it didn't take much for people who had little to do but get interested in their neighbors lives to notice the Reagans. The whispering was of the quiet and faithful wife of an alcoholic, who remained pious and determined in the face of adversity and public scorn. Jack fought alcoholism all his life until he ultimately died, having contracted heart disease from a lifetime of chain-smoking cigarettes. Small towns had their virtues as well as vices, and gossip could be just as much a force for good. Nelle's accomplishments as mother, spiritual leader and oftentimes as provider were seen in the achievements of her faith, and the work of her children, especially the second

Ronald Reagan as a lifeguard in Lowell Park, Illinois, 1927. (Courtesy Ronald Reagan Presidential Library.)

son. In addition to building a decent grade point average for college, he became a drum major, football captain and class president.

"In high school, I began to lose my old feelings of insecurity; success in the school plays in football and swimming, being the only guy on the beach with 'Life Guard' on my chest and saving seventy-seven people, being elected student body president, even the fact I could now *see* did a lot to give me self-confidence."[22] "Dutch" Reagan was Dixon's model boy. "Ordinary people remarked on his simplicity, and good manners and liked being around him, he had a knack of making them feel good."[23] As someone who was on the way up, Ronald Reagan developed a consoling sympathy for those left behind. Throughout his life, he believed that people made their own luck and deserved their fate.

To the extent that the 1920s were the age of radio, movies, country clubs, fast cars, joy riding and dancing cheek to cheek in a new mass culture—Lee County, Illinois, was not part of the Jazz Age. Nevertheless, two people had a special effect on Ronald Reagan in these years. The first was a new English teacher at Dixon High who emphasized imagination and originality in prose more than spelling and grammar. B. J. Frazier staged complete plays at the high school using scripts from recent Broadway hits. He encouraged the students to analyze the person they were portraying instead of just memorizing the lines of the character. Frazer's encouragement and his stage techniques played to Reagan's strengths, and proved invaluable to him when in the radio studio, on stage, and finally in the spotlight as a politician.

The second person of interest was Margaret "Mugs" Cleaver, the intelligent and pretty daughter of the minister of the Christian church where Nelle worshipped with her two sons. "Dutch" and "Mugs" were the perfect couple. He was president of the student body, and she was president of the senior class. They were both officers in the school Dramatic Society, acting opposite each other in a play called *You and I*. Ronald Reagan met her when he entered high school, and they dated for the next six years. She was the first girl he ever kissed, and he was quite explicit about his intentions. "I had expected to marry Margaret Cleaver since my sophomore year at Dixon High . . . I had hung my fraternity pin on her . . . I'd given her an engagement ring and we'd agreed to marry as soon as we could afford it."[24]

Before college, in a time when the wind brought the smell of new plowed earth into Dixon, separation was not a part of their plan. In 1928, it was no strange coincidence that Reagan followed "Mugs" to Eureka College. He made no effort to escape the destiny that seemed to tie them to one another. The school was set amid a heavily forested rise, with wide green lawns. Nine buildings stood starkly against the landscape with Gothic steeples and Georgian pediments floating above large windows. To students it looked as if Camelot had dropped into "the middle of the Midwest." Memorial Hall, Admin, and Chapel joined women's dorms and a central heating plant. The major buildings were covered by ivy in a semicircle at the heart of campus. The college was affiliated with the Disciples of Christ, and located 80 miles south of Dixon. "I fell head over heels in love with Eureka," Reagan later wrote.[25] It had 200 students and 20 faculty members. The football team was coached by Ralph "Mac" McKenzie, who was not impressed with the walk-on player who claimed to be the "Star of Dixon High."[26]

When only 7 percent of eligible high school graduates went to college, it was almost a miracle that Ronald Reagan even enrolled, especially given his family's economic circumstances. He had enough money to cover tuition, saved from his summer lifeguarding job, and other odd work, but he didn't have enough for room and board. He was granted a Needy Student Scholarship and provided a job on campus: washing dishes in the girls' dormitory.

Between football and his job, Reagan didn't stand out as a student. One biographer described him as "Mr. Congeniality" to Margaret Cleaver's "Young Miss Brains."[27] "Mugs" recruited her sister's boyfriend to get him into a fraternity, Tau Kappa Epsilon. Most of the time, Ronald Reagan worked to establish himself in a place where his high school accomplishments were a faint echo. Although the stock market crash was still a year away, the dark clouds of economic uncertainty were already creeping over the farmers of the Midwest. Enrollments were down, affiliated churches were not able to support Eureka, students had to leave school to return home to work, and a sense of hopelessness crept onto the campus. The college president, and his administrative council, began laying people off. When this news reached the students, a strike was called for the resignation of the president.

The administration believed the actions were an act of moral deca-
dence, but the students believed the issue was one of fairness. Ronald
Reagan was selected to give a speech on behalf of the freshmen, and
his remarks brought the crowd to its feet with a roar. "It was heady
wine," he recalled. Many biographers cited this as Reagan's first political act, but at the time it didn't seem especially auspicious to the
college freshman.[28]

Each summer, Reagan went back to lifeguarding and somehow managed to return for another year of college. "That sophomore year everything seemed to brighten all across my life."[29] Only an unbridled
optimist could make that statement given that 1929 was marked by the
greatest economic collapse in American history. "Most of my attention
was divided between Margaret Cleaver, who had accepted my TKE
pin, which was tantamount to engagement, and getting my backside
off Mac McKenzie's bench."[30] Despite a long romance, the marriage
never came and the two drifted apart when they left college. In the
words of Carl Sanburg, "For he went west, and she went east. And they
both lived."[31] Years later, Margaret Cleaver Gordon mentioned that she
gave the engagement ring back because she didn't want to raise her
children in Hollywood.[32] The fall proved good for Reagan's football career. His dramatic endeavors prospered as well. He joined the dramatic
society just as a new teacher, Ellie Marie Johnson, assumed leadership
on campus. Reagan delighted her with a willingness to memorize parts
quickly and respond to direction. For her part, she put Eureka's plays
into national competition.[33]

As the Depression deepened, money problems occupied both the
nation and Ronald Reagan. The latter made a loan arrangement with
the following pledge: "which amount will be paid in the summer following graduation as arrangements can be made with the college to
defer payments of certain bills."[34] The doubts and fears that troubled
him were not evident to his friends, who remembered an always upbeat and confident graduate. But fears were there. Years later in a 1982
address to the nation about the economy Reagan said, "I have a special reason for wanting to solve this [economic] problem in a lasting
way. . . . [When] I was twenty-one and looking for work . . . I can
remember one bleak night in the thirties when my father learned on
Christmas Eve that he'd lost his job . . . To be young in my generation

was to feel that your future had been mortgaged out from under you."[35] Back home, Jack devised a plan that allowed him to take ownership of a shoe store, but the opportunity collapsed and the family was once again adrift.

He would write years later, "a way of life was ending and it was hard for me to see that it was also a beginning."[36] The end of college was an entrance into the despair of the Great Depression, but for a time in the spring, it was good to enjoy a summer of optimism. "Dutch" Reagan was president of his class at Eureka, Margaret was awarded the highest honor for grades, and her father gave the benediction. All 45 students stood in a circle holding a rope of woven ivy from the brick walls of the school building. The future promised little, but the president of Eureka College urged them not to be bullied by it.[37] His new college degree now won him back his old job as a lifeguard.

The summer at Lowell Park meant that the chill of fall brought with it adult responsibilities. He had been taught by his mother that hard work would be rewarded, and he believed her, but no jobs were to be had. What distinguished him from others was perseverance toward his goals. A Kansas City businessman, Sid Altschuler, told him of contacts that he had with people in several businesses and offered to help. The assistance came with advice: not to base his career on the promise of money, but to find something he really enjoyed doing. Too shy to admit his real ambition of becoming a movie star, Reagan chose a more modest occupation. "I have to tell you, way down deep inside, what I'd like to be is a radio sports announcer."[38]

To understand the ambition it helps to know something about the setting. Isolated and introspective young people in the vast American Midwest learned about music, sports and life from radio broadcasts. "I remember sitting with a dozen others in a little room with breathless attention," recalled Reagan, "listening to raspy recorded music and faint voices say, 'This is KDKA, Pittsburgh; KDKA, Pittsburgh.'"[39] Through some magic they did not understand, a distant speaker became a family guest, and something invisible became audible. For someone like Ronald Reagan, who loved stories and heroic accomplishments, taking fragments of life and telling people about them was a tailor-made occupational choice. In later life, a U.S. senator recalled the power of Reagan's retentive mind. "You can tell him something just idly, tell him a joke, and he'll store it," recalled Paul Laxalt, "it's like sticking in a chip . . . and God only knows when it will surface."[40] The "follow your dream" advice from Altschuler led him to Chicago to canvass radio stations for a job.

After Labor Day, he hitchhiked to Chicago where one of his fraternity brothers put him up. In the sweltering September sun he visited the offices of NBC and CBS, but was unable to get past the receptionist. He hit the street from one radio station to another, finally, a receptionist told him to stay away from the big cities, and try small towns with smaller stations. He hitchhiked home in the rain. "Several days later, after my hopes had soared, I lost that job at Montgomery Ward."[41]

It was the bottom of the Depression, one that did not appreciate ambitious college graduates. Back home in Dixon, his father was out of work until he was recruited for a New Deal alphabet agency, the CWA, which stood for Civil Works Administration, but was really a practical arm of the Democratic Party. In 1934 Jack Reagan found work removing Dixon's streetcar tracks for use as girders at the new Dixon airport. The project was planned before the Depression and funded because it kept costs low. For a time, Jack hired Neil as a way to make ends meet for the family.[42]

In his first presidential election, "Dutch" Reagan voted Democratic, just like the rest of the family. The governor from New York, Franklin Roosevelt, seemed more likely than President Hoover to recharge the economy. Illinois went for FDR that year, but Hoover carried Dixon 52 to 48 percent.[43] Jack Reagan was caught up in the Roosevelt campaign. In later years, he worked handing out supplies of food and distributing vouchers for rations to those in need. Jack also tried to find jobs for those unemployed. For the youngest Reagan, "the sight of men lining up to receive minimal state charity doled out by his father was shocking."[44] It was also disturbing to see how clumsy the New Deal was at welfare relief, with endless forms, bureaucratic delays, and lost applications. The good intentions of government were swamped in the realities of welfare state mismanagement. The son, like his father, revered FDR and the Democrats. Reagan found himself in a situation familiar to many of his generation, unemployed with good intentions, and unsatisfied ambition.

NOTES

1. Edmund Morris, *Dutch* (New York: Random House, 1999), pp. 11–19. The weather report was ordered from http://www1.ncde.noaa.gove/pub/orders/314123401934.oaj.html (link no longer available).

2. Anne Edwards, *Early Reagan* (New York: William Morrow, 1987), p. 38.

3. Ronald Reagan, *An American Life* (New York: Simon and Schuster, 1990), p. 27.

4. U.S. Census, "Illinois," 1920.

5. Reagan, *An American Life*, p. 29.

6. Lou Cannon, *Governor Reagan: His Rise to Power* (New York: PublicAffairs, 2003), p. 12.

7. Reagan, *An American Life*, p. 7.

8. Edwards, *Early Reagan*, p. 45.

9. Ronald Reagan, *Where's the Rest of Me?* (New York: Karz, 1981), p. 14.

10. Morris, *Dutch*, p. 12.

11. Reagan, *An American Life*, p. 56.

12. Morris, *Dutch*, p. 17.

13. Reagan, *Where's the Rest of Me?* p. 17.

14. Ibid.

15. Reagan, *An American Life*, p. 42.

16. Cannon, *Governor Reagan*, p. 19.

17. Peggy Noonan, *When Character Was King* (New York: Viking, 2001), p. 38.

18. Reagan, *An American Life*, p. 35.

19. Edwards, *Early Reagan*, pp. 105–106.

20. Cannon, *Governor Reagan*, p. 20.

21. Edwards, *Early Reagan*, p. 65.

22. Reagan, *An American Life*, p. 42.

23. Lou Cannon, *President Reagan: The Role of a Lifetime* (New York: Simon and Schuster, 1991), p. 33.

24. Reagan, *An American Life*, p. 75.

25. Edwards, *Early Reagan*, p. 82.

26. William E. Pemberton, *Exit with Honor* (New York: M.E. Sharpe, 1998), p. 10.

27. Morris, *Dutch*, p. 69.

28. Pemberton, *Exit with Honor*, p. 11; Morris, *Dutch*, p. 74.

29. Reagan, *Where's the Rest of Me?*, p. 32.

30. Carl Sandburg, "One Parting," in *Honey and Salt* (New York: Harcourt Brace Jovanovich, 1953), p. 70.

31. Morris, *Dutch*, p. 121.

32. Reagan, *An American Life*, p. 51.

33. Pemberton, *Exit with Honor*, p. 13.

34. Morris, *Dutch*, p. 87.

35. Ronald Reagan Presidential Library, "Address to the Nation on the Economy," speech given on October 13, 1982, www.reagan.utexas.edu/archives/speeches/1982/101382d.htm.

36. Reagan, *Where's the Rest of Me?*, p. 40.

37. Edwards, *Early Reagan*, p. 112.

38. Reagan, *An American Life*, p. 60.

39. Reagan, *Where's the Rest of Me?*, p. 17.

40. Cannon, *President Reagan*, p. 221.

41. Reagan, *An American Life*, p. 61.

42. Cannon, *Governor Reagan*, p. 41.

43. *Dixon Evening Telegraph*, November 9, 1932.

44. Reagan, *Where's the Rest of Me?*, pp. 26–30; Pemberton, *Exit with Honor*, pp. 11–13.

Chapter 2

HOLLYWOOD

He wanted to live up to expectations, and his own most of all, but he didn't know what to do with his life and what in the world to be. Like David Copperfield, he longed to know if he would turn out to be the hero of his own story. Reagan chose Chicago because he thought he might be able to combine his love of athletics, with a vibrant social life, and at the same time become a sports announcer. It didn't work out that way, and when the sympathetic woman advised him to go out into the sticks to begin his career, that's just what he did. In October 1932, he borrowed his father's third-hand Oldsmobile and drove to Davenport, Iowa, 75 miles away from Dixon.

The station manager, Peter MacArthur, greeted him with a Scottish scowl: "Where were you yesterday?"[1] WOC, for "World of Chiropractic," had advertised for an announcer for a month, and after 94 applicants auditioned, a hire had been made. In a last minute reversal, Reagan was given the job of broadcasting a University of Iowa football game to the station's loyal weekend fans. Halfway through his initial game, where he shared the microphone with a more experience broadcaster, MacArthur slid a yellow piece of paper to his partner in the booth that read, "Let the Kid finish the game."[2] On the first page of his autobiography, *An American Life*, Reagan speculated on what his life would have like if he'd gotten a job that year at a Montgomery Ward department store. "I've often wondered at how lives are shaped by what seem like small and inconsequential events, how an apparently random turn in the road can lead you a long way from where you intended to go—and a long way from wherever you expected to go."[3] The pay was raised to 10 dollars a game, plus bus fare, with the collateral benefit being that he became a local celebrity. Both the Davenport *Democrat and Leader* and the Dixon *Evening Telegraph* praised him. He did three more games, and then in early 1933 was hired fulltime at the astonishing salary of $100 a month.

Ronald Reagan and radio were made of each other. When hired, MacArthur asked, "Could ye tell me about a football game and make me *see* it as if I was home listening on the radio?"[4] He could. The key to Reagan's success on air was his ability to use his fertile imagination and vocabulary to fill in the details for listeners. The public expected such make-believe, and he readily supplied it. When he began at WOC in Davenport, "Where the West Begins and the Tall Corn Grows," no one trained him. When he misspoke, the control room ignored his mistakes. So began the Reagan legacy of gaffes, one that would follow him throughout his presidency. If the story was compelling, and he had the ability to make most any story that way, he had a habit of putting in fiction instead of fact to make a point. After all, what mattered most was how people felt as they listened at home, not whether or not something was factually accurate.

As a broadcaster, Reagan could not have come at a better time. In 1933 the station owners merged WOC in Davenport with WHO in Des Moines. Des Moines was twice as large as Davenport and he soon became one of the most eligible bachelors when Margaret Cleaver left for France with her sister. The new 50,000-watt transmitting power made the combined station one of the most influential signals in the nation. Reagan drove around town in a Lafayette convertible coupe, dated the most attractive girls, and added to his salary by writing newspaper columns, speaking at banquets, and announcing local sporting events. He was six feet two inches tall, handsome, and full of good nature, affability, and grace. The horn-rimmed glasses gave him a serious side, belied by a wide smile. At 25, he cultivated an image, with

Ronald Reagan as he appeared in 1932 when he worked as a sportscaster for WHO radio in Des Moines, Iowa. (AP Photo.)

brown-and-white summer shoes, a pipe, a pushed-back hat, and an "aw shucks demeanor."[5]

Reagan was known about town and fairly well off financially when many people were struggling to make ends meet. "He made new friends, many at the local Christian Church college, Drake, and interviewed national celebrities [like] actors Leslie Howard and James Cagney and the charismatic religious figure Aimee Semple McPherson, joined a dance club, swam daily, and enlisted in the cavalry reserve so that he could regularly indulge a favorite hobby, horseback riding."[6] Baseball was the backbone of WHO's sports department, and Reagan broadcast hundreds of games for the Chicago Cubs and Chicago White Sox.

Sports broadcasting was a demanding occupation in the 1930s. Even a large station like WOC was not able to do live broadcasts from sporting events. Instead, they relied on telegraphed reports from the stadium press box. Reagan had to invent the weather, pop flies, and near misses into the black and silver microphone. He had to absorb material fast, manage to sound knowledgeable and at the same time give the impression of being there. Without pausing in his delivery, he would get a cryptic code like "S2C," for "strike two called," and have to say something like: "It's a called strike breaking on the inside corner of the plate." Sometimes the telegraph from the ballpark quit working, or there was a momentarily lapse, and the announcer had to manufacture even more events than usual. Reagan's imagination was so rich, and his delivery so convincing, that he was able to keep his cool and improvise until the technical problems were resolved. "Those were wonderful days," he recalled in his autobiography. "I was one of a profession just becoming popular and common."[7]

Football remained Reagan's game, and in time he broadcast the Big Ten games to become a familiar radio visitor in Midwestern homes. Reagan always said he did better with football because he knew how it felt to be on the field, even though Eureka was a far cry from Ohio State's horseshoe field or Iowa's stadium. He had an uncanny ability to memorize and recall the details of a place: the bleacher seats, the student section and the location where the band played, by kickoff, he knew the full cast of characters and the image he wanted to convey.

In February 1936, Reagan asked the station manager to allow him to follow the Chicago Cubs to their spring training on Santa Catalina Island, California. Permission was granted. In those days, William Wrigley Jr. owned the Cubs, and he insisted they hold spring practice on the island, 27 miles south of Los Angeles harbor, where he held sway as the major share owner in the island development. Reagan's idea was to enjoy a vacation, but to also feed the appetite of diehard Midwestern fans by sending back regular reports on the coaches and players before the season began. The Cubs were contenders in those Depression years; in 1935 they won the National League pennant, and lost to the Detroit Tigers in game six of the World Series. They finished second the next year, and were beginning to disclose the art of heartbreak that would become their trademark for the next 75 years.

The next season, in 1936, Reagan went to California early, and this time he wasn't interested in the Cubs. He had dinner with Joy Hodges, someone he knew from WHO, then appearing at the Biltmore Bowl in Los Angeles. "I have visions of becoming an actor," he told her. "What

I really want is a screen test."[8] She had him remove his glasses, and was impressed enough to call her agent. A meeting was set for the next morning at 10 o'clock. "I'd taken Joy's advice and not worn my glasses to the interview . . . as a result I could hardly see . . . during one of the most important interviews of my life."[9]

Max Arnow, the casting director at Warner Bros. was impressed with Reagan's shoulders and his Midwestern dialect. The actor had rehearsed his lines with Joy Hodges and felt comfortable with the scene he filmed, but his appeal was beyond what he knew. Ronald Reagan was the epitome of the Hollywood leading-man stereotype, handsome and yet smooth, with a style that merged easily with others and left a quiet impression on the audience. Despite the fact that Reagan could see no farther than he could reach, he tested well. The studio asked him to stay in California, but Reagan went back to Iowa with the Chicago Cubs. In Des Moines he laughingly told his radio cohorts about the screen test. That same Monday, a telegram arrived: "Warner's offer contract seven years, one year's options, starting at $200 a week." He flashed back a response: "Sign before they change their minds."[10]

It would become clear later than there wouldn't have been a President Reagan without his upbringing in the Midwest. It was there he learned about right and wrong, his religious values, his outlook on life, his embrace of leadership, political style and ideology were all shaped by the first 26 years of his life in Illinois hamlets. Tampico, Dixon, and Eureka experiences formed the man who followed thousands of other Midwesterners to the glittering hope that was California.

Reagan arrived in Hollywood at the end of May 1937. In Europe, the Spanish Civil War was dividing the continent, and in Asia, Japan had its eyes on China. Hitler repudiated the Versailles Treaty that year, but if any of these world-shattering events disturbed Ronald Reagan he didn't mention it. Instead, he was the center of attention. The studio was impressed with his good looks, vitality and total naturalness, but they wanted to improve him. A dialogue coach worked to change his staccato sports announcer pronunciations, and the wardrobe department changed his clothes. A cameraman complained that his head was too small for his shoulders, so they changed the cut of his suits, shirts and sweaters, and he kept that style for the rest of his life. Amid all this attention, he had to memorize his part and cope with the Hollywood dream factory.

Seven major studios dominated the movie industry when Reagan arrived. It was the golden age of American film. Stars alighted from silvery limousines, bathed in the luminescence of sky-sweeping search-lights and a thousand flashbulbs. They were a kind of American royalty, and each week, 80 million Americans—two-thirds of the country's population—went to the movie houses to watch them and escape the reality of the Great Depression. The Warner Bros. studios lay across the Los Angeles River as a gated community, complete with its own police department, fire company, power plant, hospital and school, 30 miles of streets, and even a local radio station. "Warner Brothers was a family business run by three brothers, Harry and Albert (Abe) in New York . . . [with] Jack . . . in California."[11] Nineteen warehouses stored the stuff of movie imaginations. The studio operated in assembly-line efficiency, often releasing one or more films a week.[12]

Hollywood was more than an American craze, it was an interna-tional obsession. It accounted for some 80 percent of the world's mov-ies, and celebrities had global reputations. The marketing strategy involved the double feature, with a low-budget commercial movie as a prelude to the top-billed film of the pairing. So-called B movies rep-resented a particular genre, a romantic comedy, mystery, Western, and later a horror movie, were popular. The Warners believed that all films carrying the studio label should contain a moral lesson, "by showing right and wrong, we teach the right."[13]

Ronald Reagan's first movie, *Love Is in the Air*, was a typical B movie, it took three weeks to film, had a budget of $119,000 and ran for 61 minutes. Reagan played a crusading radio reporter who ruffled the wrong feathers in his investigations of government corruption. A re-view at the time, the *Hollywood Reporter* said, "It presents a new leading man, Ronald Reagan, who is a natural, giving one of the best picture performances Hollywood has offered in years."[14] That was the plan. In the Jack Warner view of the world, the studio had a stable of stars in regular features, in the hope that one would prove to have the indefin-able, but very real, star quality. In the next 18 months, Reagan made 13 such second-tier movies and became known as the "Errol Flynn of the B Pictures."[15] Warner Bros. was the largest studio with stock con-tract players, and employed literally thousands of people. If Reagan was disappointed in the studio system, he didn't show it. The fact that he made a decent living when most Americans were unable to get a job soothed any job dissatisfactions. He became a familiar face and household name, so much so that fans came to think of him as a friend.

The people back home saw him as more than a companion. In his first months in Hollywood, Reagan wrote some 17 newspaper articles for the *Des Moines Sunday Register* about his new job, the film stars he met, the daily grind of moviemaking, his adventures of eating at the Brown Derby and dancing at the Palomar ballroom. He was the original local boy makes good, and would become as a politician what he was in the movies: an average guy peeking into a make-believe world. Reagan often played similar parts in the movies he made, that of an idealistic young man caught up in corruption or crisis.

As soon as he became a Hollywood fixture, Reagan sent for his parents and set them up with a home in Los Angeles. He had been sending them weekly checks since he came to California. His father was a shadow of the striking salesman with centrally parted hair who engaged customers in discussion back in Dixon. Jack had suffered a heart attack and every morning he had to take a prescribed walk in the never-ending sunshine. Nelle found a church and cared for her husband. When Reagan joined Warner Bros. pictures, its actors included James Cagney, Edward G. Robinson, Humphrey Bogart, Bette Davis, Errol Flynn, and Olivia de Havilland, as well as a host of others.[16] To Nelle Reagan they lacked the genuine qualities in her son. "He's no Robert Taylor," she said. "He's just himself."[17]

By all accounts being himself was enough. Reagan invariably struck people as a man of unfailing charm. Yet those who worked with him often found him distant. He was an affable and gregarious man, unfailingly nice to everyone, but not given to close friendships. His wife, Nancy, later said, "There's a wall around him. He lets me come closer than anyone else, but there are times when even I feel that barrier."[18]

In California, he was a good actor, and a quick learner. Part of his success came because he fit what Jack L. Warner was looking for: "conformity, complacency, virtue, belief in the Christian God, and loyalty to the country."[19] In a sense he was portraying the person he really was. He was the "all American good guy" whose virtues enabled him to overcome tragedy, circumstance and evil. At Warner, the work of actors like Humphrey Bogart, James Cagney and Edward G. Robinson was in the revelation of sympathetic antiheroes. Reagan and Dick Powell were their professional opposites, sugary and wholesome actors whose work was in keeping with the Horatio Alger book the boy from Dixon, Illinois read as a child.

While others in the studio chafed under the system, Reagan was happy to go along with the program. He seemed content with the roles, salaries, scripts and directors. He didn't embarrass himself or others, and always showed up on time with his lines memorized. After a time he became a little different than other actors on the set. Making films was a boring business, where technicians often worked for hours setting up scenes for a three minute shoot, which often had to be repeated. Boredom was commonplace, but not with Reagan. He seemed to relish the idle time, and frequently tried to involve his fellow actors in discussions on a host of issues, ranging from odd statistics to current events. Most of those he tried to engage were uninterested in talking; they read *Variety* and worried about their careers. It was clear that Ronnie Reagan was more interested in the economic policies of the New Deal and the Spanish Civil War than the latest movie gossip.[20]

Reagan understood the unwritten rules of dating and marriage at Warner as well. The understanding was that it was perfectly okay to become involved, as long as there was no scandal that reflected back on the studio and that affected the box office. Dutch Reagan was no one girl guy. He squired Lana Turner around town, and dated Margaret Lindsey, Mary Jane Crane, and Anita Louise. He appeared in gossip columns with a number of women on the Warner roster. Then, in 1939, he met 21-year-old Jane Wyman.

She was originally named Sarah Jane Mayfield, born in St. Joseph, Missouri, in 1917. Her parents divorced while "Janie" was still a young girl, and from age five she was raised by her neighbors, the Fulks family, while her mother was gone. They took her to San Francisco, California, with the hope of putting the little girl into pictures. The Fulks unofficially adopted Sarah Jane, and she continued to live with them until 1928, when "Daddy" Fulks died. The Fulks family was run on strict discipline; the father was on the police force and rose to the rank of inspector. The Depression years were hard on the family, and Sarah Jane dropped out of high school to take a job as a waitress at Mannings Coffee Shop to earn enough money to continue her dance lessons. She got small parts in movies, and at age 16 married a traveling salesman named Ernest Wyman. The marriage lasted less than two years, during which time she made her film debut as one of the leggy, scantily clad Goldwyn Girls, a musical stock company of female dancers employed by Samuel Goldwyn. Famous actresses whose careers included a stint in the Goldwyn Girls include Lucille Ball, Paulette Goddard, Betty Grable, Ann Sothern, Jane Wyman, Virginia Bruce, Virginia Grey, and Virginia Mayo.[21]

She was pretty, graceful and ambitious; and at Warner Bros., Jane got the dumb blond typecast. Her personal life mirrored the stereotype when she married Myron Futterman, 15 years her senior and a New Orleans-based dressmaker. Three months after the wedding, the couple separated. He was hardly around and never missed, but Myron gave her security and freedom to sample what was available, which she did quite liberally. Then, when she met Ronald Reagan, Jane Wyman filed for divorce. The grounds were mental cruelty, claiming Futterman was obsessively jealous and did not want a child while she did. The divorce was amicable, with Futterman giving her a car, furnishings and a small settlement.[22]

It was reported at the time that Wyman suffered a nervous breakdown when she fell in love with Reagan. The rumor was even uglier, that she sent him a suicide note begging him to marry her, and swallowed a lot of pills. No records survive to explain what happened either way.[23] What is clear is that Wyman found stability in Ronald Reagan's loyalty and values. "He lived in an apartment not far from his father and mother . . . [and] he never let a day pass without dropping in to see them."[24] Doubtless Jane found his optimism and trust in people infectious. Emotionally fragile herself, she was looking for a man to protect her, provide for her and probably help her with her career. "So there they were, the older-than-her-years, hard-as-nails divorcee who trusted no one and the younger-than-his-years bachelor who trusted everyone."[25] They married on January 26, 1940.

The Warner Bros. publicity department went into high gear after the wedding, explaining that the marriage was ideal for Hollywood and America. The couple fit Jack Warner's image, and Ronald Reagan had never disappointed the studio in fulfilling expectations. After a brief Palm Springs honeymoon, capped by a night of festivities at

Hollywood's Coconut Grove nightclub, the Reagans went on a studio-sponsored caravan tour of movie theatres. In the days before television talk shows, this was the best method of promoting a film. Radio had its advantages, but the fans never saw the stars face-to-face unless they went on tour.

Reagan was determined to provide for his new wife in a way his father never did for him and the family back in Illinois. His appearance in the movie *Dark Victory* was a first journey into the world of the upper-crust movies the studio had to offer, and he was optimistic that more opportunities would follow. With 18 films under his belt, he needed that breakout role to lift him into the Hollywood elite. Nine days before his wedding, he found it. *Variety* magazine announced that the studio would soon shoot *The Life of Knute Rockne*. In a coaching career that spanned the 1920s, Rockne led the "Fighting Irish" of Notre Dame to 105 victories, 12 losses and 5 national championships.

Many stories surrounded Rockne's legacy, none more memorable than that of George "The Gipper" Gipp, who died at age 25 and was sometimes the subject of Rockne's locker room pep talks to inspire the team to victory. The role of Gipp seemed perfect for Reagan. Wasn't his experience at Eureka like that of Gipp? "[Teammates] respected him for his ability, but none of them ever got close to him personally. . . . He had a great ability to relax, which was the secret of his success."[26] Jane Wyman had not had as easy an entrée into films as her husband, and she learned that the way to get a part was to campaign for it. She told him to talk to someone. Reagan approached Hal Wallis for the part, but the studio wanted a better known star, like James Cagney. "Would it surprise you that I'm five pounds *heavier* than George Gipp was when he played at Notre Dame?"[27] He presented a picture of himself when he played for the Eureka Golden Tornados. Reagan didn't have to learn the character of "The Gipper"; he had known it for years. He got the part. In the football scenes he played himself, refusing to let a double take the pounding and running required for the part. Reagan looked every inch the character he portrayed on the field. Wallis grew more enthusiastic about his choice as the shooting progressed. In Gipp's death scene, the future president murmured a line forever associated with him: "Ask 'em to go in there with all they've got; win just one for the Gipper."

While the reviews for *Knute Rockne: All American,* were good, it was not the film to propel Ronald Reagan to the starry heights he envisioned. The new studio reality was that Hollywood was changing, right along with the country. The messages in the movies took on a new urgency as the world careened into war in 1939. Much to the dismay of isolationists, movies became instruments for persuasion, and then intervention, in the global conflict on the horizon. Warner Bros. led the way. The turning point was the film, *Confessions of a Nazi Spy,* based on the real incident of German spies who came to the United States and were caught and convicted in federal court. It was the first blatantly anti-Nazi film to be produced by a major Hollywood studio prior to World War II.[28]

Reagan had no part in *Confessions of a Nazi Spy,* but he was caught in the studio controversy. His rise to A pictures was being derailed by the approaching political apocalypse. After *Knute Rockne,* and the follow-up *Santa Fe Trail,* Reagan established himself as an upper-tier actor. The time was one he would long remember, and talk about in years to come as he reflected on the Hollywood he remembered. "Their cars were big, their taxes low, their smokes unfiltered, their drinks undiluted."[29] The Reagans were beginning to rise in the estimation of both the studio and the American public. Hundreds of articles portrayed Wyman and Reagan as the film colony's perfect couple, especially after their daughter, Maureen, was born in January 1941. They became friends with actress June Allison, and her husband Dick Powell. The couples spent time together after the war, where the conservative Powell argued with Reagan about the politics of the New Deal. Years later, the story would surface that Powell wanted Reagan to run for Congress, but such a career change was unthinkable at the time.

The 1940 Gallup survey of popularity ranked Clark Gable, fresh from *Gone With the Wind,* as America's number one box office star. Ronald Reagan was number 82, and Jane Wyman was unranked. Reagan's salary per picture was only about one-fourth that of Gable's, but his accomplishments weren't bad for someone just three years removed from the Midwest. The future looked bright when he was cast opposite Robert Cummings and Ann Sheridan in the movie, *King's Row.* The story, based on Henry Bellamann's best-selling book about a small town, dealt with the seamy side of turn-of-the-century life in themes of incest, euthanasia, and homosexuality. The screenplay adaption was milder, but in the big scene for Reagan his character awakens from surgery to discover that he has had his legs, and his manhood, removed by a sadistic doctor. In the movie, Reagan sat up in bed to proclaim, "Where's the rest of me?" It was his finest performance, and the line became the title of his 1965 autobiography.

Had it not been for World War II, *King's Row* would have probably propelled Reagan into the top ranks of studio stars. Sam Wood directed the movie, and prior to Pearl Harbor was decidedly against America entering the war. The Reagan's evening dinner conversation with Wood and his wife often turned to politics. Dutch was interested, informed and argumentative, but not so his wife. "Ooh, politics . . . That's all he talks about! If you had to sit at home and listen to him like I do . . . how he's going to save the world."[30] No doubt Reagan was changing, he had a sense of history and a fascination with heroes, especially political ones.

After several deferments, managed mostly by his agent, Lew Wasserman, Ronald Reagan reported for duty to Fort Mason, California, in April 1942. Some consolation came from the fact that Wasserman had just negotiated a new seven year contract with Warner Bros. that would pay him one million dollars over seven years. It was the first seven figure deal in the industry, and reflected the faith the agent and studio had in his future. Reagan was a reserve officer in the U.S. Army Calvary Reserve, but the new mechanized army had no need for horses. Another problem was that he was nearly legally blind without his glasses. After a short time, the army assigned him to the First Motion Picture Unit (FMPU) at the Hal Roach Studio in Culver City, California. The assignment allowed him to return to his home on the weekends, and Jane to visit when she could. The FMPU, called the "Celluloid Commandos" by those so assigned, worked to produce short films educating the public about the military. The post roster numbered nearly a thousand men, including some of Hollywood's glamour and make-believe soldiers.[31] The film colony's publicity machine unfailingly depicted the Reagans as examples of the sacrifices all Americans were making for the war effort.

The best known of the FMPU movies was about the last mission of a B-17 crew in Europe: *Memphis Belle: A Story of the Flying Fortress*

(1944). It inspired a 1990 remake. The least known might have been *Recognition of the Japanese Zero Fighter* (1943), starring Ronald Reagan. The project was undertaken because of the alarming number of friendly fire downings of P-40 aircraft in the Pacific. Reagan played the part of a U.S. flier who nearly shoots down a colleague's plane after misidentifying it. Critics recalled that Reagan's main role was to stare incomprehensively into the camera, something they said he did well.

At "Fort Roach," as it was derisively called in honor of "Hal" Roach who oversaw the production operations, Reagan had his first experience with the peculiar ways of the federal bureaucracy. He still thought that government was the solution to solve postwar problems, just as it had in the Depression and the war effort. But he was noticing problems. "I discovered that it was almost impossible to remove an incompetent or lazy worker, and that one of the most popular methods supervisors used in dealing with an incompetent was to transfer him or her out of his department to a higher-paying job in another department."[32] He wanted to destroy some unwanted files, and was told that he could, as long as a copy was made of each one. Mostly, it was the incompetence, the delays, and inefficiencies that frustrated him.

After his discharge in 1945, both Reagans turned to the issue of reviving their film careers. Behind Jane Wyman's easygoing and wise-cracking exterior lurked Sarah Jane Fulks, always seeking approval and love. Her insecurities drove her to set almost impossible goals and then work furiously to achieve them. Wyman wanted to have another child, but with the revival of the studio shooting schedule, she did not want to become pregnant again and halt the momentum of her work. Instead, she convinced Reagan to adopt, and on March 21, son Michael was welcomed into the family.

For his part, Ronald "Dutch" Reagan made 22 postwar films, most of them better than his prewar efforts. His 1946 tax return put him in the highest income tax bracket, equivalent to more than one million 1990 dollars. In spite of the money, he was having a hard time reestablishing himself in Hollywood. Film production slowed down after the war, and a new generation of actors arrived, hungry for roles. While Reagan waited by the phone, Wyman's career took off. She landed a part in *The Yearling* opposite Gregory Peck, and it was rumored to be an Oscar-winning opportunity. When Reagan visited her on the set, and was addressed one day as "Mr. Wyman," he couldn't take it anymore and returned to Los Angeles. He spent his time putting up rail posts on an eight acre ranch the couple purchased in Northridge, close to San Francisco.

Reagan also became active in civic affairs. He joined the left-leaning American Veterans Committee, was on the Board of the Hollywood Independent Citizens Committee of Arts, Sciences and Professions (HICCASP). The threat of the atom bomb, and the destruction wrought by World War II, heightened his interest in politics. He joined the AFL-CIO unions in opposing Republican-sponsored Right to Work legislation and helped organize the group Californians for Truman in 1948. He supported civil rights advocate Helen Gahagan Douglas against Richard Nixon in the California race for the U.S. Senate in 1950. She lost. He was known as a conventional liberal Democrat and committed New Dealer.

Reagan joined the Screen Actors Guild (SAG) in 1938, and reactivated his membership after the war, even to the point of joining the governing board. "Like very few labor organizations . . . [SAG] can boast dozens of members who are both very rich and world famous."[33] Just when the studios were vamping up their postwar schedules, a massive stagehand strike hit the industry. At first Reagan, with his working-class roots, sympathized with the day laborers. Then he found himself in the middle of a blistering round of slander, vilification and lies. In the end, he worked against the union, and the leftist movements that supported the strike. "I began to wake up the real world and what was going on in my own business, the motion picture industry."[34]

Reagan later said the communist plan in Hollywood was to take over the industry, and control a worldwide propaganda base for indoctrination.[35] The strike had both professional and personal effects on him. The SAG work saved him from the growing shadow of Jane Wyman's blossoming career. He realized that in the postwar era, communism would replace fascism as an enemy of American culture, and he worked to halt the spread of leftist ideas. Reagan began to address large audiences on political themes. "I was blindly and busily joining every organization I could find that would guarantee to save the world. . . . I loved it."[36] And the audiences loved him. In the absence of movie debuts he found that the political circuit was a nice substitute.

The problem was that Jane Wyman didn't share his enthusiasm for such activities, and as a result, the strain on the marriage increased. In June 1947, Wyman gave birth to a premature baby that died the next day. Reagan was not even there for the birth; he was in the hospital with viral pneumonia and a six-day fever of over 104 degrees. On her release from care, Wyman resumed work on a movie at an abandoned lumber camp north of San Francisco. There she began a passionate affair with her costar, Lew Ayres, and made no attempt to hide it from others. Ayres was an intelligent, good-looking man who listened to Jane Wyman and was not interested in politics. What followed was a period of recriminations, reconciliations and separations, and finally divorce. In late 1947, Jane Wyman told Reagan she wanted to leave him, and filed for divorce in June 1948, admitting that it was her fault.[37]

Reagan read of his wife's wish to end their marriage in a gossip column. In that era of Hollywood, Louella Parsons and Hedda Hopper could make or break a career and a marriage. Parsons was a native of Dixon, Illinois, and early took a shine to Reagan. She wrote a public plea for reconciliation in April 1948, in an issue of *Photoplay*, but to no avail.[38]

Ronald Reagan was 37 years old when he and Wyman divorced. Their daughter, Maureen, was seven years old and adopted son, Michael, three. Those who supported her said politics broke them up, and those sympathetic with him said she showed her true colors in the infidelity. Whatever the reason for the split, Reagan was unprepared for separation and divorce. He admitted when he recovered that the divorce from Jane left him dead for a number of years. "The worst thing a woman can do to an actor is to announce, in public, that he bores her."[39] For a man with a string of public successes, a failure in private life was hard to take. His parents, with all their problems, stayed together. At the time of their divorce, only 18 percent of the population did so.[40] It was clear at the time, and later, that Ronald Reagan did not want a divorce, but he had no choice. The unforgiving rumor mill of Hollywood made private conversations public, and fueled gossip columns with endless speculation.

NOTES

1. Ronald Reagan, *An American Life* (New York: Simon and Schuster, 1990), p. 63.

2. Anne Edwards, *Early Reagan* (New York: William Morrow, 1987), p. 123.

3. Reagan, *An American Life*, p. 19.

4. Ibid., p. 64.

5. Edmund Morris, *Dutch* (New York: Random House, 1999), p. 124.

6. William E. Pemberton, *Exit with Honor* (New York: M.E. Sharpe, 1998), p. 17.

7. Ronald Reagan, *Where's the Rest of Me?* (New York: Karz, 1981), p. 59.

8. Morris, *Dutch*, p. 130.

9. Reagan, *An American Life*, p. 79.

10. Ibid., p. 81.

11. Edwards, *Early Reagan*, p. 163.

12. Marc Elliot, *Reagan: The Hollywood Years* (New York: Harmony Books, 2008), pp. 62–63.

13. Edwards, *Early Reagan*, p. 163.

14. Morris, *Dutch*, p. 145.

15. Reagan, *An American Life*, p. 89.

16. Pemberton, *Exit with Honor*, p. 22.

17. Morris, *Dutch*, p. 146.

18. Pemberton, *Exit with Honor*, p. 18.

19. Elliot, *Reagan: The Hollywood Years*, p. 62.

20. Edwards, *Early Reagan*, p. 171.

21. Elliott, *Reagan: The Hollywood Years*, p. 81.

22. Morris, *Dutch*, p. 162.

23. Elliot, *Reagan: The Hollywood Years*, pp. 84–85.

24. Edwards, *Early Reagan*, p. 193.

25. Elliot, *Reagan: The Hollywood Years*, pp. 84–85.

26. Morris, *Dutch*, p. 167.

27. Reagan, *An American Life*, p. 91.

28. Cass Warner Sperling and Cork Miller, *The Brothers Warner* (Lexington: University Press of Kentucky, 1994), pp. 233–234.

29. Elliot, *Reagan: The Hollywood Years*, p. 119.

30. Ibid., p. 154.

31. Morris, *Dutch*, pp. 196–201.

32. Reagan, *An American Life*, p. 102.

33. Donald F. Prindle, *The Politics of Glamour* (Madison: University of Wisconsin Press, 1988), p. 3.

34. Reagan, *An American Life*, p. 107.

35. Edwards, *Early Reagan*, p. 332.

36. Reagan, *Where's the Rest of Me?*, p. 141.

37. Lou Cannon, *President Reagan: The Role of a Lifetime* (New York: Simon and Schuster, 1991), p. 228.

38. Lou Cannon, *Governor Reagan: His Rise to Power* (New York: PublicAffairs, 2003), p. 72.

39. Morris, *Dutch*, p. 266.

40. Sally C. Clarke, "Advance Report on Final Divorce Statistics, 1989 and 1990," *Monthly Vital Statistics Report* 43, no. 9 (March 22, 1995): 1–3.

Chapter 3

REBIRTH

Years later, a contemporary remembered that "Reagan was a very lonely guy . . . because of his divorce, but a very level-headed guy."[1] The year 1948 was a difficult one, even for him, and he suffered both personally and professionally. His movie career was stalled for a more fundamental reason than his political activism—he just wasn't that castable as a middle-aged, former action star whose romantic appeal was on the wane. The divorce revealed an innocent side to his nature, rooted in his Midwestern upbringing and hometown successes, in that bad things happened to other people, not him. To make matters worse, he broke his leg in a charity baseball game that spring and spent seven weeks in the hospital. He had plenty of time to brood about Jane Wyman's Best Actress Academy Award for *Johnny Belinda*, the movie she was shooting when she became involved with Lew Ayres.[2]

He compensated by moving into politics. Reagan had always believed that the 1946 Hollywood strike was an attempted takeover by communists. "These were eye-opening years for me," he confessed in his autobiography. "I'd shared the orthodox liberal views that Communists . . . were liberals who were temporarily off track. . . . Now I knew from firsthand experience how [they] used lies, deceit, violence, or any other tactic that suited them to advance the cause of Soviet expansion."[3] He was alone now, and reading more than ever, but he was also visible to the public. His work with the Screen Actors Guild (SAG) brought him into the political world. He was horrified when he heard sympathizers at SAG events, and in related meetings, quote from the Soviet Constitution to say that "Russia was more Democratic than the United States" and that if a clash came, they would "fight on the side of the Soviet Union."[4] "Suppose we quit using the words Communist and Communism," Reagan wrote, and "substitute pro-Russian for the word."[5] The SAG was a natural venue for him to use his political instincts to counter such an eventuality. "It [was] from the beginning [a] policy not to pay its officers a salary. . . . Those involved cannot expect a boost to their careers from their years in service. . . . In other words, participants in Screen Actor Guild government are good citizens, serving their union out of a sense of responsibility."[6] Ronald Reagan was an ideal SAG subject, mostly because he needed a diversion.

Lois Maxwell, 20-year-old Canadian-born actress, receives her Screen Actors Guild member card from the new president of the guild, actor Ronald Reagan, in Hollywood, California, on March 30, 1947. (AP Photo.)

Back in 1941, SAG executive secretary John Dales recruited Reagan to the union's board of directors, and in 1947, he became president. Reagan led the SAG during several bitter postwar strikes and through it all, he became more and more interested in national and international affairs. It was the McCarthy era, and Hollywood was in the midst of blacklisting suspicious artists. The practice began in 1947 at a meeting of Hollywood producers who drew up a list of communists, including one producer, one director and eight writers.[7] The so-called Hollywood Ten would become synonymous with the red scare, which benefitted and harmed various people, depending on which side they were on. Republicans accused Democrats of being "soft on communism," and Democrats responded that Republicans were "stifling free speech." Some people had their Hollywood careers destroyed, while others, and Ronald Reagan was one of these, profited. He led the SAG in an anticommunist crusade.

In October 1947, the House Un-American Activities Committee opened hearings on the communist menace in Hollywood. Reagan appeared in a light tan suit, white shirt and blue knit tie. Under oath and before cameras, he declared that there was a "small clique" in SAG that followed the communist party line.[8] But he went on to say that the film community itself had confronted the problem and turned back the threat. Of course, this was only partially true; many in Hollywood remained sympathetic with communism, and often declared allegiance to socialism. Reagan concluded his appearance by quoting Thomas Jefferson: "If the American people know all the facts they will never make a mistake."[9] Even the liberals in the audience applauded his eloquence.

Politics was a safe sanctuary from his broken heart and personal life. He sulked, kept to himself, and dated little. On the surface the split looked amicable enough. Wyman found a house in Malibu for herself and the children. Reagan was free to visit them whenever he wished, and in the early months he did so frequently. Despite rumors to the contrary, he did not become involved with other starlets, he was "never [one] for sexpots. . . . He was never a guy looking for the bed. He was a guy looking for companionship."[10] About the only diversion he allowed himself was drinking with William Holden at Ciro's restaurant. He couldn't go back to their house on Cordell, even to prepare it for sale, so he spent his time riding horses on his ranch. His new home was a bachelor pad on at the Londonderry Apartments, the same place he moved when he first came to Hollywood. The room was furnished with a desk, some books and the bare necessities, along with lots of shoes. Reagan kept up his father's legacy, by believing that a source of one's energy came from the feet, and polished, clean shoes invigorated him.

Reagan liked to play the hero in movies, and especially loved the classic Westerns. The script of these movies was often similar, especially in the films of the forties and fifties, of a fearless man of character and rugged virtue who stood for justice and treated women with respect (think of Gary Cooper in *High Noon*). The hero used a gun only when necessary, and lived by an honor code of moral absolutes. The parts were on the wane in the sixties, with movies like *Butch Cassidy and the Sundance Kid,* and Reagan found himself on the sidelines.

He changed his personal image as well after he took over as SAG president. Where once he wore casual clothes, now he wore suits, neckties and, in the evenings, formal attire. He profited from the advances in medical science, and wore contact lenses in front of the camera. Reagan still read widely, mostly books and political columns. The charm was still there, but it was muted by his personal situation. He was still ambitious and competitive, but lacked a venue to show his gifts. The studio had almost no work for him, so he became the token celebrity actor involved in charity work. He presided over the opening of the Motion Picture County Hospital in Calabasas, California, and was especially proud of the project because it was built entirely by voluntary contributions. Reagan fretted about his lack of work, and the SAG responsibilities only occupied one regular night a week; he spent the rest of his time in recreation and meetings. His life was reduced to a cranking emptiness. Yet, he was one of Hollywood's most eligible bachelors: handsome, rich, divorced, and interested in remarriage. The movie magazines reported that he was with some of the most beautiful and eligible actresses of the time, but the one who captured his heart came to him.

Nancy Davis was born in New York City, the daughter of a stage actress and a former soldier turned insurance salesman. Anne Francis Robbins, nicknamed "Nanny," was born on July 6, 1921. Her mother wanted to continue her acting career, and the quarreling led to a divorce just after the birth. When Nancy was two years old, single motherhood proved too much for her mother, who began using the name Edith Luckett. She asked her sister, Virginia, to take the baby for a while. Nancy lived with her aunt and her uncle until she was eight years old, when Edith married Dr. Loyal Davis, a wealthy and socially prominent Chicago surgeon.[11] Davis was conservative and old-fashioned, but he had a soft side that Nancy was able to expose. "He discussed his deepest feelings with her, and answered all the questions she posed. . . . She called him 'Dad' . . . [and] refused to face the fact that Davis was not her true, her only, father."[12] The doctor's ideas about proper behavior and manners made an impression on his stepdaughter. Nancy was sent to the Girls Latin School in the Gold Coast neighborhood in Chicago where her parents lived. They sent her to private schools and to Smith College.

Dr. Davis chose Smith for two reasons: first, it was far enough from Chicago that Nancy would be on her own; and two, it lacked a theatre department. Even though Edith had a stage background, he thought acting was an unhelpful career choice. Of course, as anyone who has teenagers knows, the very prohibition of something makes it all the more appealing. Despite her stepfather's continuing disapproval, she pursued the theatre, first in Chicago, then New York, and finally with a screen test in Hollywood. On March 7, 1949, she began work on her first movie, the forgettable *Shadow on the Wall*, which she didn't even mention in her own autobiography. It was during the filming of a subsequent movie, when she was identified as 1 of 208 people who signed an amicus curie brief in support of writers John Howard Lawson and Dalton Trumbo, that she stumbled in her career. They were two of the celebrated Hollywood Ten blacklisted by the studios. Because the conservative Nancy Davis from Chicago was confused with the liberal Nancy Davis in Hollywood, MGM director Mervyn LeRoy called Ronald Reagan for help. Could Reagan, as president of SAG, please meet Nancy Davis and give her advice on how to avoid being blacklisted for the sins of another? He could.

When Reagan met Nancy Davis in November 1951, he was leaning on two canes, the result of injuries from a charity football game. She was 28, five feet four inches tall, and persistent in her affections. Unlike the first wife, Nancy found Reagan's talk about history, politics and his love of the outdoors familiar; it reminded her of the convictions of her stepfather, Dr. Loyal Davis. The truth was that she was instantly crazy about Ronald Reagan, and it showed. Reagan saw Nancy, but he also saw a number of other women. When it came to family responsibilities, Wyman was 30 miles away in Malibu, and he was increasingly delinquent in visits. He still called his mother, Nelle, frequently, but he was also busy and their visits were not as regular as they once were. What he needed was some stability in an active life, and he was about to get it in spades.

Nancy Davis became pregnant in January 1952, and a month later the couple applied for a marriage license. They were married on March 4, 1952, in a hastily arranged private ceremony in the Little Brown Church in the San Fernando Valley, a branch of the Hollywood Beverly Hills Christian Church Reagan's mother attended. He called Dr. Davis in Arizona and asked for permission, and then notified the press of the upcoming nuptials. William Holden was best man; his wife was matron of honor. Neither Reagan's mother, brother, nor his children attended the ceremony.

Actor Ronald Reagan and his bride, actress Nancy Davis, smile at each other as they pose after their marriage in the Little Brown Church of the Valley in North Hollywood, California, March 4, 1952. (AP Photo.)

Despite a shaky start, the marriage of Ronald and Nancy Reagan would become one of the great romances of American politics. "If ever God gave me evidence he had a plan for me, it was the night He brought Nancy into my life."[13] Nancy Davis was the perfect second wife for Ronald Reagan, mainly because she was willing to give up everything to help him. He would need it. At the time of their wedding, Reagan's career, already in decline, was about to collapse. To make matters worse, he had just purchased a ranch that left him flat broke, and was facing the prospect of no new pictures. He needed help fast, and his agent only had one answer: television. It wasn't what Reagan, or any Hollywood actor, wanted to hear. In the early 1950s television was a medium dominated by variety and game shows, sitcoms, clowns and comics. No self-respecting professional would be seen on it unless it was an emergency. However, Lew Wasserman knew that the future was going to be in television, and Reagan sensed it too. The money was good, even if the work was uninspiring. What they both wanted was a better platform to showcase Reagan's talents.

Ronald Reagan's marriage to Nancy Davis coincided with the end of his movie career. His last picture for Warner Bros. was *The Winning Team* with Doris Day, where he played one of his favorite characters, the baseball player Grover Cleveland Alexander. The new couple lived for a time in Nancy's apartment in Pacific Palisades. "What I wanted most in all the world was to be a good wife and mother," she wrote in her memoir. "As things turned out, I guess I've been more successful at the first than at the second."[14] When Ronald Reagan was president, and the country's leading spokesman for family values, his own home life would come in for some justifiable criticism. None of this mattered in 1952, when the wriggling Patricia Ann, known as Patti, arrived after a difficult labor.

Despite the warm California weather, Patti's father was beginning to feel the chill winds of financial insecurity. Ronald Reagan was drained financially by taxes and mortgage payments on his home and ranch. At the end of his film career he was finally in the top tax bracket, paying 94 cents of every dollar to the government. By experience, Reagan knew that high tax rates were a disincentive to working hard. He began to rethink his political beliefs, even as he searched for work. The low point in his career came in 1954, when he agreed to do a well-paying, but humiliating, stint in Las Vegas. Reagan had to do an advertisement for Pabst Blue Ribbon Beer, and don a thick German accent for a series of skits. When it was over, he vowed to Nancy he would never do that to himself again.

It was at this time that his agent, Lew Wasserman, came through for him with a job as host and pitchman for the CBS production, *General Electric Theatre*. The show was envisioned as a half-hour production on television in the popular Sunday night slot. In addition to hosting the show, Reagan would be GE's roving ambassador of good will, touring plants and giving speeches as a way to boost the company image. The idea for the show was birthed by the ad agency, Batten, Barton, Durstine and Osborne (BBD&O), who packaged shows through Lew Wasserman's company, Music Corporation of America (MCA). The idea was to lure stars to television by allowing them to choose their vehicle, and have some control over their appearance. "This meant that the stars would then own the show in which they appeared and thus be likely to draw a steady income for re-showings for many years."[15]

As the face and voice of General Electric, Ronald Reagan was offered a starting salary of $125,000, which was soon raised to $150,000, and four times the amount of money he made in his last film for Warner Bros. "I knew that having my face beamed into homes across the country every week risked the kind of overexposure that could be fatal to a movie actor's career," he wrote years later, "but I liked the idea because it offered me a chance to share in the growing financial prosperity of television while avoiding the kind of typecasting that acting in the same role week after week in a regular series brought with it."[16] No matter what the theme or the moral of that week's mini-melodrama, Ronald Reagan was there to declare that "Progress is our Most Important Product," for General Electric.

That was no idle boast in the 1950s. General Electric was one of the original 12 companies listed on the Dow Jones Industrial Average in 1896, and after more than a hundred years, it was the only one still there. The company was founded on the patents and legacy of Thomas Edison, but quickly became a multibusiness firm as native to America as apple pie and the Fourth of July. In the postwar era it was largely responsible for the electrification of the nation. GE stressed research and innovation; the first Nobel Prize awarded to a nonacademic was to a company scientist in 1932.

To Ronald Reagan, and to General Electric, the meaning of "progress and product" was more than a company slogan; it was a signature of the American experience. The initial GE tour in 1954 began at the giant turbine plant in Schenectady, New York, which was a vast factory with 31 acres under one roof. Reagan was stunned by the size of the place, and he spent the whole day touring and talking to people as they worked.[17] The intimacy of television was astonishing to him; people at the plant called him "Ron" and acted like they all grew up as neighbors in Dixon. It was on the initial tour that BBD&O agents and company executives realized how effective Reagan was at giving a speech. He gave an impromptu talk on education that held an audience of 3,000 or 4,000 workers spellbound.

Over the next decade, Reagan became the voice of General Electric, but he also became the embodiment of the credo that a better life was to be had by living in America and accepting its values. His conservative thought was based on an absolute belief in American exceptionalism, the conviction that the country was qualitatively different than other nations. In his mind the nation was less a place than an ideal. "It is nothing but the inherent love of freedom . . . it is simply the idea, the basis of this country and of our religion, the idea of the dignity of man, the idea that deep within the heart of each one of us is something so God-like and precious that no individual or group has a right to impose his or its will upon the people, that no group can decide for the people what is good for the people so well as they can decide for themselves."[18]

Reagan would help them decide, and in the process he would change as well. His conversion from liberal to conservative, from actor to politician, began in the GE years. The company had an employee relations program, known as Boulwarism, named for its founder, Lemuel "Lem" Boulware, a company vice president and labor strategist. The policy was an education initiative designed to eliminate much of the bargaining and mistrust in labor and management negotiations. "As vice president of public and community relations, Boulware developed a managed-news program that was the envy of corporate America and undoubtedly an inspiration for the Reagan White House."[19] The company published plant newspapers, issued regular bulletins, maintained book clubs for its employees and their spouses, sponsored beauty pageants, funded scholarships and facilitated the appearance of Ronald Reagan on tours of company plants.

The initial contract with GE was for five years, which was an unusually long time for a television show. Reagan proved his value when *GE Theatre* became the country's top-rated Sunday evening prime time program. Its popularity was helped by Reagan's ability to attract friends and actors from his SAG leadership contacts to appear on the show. This was a time when many movie personalities shunned television, but *GE Theatre* offered bit parts and full programs that only served to improve popularity. Reagan played a significant part in script selection, and he soon adopted the company values as his own. Working with GE allowed him to hone his antitax, anticommunism, egalitarian, individualism, populism, and laissez-faire themes.

At the time, General Electric was the fifth largest corporation in America. Ronald Reagan's tour of GE plants became his signature. In his first year on the job, Reagan asked GE head Ralph Cordiner if the company would censor anything he had to say. The company president replied they would not, so Reagan moved away from his talks about Hollywood and America, and began to discuss what was wrong with the country and what needed to be done to correct it.[20] He spent his time as a traveling ambassador visiting GE's 250,000 workers in 139 plants and speaking from civic platforms to the employees in some 40 states in the company's far-flung empire. Reagan's natural charm, wit, grace and intelligence came off well in these public appearances. Soon he found himself answering questions about day-to-day politics, and leading a company campaign against organized labor's attempts to develop grassroots political power in GE plants. Though not labeled conservative, the speeches were company oriented and presented the free market system in a favorable light. It was on these tours for 16 weeks each year that Reagan perfected his remarkable speechmaking abilities, with off the cuff anecdotes, impulsive jokes, and an ability to recall specific facts before an audience in a way that enhanced the point he wanted to make.

In time, Lemuel Boulware took GE's traveling ambassador out of the plants, and put him before civic groups, in what Reagan called the "mashed potato circuit." He was a great company man and improved town and business relations. It was before this Rotary and Lion's club audience that he developed what became known as "The Speech": an antigovernment but seriously nonpartisan talk about taxation, overregulation, the communist threat, and the fact that "freedom is never more than one generation from extinction."[21] Though he still considered himself a Democrat, Reagan began to get more and more invitations to speak at Republican dinners and fundraisers. He heard complaints from hundreds of people about how the ever-expanding federal government was encroaching on liberties they had always taken for granted. He filed away the stories for inclusion in "The Speech." "For example, I learned the government had six programs to help poultry growers increase egg production . . . [and] a seventh program costing almost as much as all the six others to buy up surplus eggs."[22]

Most Hollywood actors would find the travel and speechmaking a chore, but Ronald Reagan rubbed his hands together in anticipation of making the visits with the public relations people. He succeeded brilliantly, with standing ovations and another flood of invitations. A 1958 survey found Reagan to be one of the most recognized men in the country.[23] Audiences loved "The Speech," and so did the corporate heads of General Electric. The tours had an effect on the speaker as well. "Those GE tours became almost a postgraduate course in political science for me."[24] He believed that government was too big, and that the Democratic Party was largely responsible for the growth.

Reagan's switch to the Republican party was galvanized by the GE experience. He had crossed the track to the other side of the partisan aisle in 1952 when he boarded the Republican train to travel with Dwight Eisenhower. The Truman administration had been tainted with scandal, and Reagan was appreciating the conservative values of the GOP because of his personal financial situation. But the hands and feet of his conservatism took place in conversations with workers at the GE plants. It was those speeches that changed him the most. When he traveled he met and discussed the concerns of everyday Americans, who were having to live with the results of government policies.

He was captivated by the technology of GE. It is entirely possible that Reagan's lifelong interest in space was inspired by a visit to a General Electric plant in Santa Barbara during these years. The company was a pioneer in the production of radar defense, and on the visit he was introduced to the experimental ballistic-missile-defense project that used radar with rockets as a defensive weapon. The radar was tested on the Pacific Missile Range. Even though he had no idea what the system would look like, Reagan was intrigued by the idea of a defensive shield.

After two miscarriages, Nancy gave birth on May 20, 1958, to their second child, a boy named Ronald Prescott Reagan. The proud father nicknamed him "Skippy," but the moniker did not stick like his own father's did with him. Besides Reagan, Robert and Ursula Taylor were at Cedars of Lebanon Hospital, as was big sister Patti. Nancy raised the children in the fashionable Dr. Spock method, which encouraged parents to allow their children to experiment and learn on their own without parental intervention. Both parents did just that.

Nancy Reagan described herself as a "nester," and her husband reinforced that trait. She restored a sense of equilibrium to Ronald Reagan after his divorce, but he remained forever guarded about the subject of his first marriage. Even though he was by many standards a good father—reading to his children, singing with them, and teaching them to swim and fish—he kept a certain distance from them. As adults, the children told biographers that they knew he loved them, but "they did not think of him as a person in whom they could confide."[25]

Ten years after his divorce, everything seemed to have returned to a sane normality in the Reagan household. "Dutch" had recovered from the biggest disappointment of his life, regained his financial footing and garnered a new family in the process. But things were about to undergo a profound change. When William Holden resigned as president of SAG, the board overwhelmingly voted Ronald Reagan back into office. The powers that led General Electric were less than thrilled with their star ambassador's election. SAG was always controversial, and its political disputes, since they involved labor and management issues, could only serve to discredit the company. Their caution was well founded.

The first issue Reagan had to confront seemed innocuous enough, a proposal to create a welfare and pension plan for members. Despite the glamour of the film industry, the working hours were brutal. "Jimmy Stewart commented that when he first came to Hollywood in 1935 . . . [actors] often worked until midnight and reported back to the set at six the next morning."[26] The stars were as militant as the journeymen members of the union when it came to working hours and conditions, a pension for members who did not work regularly for the employer and compensation for television and studio production. Many of Hollywood's best known personalities were concerned they would not be paid if their films were shown on television. There were questions of agency representation and residual rights, and all these problems were Ronald Reagan's to solve.

The irony, not lost on members of the union or the Hollywood community, was that the president of the Screen Actors Guild was an outspoken conservative who favored free markets and open competition opposite union bargaining. But he was also a member of the SAG board of directors, who called for a strike against the major studio producers. Reagan recognized that the dynamics of the entertainment industry had changed. The studios no longer dominated the business, with actors held under long-term contracts. Just before the strike deadline, Universal-International studios agreed to the SAG terms, as did some 400 independent producers. Five weeks after the initial agreement, Reagan stood before the union membership and announced that the strike brought agreement with the studio moguls. One member stood up to declare: "I doubt if you will ever realize the debt of gratitude we all owe Ronald Reagan."[27]

The strike ended on April 18, 1960, and Reagan resigned from the presidency of SAG on June 7. Both he and Nancy left the Guild board, and they never returned. Dutch Reagan's approval was short-lived. While some actors thought their president stood up to the studio bosses, others, like Glenn Ford and Bob Hope, thought that the Guild gave away the worth of the older films for a pittance. All in all, it was an outcome that would become familiar to those who know American politics—a solution that ended a crisis, but really pleased no one.

While Reagan worked to solve the problems at SAG, difficulties developed at home. Adopted son Michael, who had been living with Jane Wyman and her next husband, Fred Kerger, was ordered by a child psychiatrist to start living with his father. Wyman's marriage was again unraveling and she was unable to provide a stable home environment. Fourteen-year-old Michael, who had been a regular weekend visitor to the Reagans,' was now ordered to move in with them. Maureen would have had to go as well, but she was attending Marymount College in Arlington, Virginia.

General Electric built a house for the second Reagan family in Pacific Palisades, and it had every electric gadget and gizmo the engineers at GE could devise. However, it was not large enough to accommodate a family of six. Nancy insisted that Michael attend a private boarding school and come home on weekends and holidays. She also asked her husband to take the boy to the ranch with him on the weekends. Between caring for a toddler, and Patti, who since childhood was prone to uncontrollable screaming, temper tantrums and frequent vomiting, Nancy Reagan had no time for a teenager. Within a year, Nancy and Ron added a bedroom to the house with additional space for a full-time nurse to help with Patti. Family life was not the Hollywood ideal seen on television.

Nancy Reagan may have been a mother, but she was still an actress. She maintained her size 6 figure and her air of reserve, the debutante daughter of a Chicago doctor. Her short brown hair looked immaculate, and she still kept a closetful of red dresses—her husband Ronnie's favorite. Most of all, she treasured her husband in a way few wives did. To her, he was the hero of her life and the star of her movie. Observers were always amazed that when she went with him to an event, she gazed up as he spoke as if she were hearing the words for the first time. When asked about this she always had a simple reply: "He's my hero."[28]

Ronald Reagan continued his responsible, but disengaged, role as father. He paid for his children to attend some of the best private schools around, but he let their mothers select them. None of the children would ever complete college, something he did under much more difficult conditions. Maybe comfortable circumstances made for more moderate ambitions, but for whatever reason the children floundered for a time. In the turmoil, Nancy seemed to react by longing for an extended honeymoon with her husband, while at the same time blaming Jane Wyman for her irresponsibility. In all this, the couple remained remarkably visible and photogenic.

NOTES

1. Anne Edwards, *Early Reagan* (New York: William Morrow, 1987), p. 357.

2. Edmund Morris, *Dutch* (New York: Random House, 1999), p. 277.

3. Ronald Reagan, *An American Life* (New York: Simon and Schuster, 1990), p. 115.

4. Kiron K. Skinner, Annelise Anderson, and Martin Anderson, eds., *Reagan: A Life in Letters* (New York: Free Press, 2003), p. 148.

5. Morris, *Dutch*, p. 287.

6. David F. Prindle, *The Politics of Glamour* (Madison: University of Wisconsin Press, 1988), p. 10.

7. Paul Johnson, *A History of the American People* (New York: HarperCollins, 1997), p. 835.

8. Morris, *Dutch*, p. 256.

9. Ibid., p. 257.

10. Edwards, *Early Reagan*, p. 357.

11. Marc Elliot, *Reagan: The Hollywood Years* (New York: Harmony Books, 2008), p. 228.

12. Edwards, *Early Reagan*, pp. 386–387.

13. Reagan, *An American Life*, p. 123.

14. Nancy Reagan and William Novak, *My Turn* (New York: Random House, 1989), p. 146.

15. Edwards, *Early Reagan*, p. 452.

16. Reagan, *An American Life*, p. 126.

17. Edwards, *Early Reagan*, p. 454.

18. William E. Pemberton, *Exit with Honor* (New York: M.E. Sharpe, 1998), p. 49.

19. Thomas W. Evans, *The Education of Ronald Reagan* (New York: Columbia University Press, 2006), p. 50.

20. Edwards, *Early Reagan*, p. 457.

21. Morris, *Dutch*, p. 308.

22. Reagan, *An American Life*, p. 129.

23. Morris, *Dutch*, p. 305.

24. Reagan, *An American Life*, p. 129.

25. Lou Cannon, *Governor Reagan: His Rise to Power* (New York: PublicAffairs, 2003), p. 80.

26. Evans, *Education of Ronald Reagan*, p. 130.

27. Ibid., p. 144.

28. Edwards, *Early Reagan*, p. 480.

Chapter 4

POLITICIAN

Twice, once in 1946 and again in 1952, Reagan was recruited to run as a Democrat for Congress. He refused both times. In 1948, he campaigned for Truman and others who ran under the party banner. His experiences in college, time with General Electric (GE), and his term as president of the Screen Actors Guild, gave him unique practical knowledge and widespread public recognition, but to no particular end. He was beginning to recognize that his GE service and regular speechmaking had touched something deep inside of him, as well as others in his audience. He was so moved by the commitment of prominent actors in the Screen Actors Guild strike when he was president that he said, "My education was complete when I walked in the board room. . . . I saw it crammed with the famous men of the business [and] I knew that I was beginning to find the rest of me."[1] The recently completed man moved into politics. As the fifties began to slip away, Ronald Reagan was part of a youth movement of World War II veterans making their way to the political dais.

America was undergoing an important structural change in its cultural life during the postwar era, and even though he didn't realize it at the time, Ronald Reagan was a beneficiary. It had always been a characteristic of the country that it paid little attention to formal rank, and instead respected someone who, for some reason or another—was able to achieve notoriety. Television was a great leveler, and made such people legends. The growth of TV meant that those who appeared in front of the cameras, though originally of less account for educational experience or accomplishment, became famous to millions overnight.

Ronald Reagan was one of these fortunate individuals. He was a recognized conservative spokesman even though he was not especially well read on the subject, or elected to any prominent political office. One thing he had—conviction and it came across whenever he spoke. A prominent GE executive at the time said he was more in demand as a public speaker than anyone except Dwight D. Eisenhower. His meteoric rise was no accident. From the time Reagan arrived in Hollywood, his agent, Lew Wasserman, guided and protected him. Back in 1951, when his movie career was on the wane, Reagan used his influence as president of the Screen Actors Guild to secure an unprecedented agreement with Wasserman's company, Music Corporation of America (MCA) that gave the agency a blanket waiver to produce an unlimited number of television shows. The deal turned out to be a windfall for MCA that left it as the most powerful agency in Hollywood.[2] Reagan guaranteed Wasserman's position, and their friendship survived the actor's political conversion. In each election cycle Wasserman tapped his associates for millions of dollars in Democratic causes, but that never bothered Ronald Reagan.

In 1960, the universal political cry was for youth, and both Richard Nixon and John Kennedy fit the bill. The Republican Party asked Reagan to publicly support Nixon, and the actor offered to register as a member of the GOP to do just that. But given the national disparity in party registration in those years, nearly two to one in favor of the Democrats, he was encouraged to lead a "Democrats for Nixon" campaign instead. That election year he gave over 200 campaign speeches for Nixon. "I guess it was in 1960," he wrote in his autobiography, "that I completed my political journey from liberal Democrat to dedicated Republican."[3]

The political transformation came at a price. Reagan came to believe years later that his support for Nixon made him a liability at General Electric. He had already run into trouble with his sponsors when he included a diatribe against the Tennessee Valley Authority (TVA) in his election year speeches. The New Deal TVA project consumed millions of acres of land and millions of taxpayers' dollars, yet produced little electric power and left a region mired in poverty, still in poverty. For Reagan the policy was an example of well-meaning but ultimately failed government meddling. GE was approached by a federal official who threatened to pull $50 million in business unless Reagan ceased his caustic comments. "I am sorry you found out about that," he said to the GE chairman who conveyed the threat. "It's my problem and I've taken it on."[4] Reagan removed the TVA section from his speeches.

After squeaking out a win in 1960, the Kennedy administration and the Democrats responded to Reagan's heightened visibility. The AFL-CIO tagged him as an extremist and teachers opposed his speechmaking and appearance at educational venues. The new attorney general, Robert Kennedy, declared that "price fixing in the electrical industry is a major threat to democracy."[5] Several company executives at GE

Ronald Reagan at the General Electric Theater, 1954–1962. (Courtesy Ronald Reagan Presidential Library.)

were under federal indictment for price fixing, and a prosecutor in a related investigation was about to grill dozens of witnesses in another investigation. As he became more politically controversial, General Electric tried to steer Reagan back to promoting company goodwill. He would have none of it. Reagan told the executives that he was constantly getting requests to speak on political topics and would continue to do so. "There's no way that I could go out now to an audience that is expecting the type of thing I've been doing for the last eight years and suddenly stand up and start selling them electric toasters."[6]

The antitrust investigations at GE took a toll. After a blackout in New York City on June 13, 1961, the press accused GE of collusion, and the company's stock fell by a third.[7] Reagan's sponsors in the company, Lem Boulware and CEO Ralph Cordiner, had long since retired. At the same time, *General Electric Theatre* was losing its appeal to the audience. In the early days of television, broadcast executives did not understand programming and the life span of network shows in a way that they would later. *GE Theatre* was replaced by the popular *Bonanza* as the top-rated show in the Sunday night lineup. GE wanted to hang onto the show, but change the format, while Reagan wanted to keep the format as it was. He especially wanted to stay on television. The only solution was to cancel the program, and that is what GE did in 1962. Reagan signed on as host of another show, *Death Valley Days*, with a similar format, but soon it faded as well.

When he first appeared on the political hustings in California in 1960, Reagan preached to the ideological choir. Southern California was a hotbed of anticommunist feeling and unbridled capitalist expansion. While Reagan may have finally registered as a Republican in 1962, he had been a conservative for much longer than that. The official act of political conversion occurred in the course of his campaigning for Richard Nixon as governor. In a prelude of things to come, Reagan went on television to endorse the former GOP presidential candidate. "Can you possibly believe that a man like Dwight David Eisenhower . . . whose love of country is beyond question, could have been closely associated with Richard Nixon, as he was for eight years, and now recommend him for high office, as he is doing, if he did not believe him worthy to serve?"[8] Nixon's defeat left Reagan as the most visible spokesperson for California conservatives.

In 1964, Ronald Reagan made his last movie, *The Killers*, based on an Ernest Hemingway short story. He was cast as a sadistic, unrepentant villain in the film who had to slap actress Angie Dickinson hard on the face in one scene. The movie bombed for a number of reasons, but one was clearly that the public could not accept Ronald Reagan as a rogue character. "A lot of people . . . I'm told, kept waiting for me to turn out to be a good guy in the end and dispatch the villains in the last reel, because that's how they had always seen me before. But I didn't."[9] For once, a failed picture did not mean financial despair, he was well enough off financially that he could spend his time at the ranch, chopping wood and riding his favorite horse, a dapple gray named "Nancy D."

From the time he went on the mashed potato circuit, making political speeches, Reagan repeatedly told his audiences that he had no intention of becoming a fulltime politician. His father-in-law, Dr. Loyal Davis, who lived in Chicago and knew the squalor of machine politics in that city, warned him to keep away. Reagan did not have to be convinced, he was uninterested in the wholesale commitment a campaign demanded and resented the intrusion into his privacy that a political career required. His resume was far from ideal: he was divorced in a time when it was a political liability; made his fortune in Hollywood, which conservatives despised; and he lived in California, which was no cradle of traditional values. What he did have going for him was something that would later become known as name identification. That, and a firm conviction that as a conservative he needed to do something about the problems he saw in the country, moved him to political action.

In 1962 he campaigned not just for Richard Nixon in the state gubernatorial race, but also for John Rousselot, the incumbent GOP congressman from southern California. Rousselot was defeated when his opponent used the candidate's membership in the John Birch Society as an issue in the race. The "Birchers," as they were called at the time, were antitotalitarian, particularly antisocialist and anticommunist. They wanted to limit the powers of government and defend the original intent of the U.S. Constitution, which they saw as based on Christian principles. They opposed collectivism, including wealth redistribution, economic interventionism, socialism, communism, and fascism. Reagan was unembarrassed by the revelation of Rousselot's membership. He shared a confidence in an American mission to the world, which blended with his mother's religious teaching and the patriotism of Hollywood's movies, and left him unapologetic about the national legacy. Despite his support for Nixon, Reagan was really closer to another emerging figure in American politics: Barry Goldwater.

"For conservatives, the sixties was the decade not of John F. Kennedy but of Barry Goldwater."[10] The ideological champion of conservatives was a true son of the West, who embraced freedom and independence as naturally as the Democrats did government expansion. The Arizona senator had no desire for higher office, and that made him more appealing. Senator Goldwater spoke of religion, of family and community, of the value of hard work, and of freedom balanced with power—all of which was threatened by Soviet communism. In the late 1950s, the senator separated himself from the moderate wing of Eisenhower's affiliation, and rode off into a golden conservative ideological sunset. When John Kennedy was assassinated in November 1963, the way was cleared for someone of a traditional stripe to confront Lyndon Johnson in November. The Arizona senator became the first truly convicted conservative to be nominated for president since Calvin Coolidge in 1924.

The problem was that it was easier to win the Republican nomination than the general election that year. Early polls showed Goldwater down to John F. Kennedy by a margin of 60 to 36 percent, and then after the latter's assassination it was virtually impossible for the GOP nominee to win. The American people would never accept three presidents in a little more than one year, and Goldwater knew his chances were next to impossible when he began. As a result, he engaged in an ideological campaign against liberal values, Soviet appeasement, and welfare state liberalism offering "a choice not an echo."[11] Internal polls showed that Americans were uninterested and even afraid of the blunt speech and picture of a gunslinger that Goldwater portrayed.

Ronald Reagan presented a different image. He met Goldwater in the early 1950s on a visit to Nancy's parents in Phoenix. The two men shared conservative values, but little else. Goldwater was the son of a millionaire, blunt and controversial; while Reagan came from poverty, was self-made and the ultimate people pleaser. Despite their personal differences, they shared a passionate interest in the country's future.

"I said America was at a crossroads," wrote Reagan years later. "We had a choice of either continuing on this path or fighting to reclaim the liberties being taken from us."[12] Reagan went on the stump for Goldwater. He gave essentially the same speech he had given before GE audiences, but this time it was at GOP fundraisers and rallies. After one such appearance before a frisky Republican audience, several prominent partisans in the audience asked Reagan if he would repeat his remarks on national television. "Sure," he replied, "if you think it would do any good."[13]

It was Walter Knott, the proprietor of Knott's Berry Farm in California, who called the Republican National Committee and asked what it would cost to run Reagan's message for the GOP nominee on national television. Knott then called the "Kitchen Cabinet" and raised the money.[14] At the time, Goldwater trailed badly in the polls, and the October speech appeared to be a last ditch effort to revive a failing effort. The speech was dubbed "A Time for Choosing," with the aim of drawing a partisan contrast between the two presidential candidates. It could just as easily have been called the "Collective Speeches of Ronald Reagan." It emphasized the differences between free enterprise and big government, and even borrowed language from FDR, though without attribution.

> You and I have a rendezvous with destiny. We can preserve for our children this last best hope for man on earth, or we can sentence them to take the first step into a thousand years of darkness. If we fail, at least let our children and our children's children say of us we justified our brief moment here. We did all that could be done.[15]

Reagan's filmed broadcast on October 27, 1964, was a hit with conservatives, and ultimately raised $8 million for the campaign; but it could not prevent Goldwater's landslide defeat. Lyndon Johnson carried 44 states, while the Republican candidate won 5 in the Deep South and his home state of Arizona. For conservatives discouraged about the Goldwater campaign, the Reagan speech was a highlight.

Political analysts David Broder and Stephen Hess called the address "the most successful national political debut since William Jennings Bryan electrified the 1896 Democratic convention," with his famous "Cross of Gold" address.[16] Shortly after the election, the same group of conservative activists who raised money for the broadcast prevailed on Reagan to run as a Republican candidate for the California governorship. The group, which would come to be known as Reagan's "Kitchen Cabinet," or "Friends of Ronald Reagan," included Holmes P. Tuttle, an auto dealer in Los Angeles; Italian-born entrepreneur, Henry Salvatori, who was in oil exploration; A. C. "Cy" Rubel, the head of Union Oil; Justin Dart, an heir to the Walgreen's drugstore chain; Leonard Firestone, son of the founder of the tire company; and Jacqueline Hume, a food processor whose wealth stemmed from processing dried onions, garlic, and potatoes. Despite the power and persuasiveness of the group, Reagan was initially reluctant: "After I heard what they said, I almost laughed them out of the house. . . . I said, in effect: 'You're out of your mind.'"[17] But they weren't kidding. They kept up the pressure, suggesting that there was no one else who could unite the Republicans and at the same time defeat the Democratic incumbent, Pat Brown.

The California Republican Party, of which Reagan was summoned as leader, resembled a family in divorce court. In 1954, Republicans held both senate seats, the governorship and substantial majorities in both houses of the legislature. Then a split between Senator William Knowland and Governor Goodwin Knight opened the door for big labor to back Democrat Pat Brown and gain control of the legislature in 1958. Brown was reelected in 1962, and the self-consuming fratricide in the GOP continued in the wake of the Nixon defeat for governor and the Goldwater presidential debacle. The Republicans suffered from a lack of common purpose and a vision to capture voters. The state residents seemed too busy to be occupied with political effects.

California in 1965 had a growing economy. Had it been an independent nation, the state would have ranked fifth among Western industrialized nations. Each year tens of thousands of newcomers flocked to the Golden State, and the budget for public amenities reflected the demographic realities of the growth. After the realignment of the Brown gubernatorial election, the state gave into the promises of liberal politicians who believed it was able to pay for a variety of services: parks, colleges and universities, retirement programs for state workers, welfare, medical aid, unemployment, and water storage facilities. Governor

Brown once said that Lyndon Johnson's Great Society was a reality, and it was called "California."[18]

Despite his detractors, Reagan was an ideal candidate for a statewide race. He lived in the more populous southern half of the state where his name recognition was high because of his Hollywood career. He had unusual charm and voter appeal, on the stump he was very clear and was popular with dedicated conservatives who worked hard for Goldwater and were looking for a new champion. In fact, the remnants of the 1964 calamity were a ready-made organization, frustrated and angry. As a former Democrat, Reagan had appeal across party lines, and—most importantly—he was a master of the vital television medium. According to polls at the time, he was already known to 97 percent of the California electorate.[19]

On the last day of 1965, Reagan agreed to run. In part, he wanted to prove to skeptics that the conservative sentiments of everyday voters were more widespread than the vote for Goldwater indicated. In a *National Review* article written a month after the 1964 election, he declared that "all of the landslide majority did not vote against the conservative philosophy, they voted against the false image our liberal opponents successfully mounted."[20] Holmes Tuttle, along with the other "Friends of Reagan," immediately hired the best political firm in the state—Stuart Spencer and William Roberts—to run the campaign.

When the two experienced political hands met their client, they were impressed. "We found him to be an open and candid person, easy to talk with, and a good listener," said Roberts.[21] Reagan had what one of them called a "moral core," but he lacked a thorough knowledge of state issues. Two behavioral scientists, Stanley Plog and Kenneth Holden, worked with Reagan to isolate some 17 issues into a coherent philosophical framework to which he could always refer when questioned on the stump. "Reagan [had] the most integrated political philosophy that I've seen in anyone. . . . Everything for him flows from the Constitution."[22] Soon some eight briefing books appeared, covering topics from agriculture to pollution, taxes to water use, and the candidate amazed his handlers with how quickly he assimilated facts and phrases on note cards. "I drove up and down the length and breadth of California for six months, commuting to luncheon and dinner meetings from San Diego at the southern border all the way to the coastal fishing villages."[23]

The star mystique helped. Reagan was more comfortable with reporters than most conservative Republicans. He shook their hands and eagerly answered questions they asked about his political positions, as well as his days in Hollywood. But his celebrity status was also his greatest weakness in that many voters did not take him seriously. His main primary opponent was moderate GOP George Christopher, a former mayor of San Francisco. He regarded Reagan as something of a political amateur who could not run against an experienced opponent with government experience. Christopher became the first, of many, to underestimate the competition. The veteran politician and former mayor turned out to be poorly organized, and the Spencer—Roberts team took advantage of his ineptitude.

Christopher was hindered, and Reagan helped by a quasi-scriptural admonition propounded by the previous Republican State Party Chairman, Gaylord Parkinson: "Thou shall not speak ill of any fellow Republican." Parkinson called this the "11th Commandment," and he propounded it after the 1964 Goldwater–Rockefeller primary campaign. The strategy shackled Christopher and prevented him from attacking Reagan for the latter's inexperience and mistakes in campaign appearances. Those gaffes came because Reagan was ill and in daily pain, but refused to slow down as election day appeared. In February 1966, he caught the flu, and the aftereffects lasted a year and a half. He became exhausted on the campaign trail and developed a urinary infection that led to prostate problems and finally, in 1967, to surgery. All these facts were kept from the press, who declared in print that Reagan was a "lazy campaigner."

His exhaustion led to mistakes, including a famous one in March 1966, in which he stated that California needed a common sense approach to environmental matters like preserving redwoods. "I mean if you've looked at a hundred thousand acres or so of trees—you know, a tree is a tree, how many more do you need to look at?"[24] His opponent took this as yet another example of Republican indifference to the needs of natural preservation. Even with these missteps, the Reagan campaign rolled to victory. In the June 7, 1966, Republican primary, Reagan received 65 percent of the vote. His opponent, incumbent governor Pat Brown, won the Democratic primary by 52 percent.[25]

The fall contest was destined to be a classic, and the tone was set early. When Pat Brown commissioned a television commercial in which he told a group of small children, "I'm running against an actor, and you know who killed Abe Lincoln don't you?"[26] Brown believed that he could easily defeat Reagan, and win a third term as governor, but the political winds were blowing against the Democrats two years after Lyndon Johnson's landslide win. Working class Democrats were having second thoughts about civil rights legislation that led to riots and campus unrest. For his part, Ronald Reagan welcomed Republicans of all stripes, along with a host of Independents and disaffected Democrats, aboard his campaign bus. In speech after speech, Reagan hit the Brown administration about high taxes, uncontrolled spending, the radicals at the University of California at Berkley, and the need for accountability in government.

Years after the election, Brown explained to a reporter that he had lost his zest for politics: "I think I was tired of the job."[27] The fact was that the voters were tired of Pat Brown and his administration. "He had been in office for an eventful eight years, and people blamed him for every complaint they had against government."[28] Reagan's inexperience was an asset instead of a liability. He demonstrated a talent that would baffle his liberal opponents who wanted to attack him for years to come. Conservatives usually presented their ideas in pessimistic, dour terms and seemed to relish discussing a bleak future. Reagan took a different approach. He liked to sketch an optimistic vision of California blossoming under the freedom that limited government and free markets produced.

On the stump, Reagan was flexible and reasonable, the very opposite of the Goldwater stereotype of rigid orthodoxy. The protests on university campuses proved to be a potent issue for the challenger. The counterculture was just emerging on campuses, and Reagan was able to associate the protests with Brown's permissive governance. Before audiences, he said hippies "act like Tarzan, look like Jane and smell like Cheetah."[29] What's more, Reagan was able to rise to the occasion for big events. In debates, he was relaxed and humorous; in press conferences, he engaged the press with stories and joking exchanges; in question and answer formats, he reached the audience quickly with his knowledge of facts. By October, Reagan had such a commanding

Ronald and Nancy Reagan at the victory celebration for California Governor at the Biltmore Hotel in Los Angeles on November 8, 1966. (Courtesy Ronald Reagan Presidential Library.)

lead in the polls that even the skeptics had to admit that they had underestimated him.

On the last day of the campaign, Reagan held airport rallies in six cities. Four days earlier he had been cheered by thousands in San Francisco, Brown's hometown. The candidate warned about overconfidence and urged his supporters to get out in force. "Pat Brown was one of those liberals who thought all the world's problems could be solved by throwing taxpayers' money at them, and in a way he made the campaign easier for me."[30] The last polls showed Reagan ahead by five or six points, which would translate into a 500,000 vote plurality. Reagan won by a million votes, and 15 percentage points: 57 to 42 percent. What's more, he had coattails. Republicans won every major state office but one, reduced the Democratic edge in the assembly and state senate to razor-thin margins, and picked up three seats in the U.S. House of Representatives. However, he was about to be reminded of the old saw: "Be careful what you wish for."

NOTES

1. Ronald Reagan, *Where's the Rest of Me?* (New York: Karz, 1981), p. 154.

2. Lou Cannon, *Governor Reagan: His Rise to Power* (New York: PublicAffairs, 2003), p. 112.

3. Ronald Reagan, *An American Life* (New York: Simon and Schuster, 1990), p. 132.

4. Reagan, *Where's the Rest of Me?*, p. 269.

5. Thomas W. Evans, *The Education of Ronald Reagan* (New York: Columbia University Press, 2006), p. 166.

6. Cannon, *Governor Reagan*, p. 112.

7. Evans, *Education of Ronald Reagan*, p. 162.

8. Edmund Morris, *Dutch* (New York: Random House, 1999), p. 327.

9. Reagan, *An American Life*, p. 138.

10. Lee Edwards, *The Conservative Revolution* (New York: Free Press, 1999), p. 101.

11. Ibid., p. 131.

12. Reagan, *An American Life*, p. 139.

13. Edwards, *Conservative Revolution*, p. 134.

14. Paul Kengor, *God and Ronald Reagan: A Spiritual Life* (New York: HarperCollins, 2004), p. 110.

15. Ronald Reagan, "A Time for Choosing," *Human Events*, November 28, 1964, pp. 8–9.

16. Stephen Hess and David Broder, *The Republican Establishment* (New York: Harper and Row, 1967), pp. 253–254.

17. Reagan, *An American Life*, p. 144.

18. Edwards, *Conservative Revolution*, p. 143.

19. Ibid., p. 144.

20. Ronald Reagan, "The Republican Party," *National Review*, December 1, 1964, p. 105.

21. Cannon, *Governor Reagan*, p. 135.

22. Morris, *Dutch*, p. 342.

23. Reagan, *An American Life*, p. 146.

24. Cannon, *Governor Reagan*, p. 177.

25. Ibid., p. 148.

26. Reagan, *An American Life*, p. 149.

27. Cannon, *Governor Reagan*, p. 150.

28. William E. Pemberton, *Exit with Honor* (New York: M.E. Sharpe, 1998), p. 68.

29. Ibid., p. 69.

30. Reagan, *An American Life*, p. 153.

Chapter 5

GOVERNOR

A peculiar tragedy sometimes accompanies winners of landslide elections in American politics: they take the outcome to mean more than it does. By saying an election victory is the voter's mandate for the candidate's agenda, winners run the risk of overreaching and ending up in the political wilderness. At the presidential level, this happened to both Lyndon Johnson in 1964, and Richard Nixon in 1972. It did not happen to Ronald Reagan in California for one simple reason: "When I gave in to the appeals to run for governor," wrote Reagan years later, "I had never given much thought to the possibility I might win."[1] Others did. His victory was national news, and he made the cover of *Time* magazine with his triumph.

Once elected, Reagan had just two months to rearrange his affairs and gather an administration to move to Sacramento. To friends in Hollywood he quipped that he "had never played a governor" in either television or in the movies, but he was about to do so on one of the biggest stages in the country. The task of organizing the new administration fell to two aides, working with a third, who would stay with Reagan for years. Franklyn "Lyn" Nofziger, a former newspaper reporter was recruited to the campaign as press secretary. One biographer described him as "shapeless, chuckling, squinty and wheezing over his Mickey Mouse Tie," but he was peerless when it came to strategy.[2] The group worked furiously to attract young men, most were in their forties, pro-business attorneys and corporate executives to head key agencies and departments. The most surprising and controversial find was Casper Weinberger, a San Francisco attorney with a distinguished resume whose one shortcoming was his support of Nelson Rockefeller against Barry Goldwater in 1964. That was enough for the "Kitchen Cabinet" advisors who assisted Reagan in staffing; they rejected his appointment. Weinberger would play a large part in this, and subsequent, Reagan administrations, but his initial foray as chief financial officer was delayed for a time.

"Dutch" Reagan became the 33rd governor of California at 14 minutes after midnight on January 2, 1967. He took the oath on a 400-year-old Bible brought to the state by Father Junipero Serra, who originally founded a string of missions across California.[3] The midnight ceremony was not for showmanship. Reagan was upset by the number of last minute judicial appointments made by his predecessor, so he wanted to take the reins of power as soon as possible to prevent any more. He soon found out that what the Pat Brown legacy bequeathed to him was greater than any midnight judges because the state faced a dramatic budget shortfall.

The Reagan campaign had repeatedly emphasized the failed leadership of the Democratic incumbent, but no one in the challenger's camp realized just how bad the situation was until the inauguration. "Now suddenly the state faced its worst financial crisis since the Depression, and it was up to me, as the new governor, to end it."[4] California was spending $1 million a day over the revenues it took in. In response, Reagan proposed an immediate budget cut of 10 percent, later reduced to 8.5 percent. He sold Pat Brown's state-owned airplane, slashed out-of-state travel by state employees, cancelled construction projects and stopped buying new automobiles and trucks for state agencies. "The symbol of our flag is a Golden Bear," he quipped, "it is not a cow to be milked."[5] But cutting government spending was not enough. The new governor had to do the unthinkable—accept a tax increase. No amount of budget reductions could bridge the gap to balance California's budget in 1967, but "Reagan's proposal had the distinction of being the largest tax hike ever proposed . . . [with] tax increases on sales, personal income, banks and corporations, insurance companies, liquor and cigarettes."[6] When it passed the legislature the total price was over $1 billion, with the state budget at $5.06 billion.

Why a tax increase from a committed conservative opposed to government growth and spending? Reagan said two days after his inauguration that he did not want to wait "until everyone forgets that we did not cause the problem—we only inherited it."[7] No matter how the tax increase came to his desk, it was his to wear. The positive side of the tax deal was that Reagan earned the reputation of a responsible executive who refused to let ideology interfere with effective government. The down side was that "gov-mint," as he used to call it, received a subsidy at the expense of the private sector. The former outshone the latter. He immediately gained the reputation of being flexible when he had to be, by accepting the tax package and negotiating a compromise on a Fair Housing Act opposed by the Republican base.

Reagan's practical style was rooted in the times. In the years when he governed the state, California was an attractive dreamland of highways and opportunity that welcomed a thousand residents a day. State government accommodated the increase, and even came to expect it. While developers turned orange groves into suburbs and shopping centers, government poured vast sums of money into education, aqueducts and technological and cultural centers that made it fashionable to call California a "nation-state." All the progress rebounded in a kind of cultural licentiousness that threatened the old order that was Ronald Reagan's political base. People in California were trend setters, they had more income, cars, pleasure boats, parks, beaches, patios, color television sets, and parades than those in other states. Everything was "new, fresh and improved," since Californians divorced more, drank more, smoked more, played harder, and popped more pills than other Americans. They dived into the future without a thought about the past. It was incongruous that in all the permissiveness, Ronald Reagan represented the new politics of old values.

The adversary in the fight he waged was the huge and expensive university system, with 10 universities, 19 state colleges, and 85 junior colleges. They became, beginning in 1967, the platform for antiwar protests, teach-ins, love-ins, and social experimentation the likes of which the country had never seen. Transparent and see-through dresses joined miniskirts and naked midriffs as fashion styles, and students at "Cal" flaunted convention in lifestyles as well as leading the social revolution. Drugs were as commonplace as the cigarettes of an earlier era. Undergraduates took to demonstrating about anything, and then everything. One told a political reporter, "I was a political virgin, but I was raped on the steps of city hall."[8]

The new governor had to deal with the deflowered stepchildren of the sixties, and he wasted little time in addressing them. "In all the sound and fury at Berkeley, one voice is missing, and it is the voice of those who built the university and pay the entire cost of its operation."[9] The triggering event was Reagan's demand that the University of California system reduce its appropriations request by 15 percent in the 1967–1968 budget year. This was in line with the "cut, squeeze and trim" policy applied throughout state government. What particularly upset University of California (UC) president Clark Kerr was a further proposal that UC at Berkeley start charging tuition. The idea that the Great Society should give students something for nothing was sacred, and Kerr froze admissions, predicted that the best professors would leave and warned that several branch campuses would have to close. The governor didn't budge. Reagan was willing to allow Chancellor Kerr to become a symbol of what he knew average Californians believed; that university folk were intellectually arrogant and accustomed to being coddled. The governor was not about to give into student indulgences or the administrators who tolerated them. On January 20, 1967, the Board of Regents, Reagan included, fired Clark Kerr when he demanded a vote of confidence.

Student unrest was synonymous with the Berkeley campus, but it spread to others as well, and the governor promised that students would be able to get an education and be protected "by bayonets if necessary." In Berkeley alone there were eight bombings and the discovery of thousands of sticks of dynamite along with 200 firearms. His response was clear and simple to all involved: "obey the rules or get out." Reagan sent the National Guard in to restore order on any campus whenever necessary, and his popularity soared whenever he stood up to the protestors. Polls in early 1969 showed that 78 percent of Californians thought Reagan was doing a good or fair job; only 15 percent thought he was doing poorly.[10]

Reagan enjoyed being governor, and he was good at the job. His lack of experience was actually a plus, because he learned as he went along and changed long-established policies that he disliked. In the first year mistakes were made, but they weren't fatal. "During the first year or two in Sacramento, I kept my distance from legislators," he wrote. "When I began entering into the give and take of legislative bargaining . . . a lot of the most radical conservatives who had supported me during the election didn't like it."[11] He had a hands-off management style that meant he delegated authority. Reagan believed in hiring people of proven ability who used their own expertise without interference from him. He was often uninformed on the specifics of policy, but that didn't bother him. A motto on his desk read: "There's no limit to what a man can do or where he can go if he doesn't mind who gets the credit."[12] His aides were often surprised to find out how much authority they had to do their jobs. Legislative assistants worked to improve relations with lawmakers, and the governor played the role of genial celebrity host.

In Reagan's first year in office, political scientist James Q. Wilson wrote an essay in *Commentary* titled "Reagan Country."[13] In the article Wilson declared that the political constituency that elected Reagan in California was a microcosm of what America was becoming. It was neither small-town nor urban, but suburban, homogeneous communities of detached homes and lawns and pools linked by highways to shopping centers and volunteer community associations. The people who lived in these communities were middle class, and showed common moral convictions about things like marriage, family, and economics. Unlike ethnically varied Easterners who shared an attachment to place, the inhabitants of "Reagan Country" shared "a strong, socially reinforced commitment to property." The populist conservatives valued capitalism and the future. Wilson said that the California constituency was identical to emergent neighborhoods across the South, Midwest, and Southwest, and Reagan would be a popular national candidate because he would not let government interfere with the phenomena of their faith: free, developmental, future-oriented growth.

The former actor's outspoken convictions and public visibility made him a marked man, the target of protestors and dissenters. He regularly acknowledged the prayers of his supporters, and even credited them with healing him of ulcers.[14] At the peak of campus unrest, he was the target of an aborted attempt to throw a Molotov cocktail explosive in his bedroom window. In public events admirers pushed forward, and protestors often crowded the governor as well, many times the latter chanted criticisms and threatened retaliation. At one rally, Reagan left the event after a suspicious-looking character had asked officials about the governor's schedule and his plans for leaving the venue. Reagan looked out the limousine window to see the man bent over the hood of a car explaining, "No, no, no, you fellows have it all wrong. I just wanted to *see* the son of a bitch."[15]

His greatest embarrassments, and later regrets, came from two social issues that followed him the rest of his life. In 1967, abortion was discussed in whispers, and homosexuality never mentioned at all in polite company. The former became an issue when a liberal legislator introduced an abortion bill to allow the procedure in cases of rape or incest, or when a doctor deemed the birth was likely to impair the physical or mental health of the mother, or when there was "substantial risk" that the child would be born deformed. The Catholic Church immediately opposed the bill, and flooded legislative offices with mail. Their reasoning, based on Christian tradition and seen in the birth of Jesus himself, was that children were a gift from God and the parents did not have the right to halt divine offerings. The issue divided Reagan's aides, the Kitchen Cabinet, and even his own household. Nancy Reagan, and her father Dr. Loyal Davis, favored liberalization of abortion laws. The abortion bill was foreign territory for Reagan, and neither his doctrines nor his staff offered a compass to guide him. When the bill reached his desk, he reluctantly signed it.

As abortion grew into a national scandal, it turned out to be one of the things Reagan regretted most about his governorship. The act of 1967 did what antiabortionists feared. Doctors broadly interpreted the "mental health" and "substantial risk" provisions to allow the procedure under the justification of convenience. When the law took effect, there were only 518 legal abortions in California; the year Reagan won the presidency, there were 199,089 legal abortions in state hospitals and clinics.[16] As abortion expanded exponentially, Reagan claimed that physicians abused the "loopholes of the law," especially the one about the "mental health" of the mother, to justify using the procedure for birth control. Reagan came to regret virtually every aspect of this law, and wrote in retrospect in 1983 that "the right to life is a cornerstone of all sound government."[17]

In his first year in office, Reagan also had to cope with what became known as the "homosexual scandal." One of the new governor's aides, Phil Battaglia, who was a former student body president at the University of Southern California, was also renowned as an executive secretary for the chief executive, and charged with the supervision of 87 members of the gubernatorial staff. He came in for criticism from other top members of the Reagan advising team, who set out to bring down Battaglia. The motivation for the coup was not especially opposition to homosexuality, theirs was a more prevalent emotion: jealousy. Lyn Nofziger, and other aides, resented Battaglia's liberal influence in policy issues over the governor. In August 1967, 11 aides descended on the governor when he was recovering from prostate surgery in San Diego and presented evidence of improper behavior on behalf of the executive secretary. Reagan turned pale when confronted with the evidence and asked, "What do we do now?"

It was decided that several people would have to go. In 1967 practicing homosexuals were viewed by the public as a liability for established politicians. Reagan's chief fundraiser, Holmes Tuttle, and another member of the Kitchen Cabinet, Henry Salvatori, asked Battaglia and another aide to resign. They obliged, and the governor clamped a lid on the story. Then, in a September "Periscope" column in *Newsweek*, the word popped up that a "top GOP presidential prospect," had a "potentially sordid scandal on his hands." The full story finally broke on October 31, 1967, in a column by Drew Pearson. The critique in the newspaper column was between the way President Johnson handled a similar problem, with immediate dismissals, as compared to Reagan's delay in doing something.[18]

The governor was so incensed that he immediately called a press conference. Reagan's first impulse when challenged was to always confront the issue at hand; he had great confidence in his personal ability to mute any scandal by a personal appearance. "He's a liar," Reagan declared as reporters shifted uncomfortably in their seats. The press had earlier written that the resignations were the result of an internal political power struggle, but now rumors were rife that the real reason was a sex scandal. In the end, the dispute blew over with a few

casualties. Battaglia returned to his law practice, Nofziger lost credibility with the press, and Reagan adopted an even more hands-off
management style.

After his first year in office, one reporter authored a story titled "The
Political Education of Ronald Reagan." "For much of that first year or
so, nothing went according to my plan," wrote "Dutch" Reagan in retrospect.[19] Despite the controversies of the first year, the new governor
remained personally popular. He kept his conservative base intact and
at the same time showed himself to be pragmatic when the situation
demanded it. His freshman year successes in office immediately ignited
speculation about his seeking the 1968 Republican presidential nomination.

The presidential election year was the one with Hong Kong flu and
the rock musical *Hair*, when Julie Nixon married David Eisenhower
and the American Civil Liberties Union decided to support draft evad-
ers. The style was sideburns and bell bottoms, and the young flashed
peace signs with two fingers to anyone they met. The division in the
country was generational, and the rising affluence of the time allowed
the young to create a popular lifestyle of their own. The central political focus of the youth was the Vietnam War, and demonstrations became a part of the counterculture of their lives. In the first six months
of 1968, there were 221 major demonstrations involving nearly 39,000
students on 101 American campuses. "Buildings were dynamited, college presidents and deans were roughed up, obscenities were painted on
walls and shouted at policemen."[20]

If 1968 was the "Year Everything Went Wrong," it was also the political debut of Ronald Reagan as enforcer, a role that seemed oddly out
of place on the political stage of the time. His first sortie into the presidential election revealed his surprising charm and equanimity, something that seemed to overcome the misgivings his audience had about
his conservative beliefs. He attracted the support of southern whites
and blue collar voters, and his rhetoric had the effect of bringing audiences to their feet in applause.[21] While other candidates complained
about protestors, Reagan tended to smother them with kindness. To
the frustration of his aides, he often met with opponents believing that
the meetings would help him win them to his point of view. With the
shadow of Barry Goldwater looming in his rearview mirror, Ronald

Reagan emerged as a genuine contender with conservative voters and independents alike.

The national press either ignored him or dismissed him. Throughout 1967 Michigan Governor George Romney was the presumed GOP frontrunner. Romney was regarded as a liberal Republican more acceptable to the electorate in the wake of the Goldwater debacle. For some, he was seen as a milder option to the more liberal and more personable New York Governor Nelson Rockefeller. The qualities that made Romney a successful automobile industry executive, for instance his tendency to explain his positions in detail, worked against him as a presidential candidate. He had difficulty being articulate and concise on any issue, and often rambled before the press. One reporter opined that he had added a key to his typewriter that said, "Romney later explained . . ." Conservatives longed for an alternative to the moderate stance of the leading contenders and began to sound out Reagan for a run. Like an actor facing an important audition, the California governor was reluctant to go for a role he might lose.[22] As one biographer put it, "Feels kinds premature fellows, I just don't think I'm ready."[23] Then, on August 31, 1967, Romney gave a taped interview with a Detroit television station in which he said he had "the greatest brainwashing that anybody can get" while on a visit to Vietnam. He then shifted to opposing the war effort in Southeast Asia. The queue of petitioners asking Reagan to enter the race became longer.

Reagan's reluctance to run for president aided Richard Nixon's effort to line up southern conservatives who had supported Goldwater in 1964. Despite all his indecision, Reagan was a far more appealing candidate than Nixon. The California governor was charismatic and self-confident, attracted huge crowds at fundraisers, and spoke clearly to the conservative GOP base. He believed in his ideas, while Nixon, despite his decency and generosity, had the reputation of a "ruthless political calculator."[24] On May 15, 1967, Reagan debated Robert F. Kennedy on CBS. The format allowed for people to question both participants from Europe and elsewhere around the globe. Reagan was clear, cool, and well informed, interrupting his opponents to correct their statistics and assumptions. The press verdict at the time, from sources like the *San Francisco Chronicle* and *Newsweek*, was that the governor bested the senator on the program that was mostly devoted to issues associated with the Vietnam War.[25] Reagan was able to deal with the issues and refute his questioners, while RFK seemed confused by the format and relied primarily on his personal popularity and charm. After the debate, Bobby Kennedy chastised his aides in harsh language for putting him opposite Reagan.

Reagan's aides believed their boss was destined to be president. "Funds had been coaxed out of Tuttle and Salvatori [Kitchen Cabinet members], a network of paid or pledged operatives established nationwide, and a secret campaign office opened in San Francisco."[26] The scheduler kept him on the road and in the air to give his campaign an air of inevitability. Even after Barry Goldwater committed to Nixon, allowing a host of conservatives to join the former vice president's presidential bandwagon, Reagan kept hammering away at Johnson's record and the president's morality gap on campaign promises.

The problem was not the president, but the times. "The American Flag, God, motherhood, knowledge, honor, modesty, chastity [and] simple honesty," had fallen out of favor.[27] The campuses of venerable learning institutions became disagreeable and even dangerous places. The only location more hazardous was in the public spotlight. After the assassination of Martin Luther King Jr. and Robert F. Kennedy, the country's mood turned violent. Virtually every noble principle in the American Constitution was up for revision. Nixon's remedy came on a campaign stop in Ohio, where a 13-year-old girl waved a sign that read, "Bring us Together." When Senator Strom Thurmond (R-NC) endorsed Nixon it appeared that unity, at least in the GOP, might happen. The steam went out of Reagan's campaign, but the governor's tireless political operatives refused to surrender. Behind the scenes they sounded out conservatives who had pledged their support for Nixon to see if they would switch after the first ballot if no one received a majority. Such was not the case. Nixon won on the first round of voting with 697 votes, more than enough to win, while Reagan finished behind Nelson Rockefeller for third with just 182 votes. "When Nixon was nominated, I was the most relieved person in the world . . . I knew I wasn't ready to be president."[28] The next day, Reagan encouraged the GOP faithful to support Nixon in the fall election.

Reagan's 1968 campaign proved invaluable for later efforts. On the stump he was peerless, but somehow his heart wasn't in the role all the time. He learned that a half-hearted campaign for president was really no campaign at all. Reagan and his aides garnered priceless experience in primaries and learned about delegate counting, party politics in the media swirl of a national campaign. In later years, he embraced the axiom that "defeats teach more than victories." For many conservative Republicans, their first acquaintance with the California governor was on this campaign, and it was an experience they would remember. "Reagan came out of Miami Beach a loser . . . But defeat had laid the groundwork for victory."[29]

As the sixties turned into the seventies, the mood of the country went from revolution to self-absorption. "In five years," said former hippie leader Abbie Hoffman, "from 1971 to 1975, I directly experienced est, gestlt therapy, bioenergetics, rolfing, massage, jogging, health foods, tai chi, Esalen, hypnotism, modern dance, meditation, Silva Mind Control, Arica, acupuncture, sex therapy, Reichian therapy, and More House—a smorgasbord course in New Consciousness."[30] California was the national haven for self-discovery, and the place where Governor Reagan won a second term in office.

The presidential campaign changed him. He went from a state executive to a statesman, as comfortable discussing the war in Vietnam as California water policy. In his reelection campaign he cranked up the rhetoric for conservative voters, but acted moderately when needed. For example, Reagan had a good record on environmental issues, especially when it came to preserving the state's wild rivers. He could work with legislators when he had to, and addressed problems forthrightly. He promised to make welfare reform the priority in the second term. The most surprising thing was that he ran for reelection by campaigning against government. "I can't explain it," said campaign manager Stuart Spencer, "I only know that it worked."[31]

On the hustings, Reagan still found voters suspicious of government and resentful of its expansion and bureaucratic delays. In a sense, his second campaign was an echo of "The Speech" he gave to General Electric employees, his national address on behalf of Barry Goldwater in 1964, and his military experience where he found government to be the problem, not the solution to the problem. Another part of Reagan's electoral success was accidental in that he was handed an issue by campus radicals, and able to exploit it before conservative audiences.

Events often played to his strength as a showman, with one-liners and off-the-cuff comments that deflated opponents and simultaneously made headlines. In an encounter at the Santa Barbara campus of the University of California, the governor returned to the regents meeting after a lunch break. The sidewalk was lined on both sides by students who stood in silent protest. "As Reagan reached the meeting room, he turned, put his fingers to his lips and said, 'Shhhhh.'" The students burst into laughter.[32] When a demonstrator approached his limousine yelling, "We are the future," Reagan took a piece of paper and scrawled a response he held up to the window: "I'll sell my bonds."[33]

Although student radicals were a minority on college campuses, they exerted a disproportionate and disruptive influence on the academic community as a whole. The center of the storm in California became San Francisco State College. Students had already launched tutorial programs in the surrounding black neighborhoods, and created an experimental college in which 1,500 students were enrolled in subjects ranging from black culture to guerilla warfare. The Black Students Union became the focus of the controversy when they deposed moderate and conservative students from positions of power and broke into the offices of the student newspaper.

In a subsequent demonstration on campus, the college president resigned and an outspoken conservative professor named S. I. Hayakawa was appointed in his place. Hayakawa was the child of Japanese-born Canadians, a world-class semanticist, a jazz critic, a fencer, and an excellent fisherman. When he stood up to the students who were striking on campus he described himself as "a hero to some and a son of a bitch to others."[34] To students he was the latter, but to voters he was the former. One thing was clear, at least he was consistent and knew what he was doing. Governor Reagan saw him as a champion, and backed him to the hilt. He regularly called out the California Highway Patrol to protect the universities from "criminal anarchists" and "revolutionaries," especially at San Francisco State.

In 1970 Reagan ran against Jesse Unruh, the Democratic leader of the legislature who coined the popular saying, "Money is the mother's milk of politics." Democrats had a natural allegiance in the state, given the permissive culture and the interest of the universities in social experimentation. Educators of all stripes, their faculty and students voted

Democratic, but general voters sided with Reagan. In the gubernatorial campaign, the incumbent ignored Unruh and attacked the New Left, Vietnam War protestors, and black power advocates. On the stump he described himself as a "citizen politician," opposite his opponents "professional politician" label. Unruh's strategy was to force Reagan, who ignored him, into a debate. As his Democratic opponent followed him around, making mistakes in his attacks and trying to force a confrontation, Reagan quipped to reporters: "His idea of debate obviously is cheap demagoguery."[35]

Reagan had already decided to make welfare reform the centerpiece of his reelection campaign. The incumbent governor repeatedly declared that California had 10 percent of the nation's people, and 16 percent of its welfare recipients. "Here in California," he warned, "nearly a million children are growing up in the stultifying atmosphere of programs that reward people for *not* working, programs that separate families and doom these children to repeat the cycle of their own adulthood."[36] Reagan argued that if left unchecked, welfare growth would force a huge tax increase by 1972. That was unacceptable, and he proposed a program to remove able-bodied recipients, and replace them with the "truly needy." Liberals described the "welfare reform" as a conservative war on needy children and their parents, but Reagan's rhetoric was persuasive and he overcame the shrill criticism of his opponents by calmly explaining his plans. By mid-October polls showed Regan leading Unruh by more than 10 points.

That was still not enough for his aides. California remained a trendsetting state, and most of the innovation was in social norms. A conservative was not safe in a state with a law against monkeys driving cars, and one forbidding women from going topless into restaurants. In the end, President Nixon came to the state to campaign for the governor, and Vice President Agnew came as well to attack the "radiclibs" (radical liberals) in the Democratic Party. As the demonstrators appeared with obscenities and heckling, the poll numbers for Reagan improved. William Safire, a journalist who covered Nixon at the time, described the campaign trip on behalf of the governor as "an orgy of generalized hate."[37] Reagan kept his cool throughout, and even trotted out a line that "President Dewey warned me not to be overconfident." The outcome in 1970 for the California governor was far different from that for the Republican presidential nominee in 1948. Ronald Reagan won a second term by a 53 percent to 45 percent margin, with minor candidates taking the remaining 2 percent. "I think the people had made it clear that they wanted the reforms to continue."[38]

The 1971 State of the State address was far different from the one Reagan delivered four years earlier. In the second address the incumbent appeared as a confident and experienced executive who asked the legislature to help him with fiscal matters and welfare reform. The governor's welfare plan called for 70 legislative and administrative changes to the state provisions, and he argued that only a full-scale overhaul could help the truly needy. The public response was favorable, with thousands of letters sent to Sacramento in favor of the plan. While the plan was being debated, President Nixon unveiled his Family Assistance Plan (FAP) in Washington. The FAP was characterized by the *Economist* magazine as a program that "may rank in importance with President Roosevelt's first proposal of a social security system in the mid 1930's."[39] The Family Assistance Program was more liberal than anything then in place in California, and more than what even the Democrats could imagine. The FAP proposed a more-government solution, when Reagan wanted far less government involvement.

Almost alone among prominent Republican officeholders, Ronald Reagan opposed the FAP. He told Congress that in California 1 out of every 12 persons was on welfare, and under FAP that figure would increase to one in every seven.[40] Above all, Reagan opposed the idea that the government should guarantee an income for all Americans. His aim was to reduce the number of people receiving aid, and keep government out of the provision of services, while Nixon's goals were the exact opposite.

Although his position was clear, Reagan moved to mute his criticism of the FAP. He realized that the Nixon administration needed no more public criticism and he argued that he was not against the spirit of Family Assistance. On the stump, Reagan fought hard for the welfare reform bill he had proposed for the Golden State. He pressured the legislature by setting up welfare reform committees in every county of the state. The General Assembly Speaker, Democrat Robert Moretti, kept the legislation bottled up in committee, but finally, in June 1971, the impasse was broken and a compromise reached. "Governor, I don't like you, and I know you don't like me, but we don't have to be in love to get something worked out around here."[41] Moretti recalled before the press that he was direct with the governor, but Reagan remembered the meeting differently, and the Speaker complaining that the "cards and letters" he received had influenced him to compromise. The Welfare Reform Act was generally regarded as a success; it reduced people on welfare and cut expenses by $1 billion. It also established the governor as someone with new ideas, conservative ones, for the problems at hand.

"Ronald Reagan reached the zenith of his governorship in 1972."[42] He had delivered property tax relief, welfare reform, school financing, saved and protected some of the state's wild rivers, and calmed the college campuses. In the presidential election Reagan emerged as a potent campaigner for the national ticket of Richard Nixon and Spiro Agnew. He wrote his own speeches and attacked the radicalization of the Democratic Party. Richard Nixon was resurgent that cycle, with a foreign policy peace initiative to China while at the same time playing tough with North Vietnam. Inflation was down, GNP rising, incomes up, taxes down, and the Democrats seemed intent on nominating George McGovern, who was equally zealous to give every American $1,000 from the public treasury. The Republicans carried California that election cycle by 1.2 million votes.

The only cloud in this halcyon sky happened in June, when a party of political burglars was arrested at the Democratic National Committee Headquarters in the Watergate Hotel in Washington. Reagan did not comment on the Watergate issue; he was busy enjoying the fruits of his labors in office. His popularity was reversed, when, in 1973, he overreached and suffered a rare political defeat. Proposition 1 was an initiative to write a complex tax reduction requirement into the state constitution. It seemed tailor-made for a conservative governor like Reagan, and would have galvanized his legacy for generations to come. The problem was that Proposition 1 was very complicated and not easily reduced to simple sound bite campaign phrases. Reagan worked for the initiative opposite fierce Democratic opposition. Polls showed that voters were confused about the measure and on election day it lost 54 percent to 46 percent. The governor remained popular in spite of the setback, and this defeat did not dent his legacy.

One reason for his success may have been the unfolding drama in Washington. In the words of one insightful journalist, "[Richard] Nixon seemed to accept many of the premises of his political opponents, acting more often to expand than to contract federal domestic programs."[43] The president presided over a divided nation, and his policies in Vietnam and domestically only served to widen the separation. The unraveling of the Watergate cover-up was a final act of a domestic political tragedy. It began in the courtroom of U.S. District Judge John Scirica in January of 1973, and quickly became the dominant political issue. The U.S. Senate set up a special Watergate committee at about the same time to investigate the scandal. Throughout 1973, the implications of the break-in became a national drama. "Television news, ill-suited to covering abstract issues, slow-moving national trends, and complex governmental matters, proved able to handle the concrete facts of burglary, cover-up, lying and betrayal."[44]

In 1974, two political calamities opened the path to the presidency for Ronald Reagan, though no one realized it at the time. The first one was on October 10, 1973, when Vice President Spiro T. Agnew resigned the second office under bribery and corruption charges. Had Agnew survived, he would have been very popular with the conservative movement but his absence left a void. Nixon's personal preference for a replacement was Texan John Connally, the former Democratic Texas governor turned Republican, but his hawkish views on Vietnam made him unacceptable to Senate liberals. The next two names were Nelson Rockefeller, the liberal GOP governor of New York, and Ronald Reagan, the darling of conservatives. Not surprisingly, Nixon went for a compromise candidate. The promotion of Gerald R. Ford to the office, and then the presidency itself, left the door open for a conservative champion to seize the party mantle. The second issue was Nixon's resignation on August 9, 1974, and Gerald Ford's subsequent pardon of him on September 8, 1974. Almost overnight Ford's approval ratings fell from 66 percent to 50 percent in the Gallup Poll, and he never fully recovered from this one decision.

Ronald Reagan watched the slow demise of the Nixon presidency from a distance. Gerald Ford's promotion from vice president came just as Reagan was leaving the governor's office, but he found the new president suspiciously moderate and even liberal. The Nixon years had been painful to watch, as much from spending and taxes with the growth of government as his personal failures. Nixon imposed controls over prices and incomes to counter inflationary effects, but the plan failed miserably. Reagan felt that his conservative, market-driven solutions would alleviate the nation's economic woes, but his instinct told him to wait and size up the field before attempting another run at the presidency.

In his eight years in office, Reagan made state government less costly, smaller, and more businesslike. He used his line-item veto authority 943 times, and was never overridden by the legislature. By tightening eligibility standards and eliminating loopholes, he reduced the welfare caseload and cut expenditures by hundreds of millions of dollars each year. Although many of his supporters wanted him to run for a third term, Reagan had accomplished most of what he wanted to do as governor, and left town after two terms.

NOTES

1. Ronald Reagan, *An American Life* (New York: Simon and Schuster, 1990), p. 155.

2. Edmund Morris, *Dutch* (New York: Random House, 1999), p. 355.

3. Lou Cannon, *Governor Reagan: His Rise to Power* (New York: PublicAffairs, 2003), p. 171.

4. Reagan, *An American Life*, p. 156.

5. William E. Pemberton, *Exit with Honor* (New York: M.E. Sharpe, 1998), p. 72.

6. Cannon, *Governor Reagan*, p. 194.

7. Reagan, *An American Life*, p. 157.

8. William Manchester, *The Glory and the Dream* (Boston: Little, Brown, 1974), p. 849.

9. Morris, *Dutch*, p. 343.

10. Pemberton, *Exit with Honor*, p. 74.

11. Reagan, *An American Life*, pp. 170–171.

12. Pemberton, *Exit with Honor*, p. 72.

13. James Q. Wilson, "Reagan Country: The Political Culture of Southern California," *Commentary*, May 1967.

14. Reagan, *An American Life*, p. 168.

15. Ibid., p. 174.

16. Cannon, *Governor Reagan*, p. 213.

17. Ronald Reagan, *Abortion and the Conscience of a Nation* (Nashville, TN: Thomas Nelson, 1983), p. 14.

18. Cannon, *Governor Reagan*, p. 248.

19. Reagan, *An American Life*, p. 166.

20. Manchester, *The Glory and the Dream*, pp. 1122–1131.

21. Michael Barone, *Our Country* (New York: Free Press, 1990), p. 442.

22. Stephen F. Hayward, *The Age of Reagan: The Conservative Counterrevolution, 1980–1989* (New York: Crown Forum, 2009), p. 166.

23. Morris, *Dutch*, p. 555.

24. Conrad Black, *Richard M. Nixon: A Life in Full* (New York: PublicAffairs, 2007), p. 276.

25. Lou Cannon, *Governor Reagan*, p. 260.

26. Morris, *Dutch*, p. 355.

27. Manchester, *The Glory and the Dream*, p. 1148.

28. Reagan, *An American Life*, p. 178.

29. Cannon, *Governor Reagan*, p. 270.

30. Christopher Lasch, *The Culture of Narcissism* (New York: W. W. Norton, 1978), p. 14.

31. Pemberton, *Exit with Honor*, p. 78.

32. Cannon, *Governor Reagan*, p. 285.

33. Ibid.

34. Ibid., p. 290.

35. Ibid., p. 342.

36. Morris, *Dutch*, p. 368.

37. William Safire, *Before the Fall* (New York: Doubleday, 1975), p. 328.

38. Reagan, *An American Life*, p. 185.

39. Hayward, *Age of Reagan*, p. 238.

40. Ibid., p. 241.

41. Pemberton, *Exit with Honor*, p. 79.

42. Cannon, *Governor Reagan*, p. 368.

43. Barone, *Our Country*, p. 487.

44. Ibid., p. 516.

Chapter 6

1976

By the summer of 1974, the Republican Party was in its death throes. The misfortune of the Watergate scandal opened a flood of opportunity for the majority party. "The Democratic party in Congress and in the states across the country was suddenly united under the leadership of men more consistently hostile to the politics which Richard Nixon represented for them than any Democratic leaders before."[1] Watergate eroded the liberal wing of the GOP, and demoralized conservatives. In the midterm elections that year, the largest number of new Representatives—92—in a generation were elected in the fall referendum. Democrats crossed the filibuster-proof 60-seat majority threshold in the Senate and picked up 49 seats in the House to hold a two-thirds majority. The new liberal majority campaigned on opposition to the Vietnam War, support for environmental causes, and hatred of Richard Nixon.

No Republican officeholder in the country defended the president more staunchly than Ronald Reagan. In May 1973, he said the Watergate conspirators were "not criminals at heart."[2] The governor rarely watched the televised hearings of the Senate Judiciary Committee, and privately likened the investigation to "a lynch mob." In a speech on February 12, 1974, he invoked the past to rally Republicans. "We in our party have too often been the victims of big city political machines voting tombstones, warehouses and empty lots against us in every election."[3] The words did no good. Republicans were demoralized after Watergate, and their party registration figures slipped to slightly more than half that of their Democratic rivals.[4]

Earlier, on December 6, 1973, the Senate and House confirmed Richard Nixon's appointment of Gerald Ford as vice president by votes of 92–3 and 387–35. Ford was the GOP heir apparent, and many in the Reagan circle accepted that the soon-to-be former governor was roadblocked for national office. Others were not so sure; Lyn Nofziger and Edwin Meese convened a group to explore Reagan's future options. The discussions were mostly inconclusive, but they created an informal organization of sorts that worked on Reagan's behalf.

In an assessment of Reagan's governorship, written just before he left office in Sacramento, the *Los Angeles Times* opined that "history probably will conclude that Reagan was a check-point, rather than a turning-point, in the basically liberal political direction of California."[5] Like many liberal assessments of conservative executives, this one was wrong. The Proposition 13 ballot initiative (1978) that limited property tax assessments was rooted in Ronald Reagan's support of Proposition 1, which failed at the ballot box. The belief in smaller government that led to the Prop 13 victory began in the governorship of Ronald Reagan. His accomplishments in office emboldened conservatives in California and nationwide. All this was seen in retrospect, at the time the demise of Richard Nixon was envisioned as the downfall of conservatism.

Republican misfortunes paved the path of opportunity for Ronald Reagan his whole political career. Richard Nixon's failed run for governor of California in 1962 left the office in Democratic hands, and gave Reagan an opening four years later. Barry Goldwater's landslide loss in 1964 provided the stage for Reagan's introduction to a national audience. In 1974, Nixon's complicity in the Watergate cover-up brought media attention to the California governor in his eighth, and final, year in office. The resignation of the president on August 9, 1974, placed an unelected man in the Oval Office, and his subsequent pardon of Nixon increased talk of a Reagan candidacy.

The presumed candidate was not interested. On January 3, 1975, Ronald Reagan ruefully handed the leadership of California over to

Jerry Brown, the son of his predecessor. The now former governor could hardly wait to get out of Sacramento. "Nancy and I purchased a piece of land in an isolated rural area of Santa Barbara, planning to make it our ranch-hideaway once I left office."[6] The ranch, which covered 688 acres, was dubbed Rancho del Cielo, the "Ranch in the Sky," by the new owner. The land was 2,000 feet above sea level in a big rolling range of mountains. It was a place he could go for peace, physical movement and thoughtfulness. The ex-governor had always loved the outdoors as an athlete, college leader, actor, and spokesman, he only wanted to sink fence posts in the soil of the Santa Ynez Mountains.

To that end, Reagan politely turned down an invitation from President Ford to become Secretary of Education, and continued to work on the building of his ranch. It was little more than an adobe shack and overgrown paths, but it offered the things that the ex-governor prized: elevation, seclusion, and the freedom to ride in any direction. After the purchase, Reagan lacked funds for construction of the house and improvements to the property. He had to do the work himself, and it was a task he relished. So, while he cut down trees, dredged ponds, fixed roofs and poured concrete, he joked that he did not care to ever see an executive desk again. "Yet, hardly a day passed when someone didn't call and ask me to make a run for the Republican nomination in 1976."[7]

Two of Reagan's most Washington-minded Sacramento aides, Michael Deaver and Peter Hannaford, opened a public relations agency in Westwood, Los Angeles. They had just one client: Ronald Reagan. The firm booked the former governor's speeches, sold his radio commentaries and distributed his syndicated newspaper columns. Within three months of leaving office, Reagan was making 8–10 speeches a month at an average fee of $5,000 per speech. His columns appeared in 174 newspapers, and his commentaries aired on more than 200 radio stations.[8] His estimated income was $800,000 per year, and he was having the time of his life.

With unprecedented public visibility, and a watchful public awaiting his decision, the ex-governor was maddeningly evasive about making a run for the nation's highest office. Lou Cannon, his best biographer who interviewed him during this time, said that Reagan saw himself as a kind of "watchdog who would carefully eye the Ford administration for signs of ideological defection."[9] None of this sat very well with his aides, who knew that a presidential campaign required months of planning and fundraising. Then, in an incongruous twist, a little old lady did something no one close to the presumed candidate could do. On a commercial flight from San Francisco to Los Angeles a woman turned to him on the plane and forcefully insisted, "You gotta run for President!" Reagan brooded for a while, and then turned to Michael Deaver who was sitting next to him, "Mike, I guess I really do have to run." Deaver sat speechless in the seat as Reagan explained, "I've always been the player on the bench. It's time for me to get into the game."[10]

The references to his experiences with "Mac" McKenzie at Eureka College, and as George "The Gipper" Gipp in the movies, were enough for Deaver to swing into action. He immediately set out to recruit and expand the informal Nofziger Group and develop a campaign team. One of the potential staffers Reagan met with was John Sears, a former lawyer who was widely credited with running Richard Nixon's successful delegate gathering operation in 1968. Sears had the reputation of being a straight shooter with candidates, and he believed that if Ford inherited the presidency, then Reagan should seek the Republican nomination against him in the primaries.

At the time it was a heretical notion. More than any president in the 20th century, Gerald Ford was in office because of his integrity and trustworthiness. His peers in Congress supported him after the Nixon resignation because he told the truth and kept his word. In his first 30 days in office, Ford worked diligently to restore confidence in the government. The press followed his children like celebrities, and lauded him as a dependable and sturdy replacement. The problem was that Gerald Ford, for all his virtues, was not an exceptional politician. When he pardoned Nixon, he did so to get rid of the Watergate stain and save the country a painful trial over many months, the voters were not as forgiving. His presidential approval numbers took a hit, and Republicans took another one in the midterm elections.

The impetus for a Reagan presidential run intensified when Gerald Ford selected Nelson Rockefeller as his vice president on August 20, 1974. The decision was a political disaster, and intensified the call for Reagan to come out and challenge the president. The White House had informally polled the ex-governor as to his availability for the vice presidential slot, which he declined, and then called him at 6:00 A.M. on the day of the announcement to give him the news of Rockefeller's selection. "He was furious," recalled Jim Lake, an aide at the time. "All of the Ford White House treated Ronald Reagan badly."[11] Evidently George H. W. Bush was just as incensed with the decision, because he resigned as Chairman of the Republican National Committee at the same time. The enshrinement of liberal values at the head of the ticket made his job nearly impossible. Tumbling events showed that the GOP had problems larger than the feelings of its major politicians.

The general accord among Republican strategists was that the party would be in shambles if it failed to win the presidency in 1976. The unspoken sentiment was that every party member, regardless of private misgivings, should support the president. Gerald Ford declared that he would stand for election in his own right in 1976 amid quiet nods of agreement by national Republican leaders. Polls showed that the president's announcement improved party morale, but the task of governing as an unelected president in the minority party after a scandal, remained daunting. Not to run would make Ford a lame duck president, lacking the power to threaten, encourage, or promise patronage in a second administration. In such a circumstance, the president expected the loyalty of party activists and leaders, but he was in for a surprise.

Nine years earlier, when campaigning for the California governorship, Reagan pledged allegiance to the "Eleventh Commandment: 'Thou Shalt not Speak Ill of any Republican.'" He hesitated to speak about his president, but the fact was that after just a few months in office, the wheels were falling off the Ford administration. In October 1974, Ford went before Congress to declare inflation public enemy number one and announce a series of proposals for public and private steps to affect supply and demand in the economy. In the hope of evoking a kind of solidarity and volunteerism reminiscent of World War II, the president asked people to wear "WIN" buttons for "Whip Inflation Now." Almost immediately the buttons became objects of ridicule while inflation roared on unchecked. If domestic policy failures were humorous, those in foreign policy were tragic. The fall of Saigon and South Vietnam took place on April 30, 1975. "Americans and the world saw the sorry spectacle of fleeing Americans and South Vietnamese atop the U.S. Embassy, hanging from U.S. military helicopters in a desperate attempt to escape the Communist onslaught."[12] For the first time, the United States had lost a war, and the failure cut deeply into the American psyche.

While many in the GOP counseled loyalty to the president in difficult times, others proclaimed a higher allegiance to conservative principles—ones they saw violated by the new administration. At the 1975 Conservative Political Action Conference (CPAC) in the Mayflower Hotel in Washington, Ronald Reagan brought the crowd to their feet declaring that the Republican Party should be "revitalized . . . raising the banner of no pale pastels, but bold colors which make it unmistakably clear where we stand on all issues troubling the people. . . . Americans are hungry to feel once again a sense of mission and greatness."[13] The majority of young attendees were the blasting cap of a grassroots explosion that caught fire for Reagan. There was even some talk of a third party bid by the ex-governor of California, but Reagan made it clear that he wanted a revitalized Republican Party, not a new one.

Meanwhile, the Ford administration did very little to bring conservatives into the GOP fold. New York City was $4 billion in debt; the administration wavered on a bailout and managed to alienate both liberal and conservatives in their solution. In July 1975, relations between Ford and Reagan reached a nadir when the president refused to meet with Russian dissident Alexandr Solzhenitsyn. The latter's book, *The Gulag Archipelago,* chronicled the treatment of political prisoners, including the author, in the Soviet Union. The next month Ford signed the Helsinki Accords at the urging of Henry Kissinger. The agreement with the Soviets recognized communist domination in Eastern Europe and ran opposite the staunch anticommunism of conservatives and the American people. The president's approval ratings plummeted to a meager 38 percent in the Harris poll, and 45 percent in the Gallup poll.[14] As Gerald Ford began to gear up for the 1976 election campaign, his pollster asked voters to name one accomplishment of his administration; and 61 percent of the respondents said "nothing."[15]

In California, Reagan received some 1,500 pieces of mail per month, including over 100 speaking invitations. But he still hesitated. "I spent a lot of time on Little Man riding around the ranch thinking about the future," he wrote.[16] Only twice in the 20th century had a Republican challenger attempted to defeat an incumbent president, and both had failed. In 1912 Theodore Roosevelt challenged William Howard Taft, and in 1972 Congressman John Ashbrook unsuccessfully challenged Richard Nixon. Then, on July 15, 1975, Senator Paul Laxalt (R-NV) stepped before the television cameras to announce the formation of a group called "Citizens for Reagan." He explained the new group was "exploratory," but everyone in the room knew that no assembly was possible without the knowledge of the candidate and his tacit support.

In the public eye, Reagan's soul searching continued, and for reasons other than politics. As soon as he declared his candidacy the Federal Election Commission would require him to give up his income from speeches, radio commentaries and newspaper columns. He needed the money. Reagan had a ranch to pay for and children in college. By the fall, things came to a head. In September the Citizens for Reagan committee sent out a nationwide mailing trumpeting "the Reagan Presidential Campaign is underway." It wasn't, but his supporters didn't have long to wait.

At precisely 9:30 A.M. on November 20, 1975, the 64-year-old Reagan strode to the podium at the National Press Club in Washington to announce his candidacy for the Republican nomination. He had already called Gerald Ford saying, "I'm going to run for President. I trust we can have a good contest, and I hope that it won't be divisive."[17] President Ford expressed disappointment, the first of many he would have with the former California governor. Before a skeptical audience, Reagan declared: "I believe my candidacy will be healthy for the nation and my party. . . . I am running because I have grown increasingly concerned about the course of events in the United States and the world."[18]

The experience of running for president is like no other challenge in American politics. Almost no one, regardless of experience, is able to smoothly begin the process because each election is different. For a candidate whom one supporter said "could get a standing ovation in a graveyard," the beginning of the president campaign was not auspicious. The first press question after the announcement was: "Mr. Reagan aren't you out of the mainstream of American life, and do you think the people want an extremist for President?"[19] The newly announced candidate reminded the reporter that he had been governor of California, which was a large and diverse state, twice. Two months earlier,

Reagan addressed the Executive Club of Chicago, where he promised to cut federal spending by $90 billion, balance the budget, and reduce personal income taxes by an average of 23 percent. He explained that substantial saving would come by transferring 24 programs back to the states; including welfare, education, housing programs, food stamps, and Medicaid. The press immediately labeled the whole proposal as extreme and preposterous, calling it the "$90 Billion" plan, and they kept bringing it up. Ford's experts predicted that Reagan's plan would force states and cities to raise taxes to meet their new obligations.

So it began. Reagan started his trek with an intense 15-day, 1,200-mile swing through the first five primary states. He was in the heyday of the enterprise—when new candidates experience the popularity of an announcement before being roughed up on issues and subject to follow-up questions on a speech they have just given. One national poll showed him within five points of the president, and another showed him surging into the lead over the president in conservative New Hampshire. In one three-day period he made 17 stops. He continued on in high spirits, despite the lingering problem with the "$90 Billion" speech and the continuing hostility of the press. *New York Times* columnist James "Scotty" Reston wrote that Reagan's challenge was "patently ridiculous," and Garry Wills wrote that it was "unfair to expect accuracy and depth" from the former California governor.[20] Conservative columnists wrote praiseworthy pieces about the campaign and the ideas of the candidate, but they were drowned out by the mainstream media.

The 1976 political election was the end of an era for reporters who covered a presidential campaign. The celebrity media of major television and print outlets dominated coverage and set the agenda. Their lead was everyone's lead, and their predictions gospel. In subsequent cycles the "new media" of first faxes and then the internet and bloggers, would break the stranglehold a few reporters and news outlets had on candidates in their competition for the presidency. In this last cycle they remained "The Boys on the Bus," to quote Timothy Crouse, who dominated national news on candidates and campaigns. In the words of David Halberstam, writing in the last preface of his immortal book *The Powers That Be*, "I was writing, as it turned out, about a certain kind of media era which was coming to an end."[21]

One press outlet, the *Manchester Union Leader* published by William Loeb, refused to change. It remained what it had always been, a solid conservative newspaper in a part of the country slipping into the clutches of welfare state liberalism. Loeb was squarely in the Reagan camp, and he self-edited articles in the paper on the dangers of liberalism, collectivism, and communism, as well as the virtues of American conservatism. With the largest newspaper circulation in the state, the *Leader* was a force to be reckoned with for any Republican campaign. However, in the primary of 1976, even the press were subject to a more formidable force: the weather. The temperature across the Granite State at 5:00 P.M. on Election Day was 60 degrees, in February no less, and to the surprise of everyone an astonishing 65.5 percent of the state's registered Republicans came out to vote. Most of them were party regulars who supported Gerald Ford, and the president won the primary that evening by a scant 1,317 votes out of 108,328 cast. Despite his challenger status, Ronald Reagan was portrayed as having been "upset" in New Hampshire. By winning, Ford began the process of forcing Republican voters to legitimate his presidency, and choose him as the establishment candidate over the outsider conservative.

Ronald Reagan's loss in New Hampshire was unexpected and devastating. The former governor tried to put the best face on the loss, but the fact remained that the hasty comments in Chicago and the "$90 Billion" label cost him dearly. As the two candidates looked down the road to Florida, Ford did not let up in his attacks implying that Reagan would "destroy" the Social Security system. While polls repeatedly showed that voters liked Reagan personally, they were afraid of his policy ideas. With the national focus on Florida, the states of Massachusetts and Vermont held their own primaries. The Reagan campaign had already announced it would bypass both contests, preferring to focus their attention on primaries that a Republican candidate might actually win. Not surprisingly, the two states fell into Ford's column and added to his momentum. In Massachusetts, where conservatives were as plentiful as unicorns, the president won by a two to one margin.[22]

Reagan found a new issue as he campaigned in Florida. In speeches he sharpened his attacks on the administration by charging that Ford had secretly agreed to turn over the Panama Canal to the Panamanian government. The administration immediately countered that the charge was untrue, but the differences in the two campaigns, and candidates, became obvious. Polls showed a close race, with the attacks on Ford's record beginning to take a toll. In the end it was not enough for the challenger. The president won his fourth primary in a row by a 53 percent to 47 percent margin. Ford's strategy of staying above the fray, stressing his incumbency and experience seemed to be working.

On March 16, 1976, the voters in Reagan's home state of Illinois gave 60 percent of their allegiance to the president. Ford won across the board among GOP primary voters, regardless of income, ideology, or region. An air of inevitability crept into the race, and almost immediately the White House increased the drumbeat for Reagan to leave the primary circuit for the good of the party. Some GOP spokesmen began to insinuate that conservatives were going to cause the Republicans to lose in 1976, just like they did in 1964.

After five consecutive defeats, morale in the Reagan camp reached a low ebb. Campaign manager John Sears's plan to upset Gerald Ford in New Hampshire, and then win—or exceed expectations—in Florida was in shambles. With political defeats came resignation. Ford was raising 2.5 times more money than Reagan.[23] In the month of February he seemed destined to win the nomination, and staffers on the governor's campaign were either laid off or worked for no salary. It didn't matter, the conservatives were so convicted that they refused to quit and worked without pay. Rumors circulated that John Sears had opened back channel communications with the Ford campaign to negotiate a graceful exit. The candidate seemed determined to go on. To several hundred people on the tarmac of the Raleigh, North Carolina airport Reagan asked if they wanted him to quit: "The people in the White House seem to think I should be withdrawing." To a chorus of no's, he responded, "You took the words right out of my mouth. . . . I'm not walking away from this."[24]

Reagan threw himself into a desperate effort to win the North Carolina primary. Three important factors came into play in the Tar Heel state, and they each helped the challenger's campaign. First, the American Conservative Union authorized some independent expenditures on behalf of the governor. Second, Gerald Ford slipped back into his habit of botching opportunities and misreading the public mood. While Reagan allied himself to the Jesse Helms wing of the party in

North Carolina, Ford chose establishment figures without grassroots influence. Third, the campaign itself was able to better target primary voters, and then motivates them to get to the polls. In the last two weeks before the primary, mail from the Citizens for Reagan campaign went out on time, phone banks hummed, volunteers went door to door distributing handbills, and Jesse Helms tore into Ford, Kissinger and their company with unmitigated zeal. Local conservatives found film of a speech Reagan gave in Florida, and they rebroadcast it on the 13 television stations in North Carolina. Everything came together on March 23, when Ronald Reagan defeated Gerald Ford for the first time—53.4 to 46.6 percent.

The win paid huge dividends for Reagan. Prior to the North Carolina primary, Ford was able to use his position as the incumbent president and consistent primary winner to convince skeptical party activists that his nomination was certain. The defeat shattered this aura of inevitability. Once Ford was defeated, Republican voters and convention delegates no longer believed in the sureness of his nomination, and were free to consider other candidates. In any comparison, Ronald Reagan was likely to emerge as the winner. The words of assurance came from a man who was warm and genial, not arrogant or overbearing like so many politicians. People who met him often commented on his size; he was tall and trim with dazzling white teeth. His face was lined with tiny wrinkles, like leather, and he was always tan from working in the sun.

Credit for the resurgence in the Reagan campaign belonged solely to the candidate. Michael Deaver, his longtime aide, recalled the exact day when Reagan's demeanor changed. It was when the Ford campaign had mayors and governors call and ask him to get out, and when the president himself suggested he get out. "That was it for him. . . . He became more aggressive, more confident."[25]

North Carolina was the turning point of Reagan's political career. It showed him as a viable, full-fledged candidate, opposite the fading president. After the victory, Reagan made a 30-minute nationally televised broadcast to take his message to the American people, and appealed directly for contributions. Only NBC would sell time to him for this, but the outcome was reminiscent of when he went before the cameras in 1964, with $1.5 million raised and a 20 percent share (meaning one

of every five television sets in America) tuned in to hear candidate
Reagan. The momentum was undeniable, and the belief was that Reagan was destined to do much better in later primaries because they were
in the South, Southwest and Far West, an area now designated as "Reagan Country." A new pattern emerged; a small group of dedicated conservatives backed Reagan and worked overtime, while the state GOP
machinery and local party chairs gave titular allegiance to Ford.

Six days after his national speech, Reagan lost the Wisconsin primary to the president. He won 45 percent of the popular vote, but
because of party rules did not win a single delegate. The outcome was
different in South Carolina, where he won 27 of 36 delegates. The
Pennsylvania and New York delegations officially were listed as "uncommitted," but the vast majority would eventually go to Ford. These
victories and defeats had the effect of heightening the importance of
the Texas primary. Ford spent more time and money in Texas than
any primary before, and with less effect. He was photographed at a
Texas event eating a tamale without first removing the corn husk, and
his personal attacks on Reagan appeared desperate. "On primary day,
Reagan won a crushing victory over Ford in Texas, taking ninety-six
delegates . . . and winning most of the twenty-four congressional districts by better than two to one."[26] It was the worst primary defeat ever
inflicted on an incumbent president.

Four days after Texas came three state primaries in Georgia, Alabama, and Indiana. Reagan won all three, receiving an astonishing 71 percent of the vote in Alabama, 68 percent in Georgia, and
squeaking by in Indiana with 51 percent. The latter victory was especially sweet, since the state party chairman predicted a 10-point
spread for Ford just two days before the vote.[27] The president's campaign was in shambles, and on the night of the debacle an aide gave
one the more unfortunate comments about the situation in the history of American politics: "I'm not going to rearrange the furniture
on the deck of the *Titanic*."

What ensued was not a listing campaign, but a seesaw battle for
delegates to the GOP summer convention. After 30 Republican primaries in which over nine million people voted in a six month period,
with thousands of volunteers and millions of dollars spent by the two
campaigns on television and mail, the party was no closer to deciding

on a nominee than it was on the first day of January, 1976. With the primaries over, Ford was uncomfortably ahead in the delegate count, 961 to 856, with 1,130 needed to nominate.[28] Many of the remaining uncommitted delegates were in "Reagan Country," meaning that their allegiance was suspect. The state conventions in June and July became the focus of a close, brawling finish where Reagan inched up on the president in the delegate count. On the Wednesday before the final round of state conventions, Reagan again took to the airwaves, this time on ABC, in a nationwide half-hour address. The results were not as spectacular financially as the earlier address, but in terms of Reagan's image as a leader, it did wonders. The final delegate counts for each campaign varied, with the *New York Times* showing a difference of only 24 delegates by the time of the convention, and the president short of his goal of a first ballot victory by 30 to 40 delegates.[29]

While the Republicans fiddled, the Democrats ended their harmonious convention in New York City by nominating James Earl Carter of Georgia for president, and Walter Mondale of Minnesota for vice president. Postconvention polls showed the ticket trouncing either Reagan or Ford by 15 to 20 points.[30] Then, on advice of his campaign manager John Sears, the governor overreached in his strategy with the hope of attracting Democrats and Independents as well as dissident Republicans to his side. He made an overture to have liberal Pennsylvania senator Richard Schweiker share the ticket as vice president.[31] The move was designed to keep the Ford campaign off balance until the convention, but it had the effect of alienating Reagan's conservative base. The ploy proved the last straw in the drama, as the remaining uncommitted delegates flocked to President Ford. The president invited delegates to the White House and placed calls to those bound for Kansas City. In the Magnolia State of Mississippi the two contenders engaged in a shameless battle of promises and vote trading worthy of their Democratic adversaries. The final tally was 1,187 for Ford and 1,070 for Reagan.[32]

At the time, the defeat was seen as an obituary for any future Reagan candidacy. The *New York Times* summarized conventional wisdom when it declared that "at 65 years of age . . . [Reagan was] too old to consider seriously another run at the Presidency."[33] In a speech to loyalists he sounded typically upbeat, and dismissive of past good judgment. "The cause is still there. Don't give up your ideals, don't compromise, don't turn to expediency, don't get cynical. . . . The cause will prevail because it is right."[34] In obedience to his own 11th Commandment, the Reagans were in a convention skybox when Ford addressed the delegates. He had earlier told Tom Brokaw of NBC News, that he would not give any interviews and would not speak to the convention.

Then, in one of those strange ironies that change political history, President Ford himself, before a nationwide television audience, asked his "good friend" Ron Reagan to come down and speak. The defeated challenger paused, and then stepped out of the skybox and into the future. On stage he mentioned in unprepared remarks that he had been asked to write a letter for a time capsule to be opened in Los Angeles 100 years later. He asked if, "They will know whether or not we met our challenge. Whether we will have the freedom that we have known up until now will depend on what we do here. . . . And if we fail, they probably won't get to read the letter at all because it spoke of individual freedom and they won't be allowed to talk of that or read of it."[35]

On the floor of the convention, the words took hold. Gerald Ford had just delivered the best speech of his life, and in the years to come no one could remember what he said. The seven minute impromptu remarks by Reagan were a legacy for the political ages. Behind one reporter, a dedicated Ford supporter gasped, "Oh my God, we've nominated the wrong man."[36] The audience of 15,000, with millions more watching on television, never forgot what they had just witnessed. In the time it took for Reagan to speak, the Republican Party moved from the clutches of moderation into the embrace of conservatism.

NOTES

1. Michael Barone, *Our Country* (New York: Free Press, 1990), p. 521.

2. Lou Cannon, *Governor Reagan: His Rise to Power* (New York: PublicAffairs, 2003), p. 385.

3. Ibid.

4. Harold W. Stanley and Richard G. Niemi, *Vital Statistics in American Politics* (Washington, DC: Congressional Quarterly Press, 1988), p. 124.

5. Tom Goff, "Legacy for State," *Los Angeles Times*, September 29, 1974.

6. Ronald Reagan, *An American Life* (New York: Simon and Schuster, 1990), p. 192.

7. Ibid., p. 195.

8. Cannon, *Governor Reagan*, p. 399.

9. Ibid.

10. Edmund Morris, *Dutch* (New York: Random House, 1999), p. 588.

11. Craig Shirley, *Reagan's Revolution* (Nashville, TN: Nelson Current, 2005), p. 27.

12. Ibid., p. 34.

13. Ibid., p. 36.

14. Ibid., p. 48.

15. Ibid., p. 66.

16. Reagan, *An American Life*, p. 195.

17. Shirley, *Reagan's Revolution*, p. 88.

18. Ibid., p. 91.

19. Ibid., p. 93.

20. Ibid., p. 106.

21. David Halberstam, *The Powers That Be*, 4th ed. (New York: Random House, 2000), p. xi.

22. Shirley, *Reagan's Revolution*, p. 139.

23. Ibid., p. 159.

24. Ibid., p. 162.

25. Ibid., p. 177.

26. Ibid., p. 196.

27. *New York Times*, May 3, 1976.

28. Shirley, *Reagan's Revolution*, p. 240.

29. Ibid., p. 262.

30. Ibid., p. 260.

31. J. David Woodard, *The America That Reagan Built* (Westport, CT: Praeger, 2006), p. 23.

32. Shirley, *Reagan's Revolution*, p. 328.

33. *New York Times*, August 20, 1976.

34. Shirley, *Reagan's Revolution*, p. 329.

35. Ibid., p. 333.

36. Ibid., p. xxiii.

Chapter 7

1980

Ronald Reagan was exhausted as he left Kansas City to fly back to California after the 1976 GOP convention. From the time of his announcement in November 1975 until the end of the convention in August, he had been on the road constantly. He traveled over 100,000 miles, eaten on the run, slept in hotels, worked early to late schedules, shook innumerable hands of strangers, and given countless speeches.

It was all for naught.

Gerald Ford won the GOP nomination on the first ballot by 57 votes, and the only thing the press could talk about was Reagan's age. He had run for the presidency twice, lost twice, and would be 70 years old by 1981. As far as anybody was concerned, he was finished as a prospective candidate for president. On the way to the airport, the Reagan entourage passed a hand-painted sign in a bakery that read, "Goodbye, Republicans. You picked the wrong man."[1]

In retrospect the baker was right. For conservatives, the bicentennial of 1976 stood out as a high point of a dismal decade. The issues that they had warned about for years—like excessive government spending, more regulations, a stagnant economy, a shrinking dollar, inflation, Soviet expansion, decaying cultural standards, and weak leadership—all culminated in the decade that writer Tom Wolfe labeled as "Me." Social indicators joined economic ones to convey the magnitude of the change over the previous decade. The crime rate at the end of the decade was three times higher than in 1960. "Since the causes of crime were increasingly attributed to society, rather than the criminal, the federal government and the states very logically hurled themselves with enthusiasm into the task of social reform."[2] The number of people murdered in the United States in the decade was twice the number killed in the Vietnam War.

Conservatives feared that the sexual and cultural experiments of the 1960s had been legitimized by the promiscuous ethic of the 1970s. A majority of Americans approved of premarital sex, and the divorce rate went from one in three to one in two. "The number of single parent families increased 50 percent during the decade, and the number of unmarried couples jumped by 300 percent."[3] The *Roe v. Wade* Supreme Court decision in 1973 unleashed a torrent of sexual permissiveness with fateful consequences. Virtually every pop song in the decade was about sex; whether it was "Afternoon Delight" or "Shake Your Booty," the subject was always the same. The previous generation's faith in reason and planning gave way to a new trust in feelings. The point was this: the character of the nation was changing, and not for the better.

Ronald Reagan remained the same, like a rock in the middle of rapids. The theme of his 1976 campaign was the same one he used in 1980: the belief that government, particularly the federal government, had the answer to societal problems was false; and the collectivist, centralized approach created more problems than it solved. His solution was to shrink the size and scope of government, transfer power from the public to the private sector, and move programs from Washington to the state and local level. This was exactly the opposite of the popular trend at the time. It was not clear how the values of smaller government could alter the social disintegration of marriage and crime, but the longing for someone to halt the slide was palpable.

In the fall of 1976, Jimmy Carter became the 39th president of the United States with 297 electoral votes, besting Gerald Ford's 240. In the popular vote, the margin was even closer, 50 to 48 percent. The Carter presidency opened on a high note when the president stepped out of his limousine on the slopes of Capitol Hill and walked down

Pennsylvania Avenue, with his wife at his side, exulting in the cheers and the sunshine. The hope was that he would erase the stain of scandal and improve the functioning of the office, but the euphoria did not last long.

Carter thought the American people wanted someone with a common touch for their president, after the pomp and circumstance of the Nixon misfortune. He tried to give it by wearing a light-colored cardigan sweater on television in front of a roaring fire in the White House, eliminating limousines for the use of the senior staff, banning the playing of "Hail to the Chief," and carrying his own suit bag slung over his shoulder. The new administration found out that the changes weren't helping: people wanted their president in a suit, liked the trappings of office, and discovered the suit bag was empty. Even the *New York Times* called Carter's behavior "showboat populism."[4]

The dissatisfactions of the country went deeper than having a next-door-neighbor president. Beginning in 1977, Cuban soldiers took up positions in Ethiopia. A pro-Marxist faction rose up in Yemen, on the Arabian Peninsula. Vietnam, Laos, and Cambodia fell into communist hands, and in the Caribbean, a Cuban-backed group took power in Grenada. In Nicaragua, a guerilla army known as the Sandinista National Liberation Front (FSLN) gained strength. In all these matters, Jimmy Carter was alternately indignant, dismissive, and apologetic—never confrontational.

The Soviet successes, and Carter's inept responses, pushed Ronald Reagan out of any thought of retirement and back into the political fray. By the summer of 1977, in Carter's first year in office, Reagan emerged as the most high profile and vocal critic of the administration, excoriating it on policy, politics and hypocrisy. "In the month of June alone, Reagan made thirteen major policy speeches in New York, Washington and other locations."[5] He renewed his candidacy for president by maintaining a vigorous travel schedule, speaking to audiences around the country, meeting with visitors, and reaching thousands of listeners with newspaper columns and weekly radio commentary.

Radio was an ideal medium for the discussion of values, and Reagan knew this better than anyone. From his time at WOC Reagan learned, just like Roosevelt before him, that with the right tone of voice and choice of words, a radio personality could develop intimacy with an audience. The descriptions and stories he told on the air, later compiled in the book *Reagan: In His Own Hand,* stimulated the human imagination and had the effect of endearing the listener to the speaker. "I love America because people accept me for what I am," he said. "I don't have to show an identity card to buy a pair of shoes [and] . . . my mail isn't censored." "Those who labor from sun up till late in the summer evening must now put up with government paper work growing out of multitudinous and unnecessary regulations."[6] Nancy Reagan recalled in an interview that her husband took long showers "where he got a lot of his thoughts," and then "he'd sit down and write." She remembered that he did not watch much television, but would "sit behind that desk in the bedroom, working."[7] His box of notes and clippings was from a variety of popular sources, like the *Los Angeles Times, National Review* and *Reader's Digest,* along with lines from his favorite movies. By 1978, Reagan was in 226 newspapers, and on 286 radio stations, with an estimated audience of 20 million each week.[8]

His candidacy was helped by events, and Carter's response to them. In April 1978, the Senate approved the Panama Canal Treaty by one vote more than the two-thirds necessary to pass, and in June of the same year California voters approved Proposition 13, which limited property taxes. The vote wasn't close, proponents won by a 65 to 35 percent vote margin.[9] A conservative, populist, middle-class revolt was washing across the country, with an outpouring of opposition to government growth, the Panama Canal treaties, and the Equal Rights Movement, which enshrined feminism in the U.S. Constitution. All these missteps by Carter and establishment GOP politicians were fodder for Reagan articles and speeches.

In the spring of 1979, Reagan began to accelerate his campaign by gathering conservatives into meetings and bringing political operatives into his corner. He made a tactical decision to bring John Sears back as campaign manager, a choice that did not please some veterans of his 1976 effort. One of Sears's first decisions was to take Reagan off the road and limit his public exposure. The reasoning was that Reagan was the frontrunner, and by putting him under wraps his nomination would appear "inevitable," and he would be the "mainstream" candidate. But the decision only encouraged reporters to write stories about Reagan being too old for one more try. Those who had been with the governor in Sacramento knew it deprived the campaign of one of its great strengths—Reagan's public speaking abilities and upbeat personality.

The ploy to put Reagan on ice opened the door for other candidates like George H. W. Bush, John Connally, and Bob Dole to step up their campaigns in crucial primary states. While the Reagan effort struggled with infighting among the staff and lagged in fundraising, Jimmy Carter floundered in Washington amid gas shortages, double-digit inflation and interest rates, a growing tax burden, high unemployment, and apologies for Marxist-Leninist regimes. The president seemed to be giving away his office, and on July 15, 1979, he just about succeeded. "As you know, there is a growing disrespect for government . . . the churches . . . the schools, the news media and other institutions."[10] The irony is that Carter never actually uttered the word *malaise* in his speech, but he did say that the energy crisis was a "fundamental threat to American democracy," "a crisis of confidence," and a "calamity . . . that strikes at the very heart and soul and spirit of our national will."[11] The president's pessimistic tone suggested that America's greatest were long gone, and that the only solution was to accept a slow, steady, dignified decline.

While his intentions may have been laudable, Carter had nothing to offer as a clear direction out of the morass. Reagan did. He immediately denounced the speech, saying, "There isn't any crisis in the country. There's just a crisis in the White House."[12] Some Democrats agreed. Senator Edward M. Kennedy reportedly dropped 20 pounds and planned to challenge Carter for the nomination. Just when it seemed the situation could get no worse for the president, things went from bad to catastrophic. On November 4, 1979, radical Islamic students charged the American embassy in Tehran, Iran and took 66 American hostages. The number was later reduced to 56 when some were let go, but the slide on the screen behind the national news broadcasts each night said it all: "America Held Hostage."

One year before a presidential election, the nation found itself in the clutches of both a domestic and foreign crisis. The December 30, 1979, cover of *Time* magazine was titled "The Cooling of America," and showed a family huddled around a television fireplace with a newspaper headline that read, "Cold Wave Hits: Fuel Prices Up."[13] That winter home heating oil prices nearly doubled, and wood stove manufacturers and importers said their business was up more than 100 percent. But no event in politics or economics was more important than the hostage crisis. It stimulated a wave of patriotic fervor and national frustration. Iran's leading Islamic cleric, Ayatollah Ruhollah Khomeini, whipped up anti-American sentiment and threatened revenge against the "Great Satan" of the United States. Khomeini's criticism gave President Carter a breath of fresh respect, and he was soon getting 70 percent approval ratings from the American people for his handling of the crisis.[14] While no one knew exactly what to do, the feeling was that enough wasn't being done, but they wanted to support the president anyway. Military recruiters looked up to see young men across the table who cared little about Vietnam, but wanted to avenge the kidnapping of the American diplomats.

It was in this atmosphere of domestic insecurity and foreign terrorism, that Ronald Reagan announced for the presidency in the New York Hilton Hotel. He gave a fresh address on the national mood before 250 reporters and a crowd of invited guests. Unlike Carter, he blamed the government instead of the American people. "The crisis we face is not the result of any failure of the American spirit; it is a failure of our leaders to establish rational goals and give our people something to order their lives by."[15] In the climax of the speech, he invoked a favorite phrase, saying that Americans had a "rendezvous with destiny" ever since that moment in 1630 when John Winthrop told his followers, "We shall be a city upon a hill." The speech was written in Reagan's own hand, and original in insight, uplifting in tone with new content—and almost nobody heard it. When he left the next day for a five-day, 12-city tour, reporters asked him why he refused joint appearances with other candidates and bypassed debate opportunities.

As the nation plunged into an election year, Ronald Reagan dropped in the national polls among GOP primary voters. The age issue had grown to alarming proportions and the permanent class of reporters and consultants appeared unimpressed with his blundering start. They labeled him the "Front Walker," instead of "frontrunner." Inside the campaign, the power struggles intensified between John Sears and the older California loyalists. Lyn Nofziger, for one, understood that Reagan had an uncanny ability to connect with voters. The governor's charm, candor, self-deprecating humor, and his utter belief in the rightness of his ideas allowed him to motivate and touch people in a manner that left his jealous opponents in awe. But Reagan was not getting an opportunity to do what he did best. Michael Deaver, a longtime aide and favorite of Mrs. Reagan, left quietly after a clash with Sears. The dissidents wanted the campaign manager to "let Reagan be Reagan" and raise his visibility, but Sears declared that he had poll data showing Reagan far ahead in the initial primary states of Iowa and New Hampshire, and he refused to change course.

On January 21, 1980, with the nation in a full-blown recession, inflation rising one point a month and again in double digits, and with gas and oil prices at an all-time high, Ronald Reagan lost to George H. W. Bush in the Iowa primary 31.5 to 29.4 percent. The difference was 2,182 votes, but they made the defeat into a cataclysm. The state where Ronald Reagan got his radio start 40 years earlier, voted for someone who had campaigned there for 40 days. The problem was that Reagan had only campaigned for 40 hours. Now the worst fears were realized in the Reagan camp. They had misjudged the electorate and relied on inaccurate poll data. Bush was able to boast that he now had momentum, "Big Mo" as he called it, 35 days before the crucial New Hampshire primary.

The only consolation, and it was a negligible one, was that one-time Democratic favorite and sentimental choice Ted Kennedy was routed by 28 percentage points in Iowa as well. The embarrassing image of Carter as a loser was banished. The president inflicted the worst loss ever sustained on a member of America's reigning political dynasty. The Kennedy family was humiliated, as were the liberals who believed the Camelot legacy was sacred and could survive any challenge. It appeared that Jimmy Carter would be the Democratic nominee in spite of the divisions within his own party and his own inept policies.

As was his habit, Reagan blamed himself for the loss, and stepped up his criticism of the Carter administration in response. He also found himself the beneficiary of a turn of fate only he thought possible. A New Hampshire paper, the *Nashua Telegraph*, arranged a debate between Reagan and Bush at the local high school. Senator Bob Dole, Gerald Ford's vice presidential running mate in 1976, cried foul. He believed the debate gave an unfair advantage to the two frontrunners and violated the provisions of the Federal Election Commission. Dole complained accordingly. And Reagan promptly agreed. The governor declared that the other five candidates, Bob Dole, Howard Baker, John Anderson, Phil Crane, and John Connally, should be invited to the debate. When the Bush campaign refused to cofund the event if others came, the Reagan campaign agreed to pay for the whole thing.

On the night of the debate, the auditorium was set for just two candidates, and the G.H.W. Bush campaign insisted that the others were unwelcome. Bush took his seat and remained silent while Reagan explained to the audience what was going on. Then, the governor was interrupted by John Breen, the editor of the *Telegraph*, who said, "Turn Mr. Reagan's microphone off." In anger, Reagan blurted out to everyone, "I am paying for this microphone Mr. Green."

It became a part of American political folklore that Ronald Reagan's remark and mispronounced name revived his campaign. "For some reason my words hit the audience, whose emotions were already worked up, like a sledgehammer. The crowd roared and just went wild."[16] Ronald Reagan finally got angry, and it invigorated his campaign. In a time right after the American hockey team upset the Soviets in the Lake Placid, New York Olympics, and sportscaster Al Michaels joyously cried out in the last seconds of the game, "Do you believe in miracles?" those who supported Reagan and believed in American exceptionalism shouted out, "Yes!" For a brief shining moment, the country celebrated its heritage. The USA was a good and great country, where underdogs could triumph, opposite the brutish USSR. No one believed this more than Ronald Wilson Reagan.

In the final 13 days before the New Hampshire primary, Reagan spent 10 of them in the state. On election day he fired John Sears, and two of his protégés, Charlie Black and Jim Lake. "A change was necessary at the top of the campaign staff. I knew I had to do it before the results were in from New Hampshire because if I lost and then fired Sears, people could say I was trying to make him the scapegoat for my loss."[17] He didn't have to worry. Reagan won the primary in a blowout, 50 percent to 23 percent for Bush. "Overall Reagan took all ten counties in New Hampshire and eleven of the thirteen cities."[18] He won among blue collar voters, those making less than $10,000 a year, and white collar voters. When the numbers were in from rural areas and urban centers, Reagan took more votes than all the other candidates put together.

Reagan soon opened up such a substantial lead over his Republican rivals that they all dropped out except Bush, who hung around for another month. The new official frontrunner candidate told his audiences: "This isn't a campaign anymore. It is a crusade to save America."[19] Millions of Americans seemed to agree. William J. Casey replaced Sears as campaign chairman, along with Ed Meese and Peter Hannaford from the California days, and soon a number of other aides from abandoned campaigns joined the Reagan bandwagon. Lyn Nofziger, Marty Anderson, and Mike Deaver returned to the fold. Without the constraints imposed by his own campaign, Reagan spoke freely about the danger of the Soviet Union, the creeping intrusion of government, and the debilitating effect of high taxes. The message was tailored directly at the indolence of the Carter era. Michael Barone would later write, "He spoke the language of Franklin Roosevelt," meaning that Reagan was gushing with enthusiasm; he was confident, cheerful, theatrical, and larger than life.[20]

But it wasn't over. In the early spring, former president Gerald Ford gave an interview with reporter Barbara Walters of ABC where he said there was a "50–50 chance" that he would get into the race for the GOP nomination. "Every place I go and everything I hear, there is the growing, growing sentiment that Governor Reagan cannot win the election."[21] The inevitable comparison was being made in the press to Barry Goldwater's crushing defeat in 1964 because he, like Reagan, was "too conservative." The frontrunner counterpunched that he had been twice elected governor of a state with a two to one Democratic registration edge. No matter, the issue of Reagan's electability was now front and center. A poll in the first week of March showed Ford defeating Reagan among Republicans 36 to 32 percent. When independents were thrown into the mix, Ford widened his lead to 33 to 27 percent.[22] All waited with bated breath to hear the former president's decision about another race. It came on March 16, 1980, when Ford declared, once and for all, that he would not run for the nomination.

Throughout the early months of 1980, Reagan had an almost evangelistic fervor about his campaign. Religious conservatives became fully engaged in the campaign that year, motivated mainly by their disappointment with Jimmy Carter. They thought the Baptist from Georgia would oppose abortion and the Equal Rights Amendment, but they were wrong. That year a number of training sessions were held in churches across the South, where one minister after another took the microphone to complain about the Carter presidency. Bob Novak, a reporter, attended one of these meetings in the president's home state of Georgia and concluded, "Jimmy Carter's goose was cooked because I saw the intensity of [those] people."[23] Ronald Reagan seemed an unlikely hero for what was becoming known as the "Christian Right," but he had a feel for the evangelical constituency that Carter lacked. Maybe it was his Disciples of Christ background learned at 123 South Hennepin Avenue in Dixon, Illinois, or his mother's legacy of regular Bible instruction. Whatever it was, he was the one candidate who spoke directly and effectively to the born-again voters. Despite the fact that he was divorced, had once supported the Equal Rights Amendment, and as governor signed into law a liberal abortion measure, which he later regretted, Ronald Reagan was seen as God's appointed man at the appointed time.

If not the Almighty, then at least events seemed to be confirming the belief in Reagan's inevitability. "In April of 1980, a *New York Times*/CBS poll found that the president's approval had dropped from a high of 77 percent in December of 1979, to 49 percent in March."[24] Carter had to do something and on April 24 he did. Plans for a possible rescue of the American hostages had been in the works within hours of their capture, but the impossible logistics made any raid risky. Not surprisingly, the joint military operation was dubbed "Desert One," and it failed ignominiously in the sands outside Tehran. One of the rescue helicopters with a flattened nose wheel slammed into a parked C-130 plane and ignited a raging fire. Eight men lost their lives, and others were injured by projectiles flying from the flaming wreckage.

The next day the worldwide press was treated to pictures of burned-out American helicopters being inspected by Muslim mullahs. *Time* magazine's coverage was titled, "Debacle in the Desert," and asked if the president's "image as inept had been renewed."[25] Secretary of State Cyrus Vance resigned on principle in opposition to the raid. Joseph Kraft, a columnist for the *Washington Post*, called the rescue mission, "a half-hearted, second-best spirit."[26] American morale, and that of the besieged hostages in Iran, sank to an even lower level.

The failure in the Iranian desert underscored one of Reagan's main campaign themes: the need for upgraded military strength. A Pentagon investigation found that the helicopters used in the mission were old and shoddy—this at a time when the Carter White House was again trying to cut the military budget. The disappointment of the Iranian rescue mission opened the ears of voters to hear the conservative message of "peace through strength," something they were deaf to since American failures in Vietnam. He went after the administration on the issue of military preparedness, stating that about half the ships in the American navy couldn't leave port because of a lack of parts or crew, and the depleted readiness of the air force was for the same reason. The everyday military personnel were high school dropouts for the most part, and were paid so little that they received food stamps as a supplement. Diplomacy had its merits, but most people in the country wanted action, not explanations, when it came to the hostage crisis. As a candidate, Reagan promised to act boldly to overcome the contradictions of past administrative actions.

The Reagan campaign began to prepare for the Republican convention in Detroit. Most polls over the spring of 1980 showed a close race between Carter and Reagan. Estimates varied, but one calculation in June showed Carter ahead in 16 states and the District of Columbia with 154 electoral votes, and Reagan leading in 22 states with 160 votes. Twelve states, with 224 electoral votes were too close to call, but would decide who received the 270 electoral votes necessary to win.[27] The main issue on the minds of voters was the sick economy, with dropping economic indicators, inflation at 18 percent per annum, and gasoline prices, which were at 58 cents a couple of years earlier, rising to $1.20 per gallon.[28] Of course, the foreign policy disaster remained fresh on the minds of voters as well, but it was secondary to the economic woes. Just before the GOP convention, the president made a trip to Detroit to decry the economic situation and call for more relief. One Republican likened the visit as "Sherman visiting Atlanta" after he burned it in 1864. The speech stimulated an avalanche of bad media for the administration; news reports used the visit as an opportunity to remind the public of the economic despair of the city.

Even the press was beginning to catch on to the new reality, as the GOP began to earn praise for articulating a coherent philosophy,

confidence, and the will to win. The Republican platform that year reflected the conservative mood. Gone was earlier support for the Equal
Rights Amendment, and in its place was a plank supporting a constitutional amendment to outlaw abortion and a recommendation that
opposition to abortion be a prerequisite for any federal judgeship. In
contrast to earlier GOP conventions, this one left fewer ideological
victims bleeding in the aisles. The Reagan team consistently patrolled
the floor and played the role of party unifier. Dissident delegates got
little or no time on television to decry the nominee or his actions.
While many thought the final platform too conservative, the party as a
whole was able to unite behind it.

Of course full party unity could only come when Reagan picked a
running mate. He needed someone who was qualified and comfortable
with the nominee's conservatism, but also someone who could reach out
to party moderates and independents. On the floor of the convention,
the buzz was going around about a "Dream Ticket," of Ronald Reagan
and Gerald Ford. In the middle of convention week the two men met,
and Reagan made a gracious request for Ford to join the ticket. For a
24-hour period, rumors and speculation about the likelihood of a former
president joining up as vice president—which he had already been—
sent the media and the convention into a frenzy. In the end, nothing
happened. Ford turned down the request, and Ronald Reagan called
his most persistent adversary, George H. W. Bush to join him on the
ticket. Why Bush? "We had been through a competitive and sometimes
rough primary battle, but I had always liked him personally, and had
a great respect for his abilities and breadth of experience; and I knew
he had a lot of support within the party."[29] The Texan was stunned by
the request. He was expecting Reagan to give him a courtesy call saying that Ford was the choice, but accepted on the spot. Reagan's actor
sensibilities led him to walk across the street to the convention in Joe
Louis Arena after midnight. There he said that he had chosen "a man
who was a candidate, a man who had great experience in government,
and man who told me he could support the platform across the board."[30]

That one phone call changed American politics, and the Republican Party, for the next 25 years, with G.H.W. Bush winning in 1988,
and his son, George W. Bush, serving for two terms from 2000 to 2008.

The last minute pickup of Bush was beneficial for the ticket. "Running alone against Carter, Reagan was ahead 38—32, but the ticket of Reagan/Bush versus Carter/Mondale was leading 43–34."[31] In his address to the convention, Reagan struck a familiar theme:

> They say that the United States has had its day in the sun, that our nation has passed its zenith. They expect you to tell your children that the American people no longer have the will to cope with their problems, that the future will be one of sacrifice and few opportunities.
>
> My fellow citizens, I utterly reject that view.
>
> The American people, the most generous on earth, who created the highest standard of living are not going to accept the notion that we can only make a better world for others by moving backward ourselves. And those who believe we can, have no business leading this nation.[32]

The new tenor of presidential politics was set at the end of Reagan's acceptance speech, when the newly nominated standard-bearer asked for a moment of silent prayer, and then closed with a benediction: "God Bless America." Peggy Noonan, who was in the convention hall working for CBS radio that night, recalled, "He knew what he was doing, and took a chance. I liked him so much at that moment."[33]

Even though the country was in a bad mood by August 1980, they were not ready to fire their president. Jimmy Carter had held off the crown prince of the Democratic Party to win renomination, and the core base of the coalition that had dominated American politics for nearly 50 years (labor unions, urban ethnics, Jewish and black voters, women's groups, the South, and intellectuals) was coming home. The campaign strategy for the Democrats was to use the Rose Garden, the presidential office, to maximum advantage. The incumbent would paint Reagan as a warmonger, a dangerous trigger-happy nuclear cowboy (think Barry Goldwater in 1964) unfit to hold higher office. "A Carter campaign memo clearly spelled out this agenda: 'Our goal must be to establish the shadow of doubt about Reagan's ability to handle the Presidency.'"[34] Walter Mondale told reporters that he thought the GOP nominee would "fall like a crowbar . . . awfully fast," once the fall campaign got under way.

The Reagan campaign worried that the White House would spring an "October Surprise" on the electorate with Carter going on television to announce that the hostages had been released from Iran. The imagined scenario had President Carter greeting each returning American at the bottom of a ramp at Andrews Air Force Base, followed by a ceremony on the South Lawn of the White House, and a procession up to Capitol Hill. The incumbent president would get such a boost from the grateful American voters that he would leap right over Reagan and into a second term. Each day's news events brought with it the possibility of such a revelation, and there was absolutely nothing the Reagan campaign could do about it.

Another worry was the third party candidacy of John Anderson, a liberal Republican from Illinois who teamed with former Democratic governor Patrick Lucey of Wisconsin to mount a third party challenge in 1980. Most of Anderson's support in the GOP came from so-called Rockefeller Republicans who were dissatisfied with Reagan's takeover of the party. After winning no primaries, the Illinois congressman remained a nuisance through the fall, and the only questions asked about him was: Who was he hurting the most, Carter or Reagan?

"Every American election," wrote Theodore White 20 years earlier, "summons the individual voter to weigh the past against the future."[35] Republicans liked their odds in any comparison, but they didn't know if events would allow voters to make a choice. The traditional opening gambit in the presidential sweepstakes every four years is Labor Day, with Democrats gathering at a parade and Republicans choosing a different venue. Ronald Reagan began his campaign in New York with the Statue of Liberty in the background, and the wind tousling his hair. He chanted a refrain that would become familiar that election year. "A recession is when your neighbor loses his job, a depression is when you lose yours and a recovery is when Jimmy Carter loses his!"[36] A mid-September poll published in the *Washington Post* showed the two candidates deadlocked at 37 percent apiece.[37]

Then the Carter campaign began to try to define Ronald Reagan for voters. It was the standard Democratic strategy to identify conservative Republicans as being out of touch with the mainstream of political life. Barry Goldwater was the first among many COP candidates to be labeled as "extreme." The opposition believed the electorate was still trying to figure out who Reagan was, so they went hard after the Republican in speeches. They also rolled out attack ads designed to raise questions about Reagan's ability at age 69 to handle the job. The problem was that Ronald Reagan was a well-known and accepted television personality. The Carter campaign fell into the trap of treating their opponent as a political candidate instead of a television celebrity. They failed to realize that the persistent optimism, uncomplicated policy proposals and emotional rhetoric he always used connected with voters. The Carter campaign kept waiting for the crowbar to fall, and it kept wrecking their plans.

By October, a dozen battleground states were considered toss-ups. President Carter believed the key to winning them was to get Reagan into a television studio for a debate. The Democrats were contemptuous of Reagan and believed they could win the election if they could expose him as a "grade B actor" in public. Patrick Caddell, the president's pollster, later said, "I don't think the president . . . felt Ronald Reagan was well informed. I think that's a nice way to put it."[38] The Reagan team was split on the subject of a debate, but given the closeness of the race, sentiment gradually favored a face-to-face showdown. The League of Women Voters immediately issued an invitation at the Cleveland Convention Center for October 28, only one week before the election.

The president's plan for the debate was to go right at Reagan, hitting him on several issues where they thought he changed his mind. The Republican strategy, in the words of Lyn Nofziger, was to again just "Let Reagan be Reagan." The most memorable line from the debates was when Carter attacked Reagan on the issue of Social Security and Medicare. The GOP nominee emitted a low chuckle and said, "There you go again," and the audience forgot an earlier admonition to be silent and laughed. If that line did not finish Carter off, the summation did. Reagan suggested in his ending that when voters went to the booth, they should ask themselves: "Are you better off than you were four years ago? Is it easier to buy things in the store than it was four years ago? Is there more or less employment than there was four years ago? Is

America as respected throughout the world as it was? Do you feel that our security is as safe? That we're as strong as we were four years ago?"[39]

Television demonstrated, yet again, its primitive power in politics. More than 105 million people watched the debate, and reporters who covered the campaign felt a quantum leap in the enthusiasm for Reagan at its conclusion. While both sides claimed victory and the polls were inconclusive, it was clear that a gloom was enveloping the president's campaign. Reagan told the crowds in the final days that Carter reminded him "of someone who can name the fifty parts of an automobile—he just can't drive it or fix it."[40] One campaign ad that ran nationally growled, "Do you really think the Iranians would have taken American hostages if Ronald Reagan was president?" Polls in the last week still had the outcome a toss-up, but in the end Ronald Reagan won a landslide victory.

The Reagan conservative coalition united the South and Midwest, drained conservatives from labor unions and Jewish voters from their historic Democratic allegiance, added evangelical voters, and stirred enthusiasm with younger and new voters. That coalition would define politics for the next 20 years. The Republican presidential nominee garnered 489 electoral votes to Carter's 49. Reagan was elected with a sweep of all but six states and the District of Columbia. John Anderson, the third party candidate, won no electoral votes, but had over five million popular votes. The nation had over 200 media markets, with about half the national population in the top 30, and Reagan won 24 of them.[41] Reagan won 51 percent of the vote compared with incumbent Jimmy Carter's 41 percent, and John Anderson's 7 percent. "It was the biggest repudiation of an American president since Herbert Hoover lost in 1932, and perhaps the most stunning too."[42] Even Hoover, crushed by FDR in 1932, took 10 more electoral votes than Carter managed. Reagan made Jimmy Carter the first president in 48 years—and the first Democrat in 92 years—to lose a bid for reelection. The GOP picked up 13 seats in the U.S. Senate and took the majority.

As for the candidate himself? He was taking a shower when Jimmy Carter called to concede; the polls in California would not close for another two hours.[43] The 1980 election was a turning point in American politics. Reagan's success led to a new party realignment with liberal

Republicans and conservative Democrats changing party affiliation, and it signaled the new power of Sun Belt suburbs in politics.

NOTES

1. Craig Shirley, *Rendezvous with Destiny* (Wilmington, DE: ISI Books, 2009), p. 13.

2. David Frum, *How We Got Here* (New York: Basic Books, 2000), p. 17.

3. Stephen F. Hayward, *The Age of Reagan: The Conservative Counterrevolution, 1980–1989* (New York: Crown Forum, 2009), p. 611.

4. Shirley, *Rendezvous with Destiny*, p. 20.

5. Ibid., p. 25.

6. Kiron K. Skinner, Annelise Anderson, and Martin Anderson, eds., *Reagan: In His Own Hand* (New York: Free Press, 2001), pp. 227, 468.

7. Ibid., p. xv.

8. J. David Woodard, *The America That Reagan Built* (Westport, CT: Praeger, 2006), p. 24.

9. Shirley, *Rendezvous with Destiny*, p. 30.

10. *Vital Speeches*, July 15, 1979.

11. Ibid.

12. Shirley, *Rendezvous with Destiny*, p. 54.

13. *Time*, December 30, 1979.

14. Shirley, *Rendezvous with Destiny*, p. 64.

15. Ibid., p. 73.

16. Ronald Reagan, *An American Life* (New York: Simon and Schuster, 1990), p. 213.

17. Ibid., p. 214.

18. Shirley, *Rendezvous with Destiny*, p. 162.

19. Ibid., p. 170.

20. Michael Barone, *Our Country* (New York: Free Press, 1990), pp. 594–595.

21. Shirley, *Rendezvous with Destiny*, p. 191.

22. Ibid., p. 201.

23. Woodard, *The America That Reagan Built*, p. 29.

24. Ibid., p. 11.

25. *Time*, May 5, 1980.

26. *Washington Post*, May 5, 1980.

27. *U.S. News and World Report*, June 16, 1980.

28. Shirley, *Rendezvous with Destiny*, p. 302.

29. Reagan, *An American Life*, p. 216.

30. Shirley, *Rendezvous with Destiny*, p. 367.

31. Ibid., p. 374.

32. Ibid., p. 379.

33. Peggy Noonan, *When Character Was King* (New York: Viking, 2001), p. 131.

34. Shirley, *Rendezvous with Destiny*, pp. 449–450.

35. Theodore H. White, *The Making of the President, 1960* (New York: Atheneum House, 1961), p. 243.

36. Shirley, *Rendezvous with Destiny*, p. 459.

37. Barry Susman and Paul Ferber, "Economic Prospects Give Carter Edge," *Washington Post*, September 14, 1980.

38. Shirley, *Rendezvous with Destiny*, p. 506.

39. Ibid., p. 544.

40. Ibid., p. 553.

41. Ibid., p. 32.

42. Barone, *Our Country*, p. 596.

43. Reagan, *An American Life*, pp. 221–222.

Chapter 8

PRESIDENT

A neighbor once said of Ronald Reagan that "nothing ever changed him." What she meant was that he wasn't given to self-importance like so many other politicians. He didn't play with people, like showing up late because he was the most important person invited. He had humility; he didn't think he was better than others. In December 1980, one month after being elected president, and just before he left his California home to move into the most important address in America, he called his longtime personal aide to help with an important task. What was the pressing issue for the president elect? Dave Fischer was needed to help put the Christmas lights up on the Reagan ranch house. Fischer recalled, "There were Secret Service there but that wasn't their job. It was a husband and father's job to do that for his family . . . so that's what we did that afternoon."[1]

When the Reagans came to Washington, the Carters broke with tradition and did not give them a personal tour of their new home. Instead, the outgoing tenants greeted them a few days before the inauguration, and then turned the incoming residents over to the staff. The night before the swearing in, at a gala ceremony in Landover, Maryland, actor Jimmy Stewart, himself a brigadier general from World War II, appeared onstage with General Omar Bradley, the nation's only re-maining five-star general. Bradley was in a wheelchair, and together the two men stopped in front of the president elect and saluted. Ronald Reagan stood in response and returned the salute. When he sat down, the next president leaned over to his wife and said, "I think it's finally sunk in."

Jimmy and Roslyn Carter greeted Ron and Nancy Reagan the next morning in the limousine on the way to the inauguration. Carter was si-lent, exhausted and depressed, after a night of dealing with last minute problems in the release of the American hostages in Iran. The feared "October surprise," of a negotiated liberation of the captives before the election to boost the president's reelection, never materialized. Instead, the hostages would be freed moments after Reagan was sworn in, a final humiliation for the past president. At the time, Reagan thought Carter rude in the limousine, "but eight years later I think we could sense a little of how President Carter must have felt that day—to have served as president, to have gone through the intense highs and lows of the job, to have tried to do what he thought was right, to have had all the farewells and good-bye parties, and then to be forced out of the White House by a vote of the people. . . . It must have been very hard on him."[2]

The inauguration that year broke tradition. Previous swearing-in ceremonies were held on the east of the Capitol, where the shade from the marble building overlooked a dull parking lot. Reagan wanted to look west, to his boyhood home in Illinois and his ranch in California, and into the sun. The view was spectacular, a vista framed by librar-ies and museums stretching down the Mall to the Washington Monu-ment. It took a month to build the scaffolding, painted white to reflect the bright sun of January 20, 1981. The weather cooperated; it was 55 degrees, the warmest on record. The president wore a club coat, striped pants, and a gray vest, and Nancy wore a red dress and a coat by Adolfo. Chief Justice Warren E. Burger administered the oath of office on the Reagan family Bible, in which his mother had inscribed, "You can be too big for God to use, but you cannot be too small." Nancy Reagan wrote in her memoir that "it [the Bible] was old and crumbling and taped together, and it seemed just right for the occasion."[3]

With the sun in his face, Ronald Reagan spoke down the sweep of the Capitol steps and corridors of the buildings into history. The financial heart of the country was about to stop beating, and the arteries were clogged with government regulations and taxes. "In this present crisis," he said, "government is not the solution to our problem, government is the problem."[4] He wrote most of the 20-minute speech himself, it was not soaring or lyrical, but declarative and explanatory. It had the avowed purpose of shedding the politics of past despair, and getting the country to believe in itself again. "The economic ills we suffer have come upon us over several decades. They will not go away in days, weeks or months, but they will go away."[5] The country needed reassurance, which Reagan provided, but no one was certain what would happen next.

The day was more emotional than most because at the moment Reagan took the oath of office, the American hostages were loaded aboard a Boeing 727 and flown out of Tehran's blacked-out airport. The 444 days of the national nightmare were at an end, and America had a new president. In Washington, Mr. and Mrs. Reagan traveled from the Capitol to the White House down Pennsylvania Avenue in an open-top limousine as people stood 10 deep along the parade route to wave and cheer. The Reagans watched the inaugural parade from the grandstand, and waved to the Dixon High School band. After the parade, they entered the executive mansion holding hands. In the Oval Office, Reagan offered a brief silent prayer and leaned over to his aide, Michael Deaver, to ask: "Do you have goose bumps?" Deaver laughed and confessed that he did.

That night the new president dressed in a white tie and tails, turned to one of his children and comically clicked his heels and declared, "I'm the president." Nancy Reagan set tongues wagging with an inaugural wardrobe said to cost $25,000, all privately raised. They went to every one of the 10 inaugural balls. A seven-foot-tall, 3,000-pound inaugural cake, baked in six sections in Quincy, Massachusetts, arrived in Washington too soft to be reassembled and too big to fit through the Kennedy Center doors. The whole thing had to be taken to the Army and Navy Club, where it was consumed by generals and admirals.[6]

Ronald Reagan began to change the country the next morning. It was in a fiscal crisis similar to the one California faced when he took over as governor 13 years earlier, but this one was much worse and could not be solved by a tax increase. It was one thing to quote Thomas

Paine on the political campaign trail that "we have it in our power to start the world all over again," but it was another thing entirely to actually do it. Interest rates were the highest since the Civil War; the prime rate was at an astonishing 21.5 percent. In his campaign four years earlier, Jimmy Carter developed a concept called the "misery index," defined as the sum of inflation and unemployment. In 1976 the figure was around 13 percent; by 1981 it was more than 20 percent. There was plenty of sadness to go around.

The nation's population in 1980 was a little more than 227 million, just about double what it was when Nelle Reagan scribbled that thought for the day in her Bible at the height of the Great Depression. Demographers wondered if it would get much larger, since more and more women were working and couples were consciously deciding not to have children. Eighteen percent of births were outside of marriage in 1980; the number of singles in the population along with the number of couples living together without bothering to marry was on the rise.[7]

The Gross National Product was about $3.0 trillion. The Dow Jones Industrials average drifted back and forth around the 900 mark. It would reach a low of 776 in August 1982.[8] America's economy was, in the words of the time, "soft"; but for most people the words was a misnomer. The country was in a recession, and it seemed insoluble. The federal budget was somewhere around $500 billion, with the Defense Department taking the largest chunk, some $134 billion. Still, it was not enough, and the government was constantly either borrowing money or asking for a tax increase. The average salary was $24,500, and in more and more families both spouses worked to pay the bills. Movie tickets cost $2.69, a Burger King Burger was $1.40, a gallon of gas cost $1.25, and *Time* magazine sold for $1.75 at the counter.[9]

The Reagan team began putting together an economic recovery package on the day after the election. The press called it "Reaganomics," and it was the most ambitious reform effort of American capitalism since the New Deal of the 1930s. The four key parts of it were income tax cuts, new expenditure priorities, monetary restraint, and regulatory reform. Without a doubt the most controversial part of the package was the tax cuts. Historically the government did not cut taxes in a time of recession; it cut them in a time of budget surpluses. The problem was the country had not had one of those since the Eisenhower administration. The Reagan proposal suggested that when taxes were cut the money they generated for business and upper-income groups would be used for capital investments. The economy would recover and the tax losses would be reclaimed by the resultant expansion. This approach, variously called trickle down or supply side, would reinvigorate spending and consumption. The expectation was that fiscal cuts, along with a diminished role for government in the system, would end what Reagan criticized in his inaugural: "a tax system which penalizes successful achievement and keeps us from maintaining full productivity."[10]

The "Reagan revolution" set the spending priority for the military, not social programs. Monetary policy had to be tightened enough to bring down inflation, but not so much as to create a recession. Regulation had to be cut to boost productivity, but without eliminating public support for the controls that caused their enactment in the first place. Taxes had to be cut, but without raising the specter of bulging deficits. The president was confident, but the details remained murky.

The new president's first official act on moving into the White House was to take out the solar water heating panels on the roof placed there by Jimmy Carter. Eight days later he ended oil price controls. Ronald Reagan changed the mood of the country on the premise that if you improved the national disposition you improved the nation.[11] Up at 7:00 or 7:15 A.M., Reagan began the day by reading the papers as he drank Sanka or brewed decaf. He was in the office by 9:00 A.M. for a 15-minute meeting with the senior staff, then worked straight through the day, taking his lunch on a tray, until 5:00 or 6:00 P.M. In the evening he took calls, wrote letters and ate an early dinner with Nancy. A dinner, a speech, an interview or a personal appearance changed the evening routine.

In those first months, they all worked hard. James A. Baker, the newly appointed Chief of Staff, who came over from the George H. W. Bush campaign, remembered, "The power of the presidency . . . is hard to resist, so the president regularly invited key Democrats to the Oval Office, to state dinners, even to Camp David."[12] To pass the program, Reagan cobbled together a coalition of Republicans and conservative Democrats. The new mood in Washington was political capital with a confederate legacy that could be spent in any state south of the Potomac River. For example, Reagan carried Texas by 600,000 votes, while Democrats won 19 of 24 congressional districts. Democratic Party loyalty was suspect in Texas and other parts of Dixie as well, where in 1980 the GOP carried every state in the region with the exception of Jimmy Carter's home state of Georgia.[13] Reagan "personally lobbied hundreds of Congressmen and opinion-makers."[14] James Baker worked 16-hour days courting congressmen. "During the first hundred days of his presidency, Reagan held 69 meetings with 467 members of Congress, promoting some of them to say that they had seen more of Reagan in four months than they had of Carter in four years."[15]

Catastrophe came in the middle of the budget lobbying process. On the afternoon of March 30, 1981, Reagan had been in office just nine weeks. He accepted a speaking invitation before 3,500 members of the AFL-CIO's Building Workers Union at Washington, D.C.,'s Hilton Hotel. The topic was his favorite, tax cuts and economic growth. As the only president ever to be an AFL-CIO member, he knew from the campaign that he would get a warm reception from what was usually a hostile audience for Republicans. He wore a new blue pinstripe suit and roused the crowd with a standing ovation. After the speech, Reagan exited the hotel by the VIP entrance where a black Lincoln limousine awaited him, and police stood at a rope barrier restricting reporters, onlookers and cameramen. As he walked to the limo, Mike Putzel of the Associated Press called out, "Mr. President!" The reporter wanted to ask a question about the Solidarity movement in Poland.

With his arm raised in a wave, the president began to turn toward Putzel, just as Michael Deaver put his hand on the back of press secretary Jim Brady to direct him to intercept the press and get between them and the president. At that moment everyone heard what sounded like firecrackers. In the crowd was 25-year-old John W. Hinckley Jr., carrying a .22-caliber Rohm RG-14 revolver loaded with Devastator bullets designed to explode on impact.[16] In a bizarre attempt to live up to his family's expectations, and at the same time impress actress Jodie Foster, Hinckley had decided to kill the president.

Six shots rang out.

Press Secretary Jim Brady collapsed with a bullet to the head. Secret Service agent Timothy McCarthy and policeman Thomas Delahany were also hit. Agent Jerry Parr pushed President Reagan into the limousine, slamming his head on the doorjamb in the process. The presi-

The Secret Service moves in after the assassination attempt on President Reagan on March 30, 1981. (Courtesy Ronald Reagan Presidential Library.)

dent fell onto the car's transmission bump and did not believe that he had been hit, even though he felt an acute pain in his chest. "Jerry, get off, I think you've broken one of my ribs."[17] Parr noticed that blood was coming out of the president's mouth and he ordered the limousine to go directly to George Washington University Hospital.

Reagan complained of difficulty breathing on the way, but when the limo arrived at the emergency room he walked into the hospital without assistance—only to collapse once inside. He faced two hours of surgery as doctors removed a .22-caliber bullet that struck his seventh rib and lodged less than an inch from his heart. The president had a partially collapsed left lung and received eight units of blood. Dr. Dennis O'Leary of the hospital staff said he was "right on the margin" of death, losing about 40 percent of his blood volume.[18] Four days later the president's temperature soared to 102 degrees.

Days later, what had happened outside the Hilton became clear. The president was hit by the fifth shot, "which ricocheted off the armor of the limousine, flattened out, went through the half-inch space between the open door and the car, and then sliced into the president, hitting him under his left armpit."[19] After the surgery, more bad news awaited.

Although the White House wrapped the 12-day hospital stay in optimism, interspersed with Reagan's jokes, the president had a secondary infection that was as serious as his initial gunshot wound.

In sum, it was a close call, closer than the American people were told, and things were even worse than reported. Part of this was because of Reagan himself. He made news through his surrogates. When James A. Baker walked in the emergency room, the president winked from behind his oxygen mask and asked, "Who's minding the store?" His greeting to his wife was just as light, "Honey, I forgot to duck."[20] The truth was that John Hinckley nearly succeeded in killing the president. If six-foot-tall Jim Brady was five-foot-five Michael Deaver, Ronald Reagan would have been dead. The bullet destined for Reagan hit Brady in the head instead.

News of the shooting traumatized the country. Television coverage was live, but the news reached others third or fourth hand, from a passing stranger or a telephone call, or a waiter in a restaurant. Nancy Reagan recalled the "scenes of Parkland Hospital in Dallas and the day President Kennedy was shot."[21] The whole country remembered, and held its breath. Michael Deaver believed that President Reagan was not in any real danger, until "I ducked into the room where the president had been taken . . . [and saw] my president, was stripped to the skin and one of the doctors was holding his coat up to the light, evaluating the tiny bullet hole under the left sleeve."[22] Around the nation, people wanted the news to be false. They gathered around television sets and car radios and talked to strangers in bars. The unspoken fear was that the shooting continued a string of national disasters stretching back to the 1960s and signifying some sort of decline in American society and the unraveling of society.

That did not happen. Reagan's quick recovery, more remarkable given that he was 70 years old, was seen as symbolic of a revitalized national spirit. "It took me forty minutes to cut through that chest," Dr. Aaron the operating surgeon told Michael Deaver. "I have never in my life seen a chest like that on a man his age."[23] His job approval rose to 73 percent, and his courage and humor earned him the admiration of the nation. "Please tell me you are all Republicans," he quipped to the doctors when he was wheeled into the operating room.[24]

He was different after the assassination attempt. "I know it's going to be a long recovery," he wrote on the first evening back in the White

House. "Whatever happens now I owe my life to God and will try to serve him every way I can."[25] The attempt on Reagan's life was one of the major factors of his becoming a popular president, not just that he survived but the way he recovered with grace and élan. The assassination created a bond between him and the American people that was never really broken.

In June the work paid off, and Congress passed Reagan's budget without major alterations. It was the largest tax cut in U.S. history, and most of the press concluded that with it, Reagan had ended 50 years of liberal government.[26] Subsequent years would show that wasn't the case, but he had substantially derailed the welfare state momentum. The *Wall Street Journal* commented on the "spectacular tax victory."[27] More importantly, Reagan showed a sophisticated grasp of the issues and the legislative process. He knew how to use television, and his personal popularity, to get what he wanted. It became clear that he would stick to his convictions, and not moderate under pressure.

The coalition of conservative Democrats called "boll weevils" (because many of them came from the South and their abandonment of the Democratic Party had a debilitating effect on the majority party in

President Reagan celebrates with his staff in the Oval Office on the passage of federal tax legislation in 1981. (Courtesy Ronald Reagan Presidential Library.)

Congress), and Republicans formed again in August to enact a series of tax reductions on individual incomes that amounted to 25 percent over a three-year period. It also lowered the tax on estates and provided for Individual Retirement Accounts (IRAs), in the hope that the proposed reductions would lead to more savings, diminished consumer debt and less inflation. So-called Reaganomics was the essence of the first-term presidency. In passing the legislation, Ronald Wilson Reagan changed the economic philosophy in Washington and in the country at large.

In the next few months, the stamina and determination of a still-recovering Ronald Reagan was put to the test. In August, the 13,000 members of the Professional Air Traffic Controllers Organization (PATCO) decided to go on strike until their demands for reduced workloads and higher salaries were met. As federal employees, the controllers were violating a written pledge in the no-strike clause of their employment contract. Unlike a walkout of automobile workers or coal miners, this one was less a threat to the economy than to the safety of the nation's airline passengers.

The president responded in the Rose Garden with an ultimatum that was clear, return to work within 48 hours or face termination. Ironically, PATCO was one of the few unions that supported Reagan's candidacy in the 1980 election. To the surprise of the PATCO strikers, and labor union loyalists in the Democratic Party, the public sided with the president and had little sympathy with the controllers. When the federal employees did not show up for work, Reagan fired them, and directed Transportation Secretary Lewis to hire replacements.[28]

The controllers were tough professionals who manned airport and control towers and radar centers around the country. Their jobs required concentration, precision and endurance. If an aircraft crashed, they were usually to blame. The PATCO argument was that the pressure of the job justified an 11 percent pay increase. Reagan said that his SAG years made him the best friend they would ever have in the White House, but there was no way he would accept their demands, and he would not negotiate if they went out on strike. Lane Kirkland, president of the AFL-CIO, joined a picket line with members of the striking controllers. In Toronto, three controllers were suspended for showing sympathy in refusing to clear flights to the United States. PATCO appealed for other unions in the United States and abroad to honor their strike and boycott sending planes to U.S. airports.[29] The press and union workers openly speculated that airplanes would crash when they were directed by inexperienced controllers. If there had been an accident, of course, then the consequences for Reagan would have been catastrophic, but no accidents happened. For the new president, fresh from victories in Congress and a remarkable recovery attempt on his life, a new principle was now at work in Washington declaring that people should be held accountable for their oaths. The decisive way Reagan handled the PATCO strike convinced many Americans that he was, in the words of *Washington Post* reporter Haynes Johnson writing about sports figures, "a hero" when the country had forgotten there were any.[30]

The city of Washington was finding out more about the president in bits and pieces, and discovering that he was very different from his predecessors. For example, he was not the type of leader to consult polls to guide his decisions. Instead he used public opinion to find out what people were thinking, and then summoned his powers of persuasion to get them to change their minds. In September before he took office, 60 percent of those surveyed by the Gallup poll thought that the high cost of living and inflation were the most important problem facing the country. No respondent had ever heard of tax cuts as a solution for the budget crisis. In the fall of 1981, Gallup found that 87 percent of Americans had heard of the administration's tax cut program, and 59 percent favored it as a solution. Not all of this was Reagan's doing, of course, but much of it was, and he got the credit.[31]

Reagan recuperated in the Lincoln bedroom after being shot. He had a lot of time to think in his robe and pajamas as he watched TV from his hospital-type bed. In this time, he decided to write a personal letter to Leonid Brezhnev, the Soviet leader. The United States had a grain embargo to the USSR, imposed by Jimmy Carter in 1979. Reagan wanted to lift it. The State Department, and several of his advisors, opposed lifting the embargo as well as writing a personal letter. Reagan wrote the letter anyway. He got a blunt response, but it was typical of him to trust his own instincts over those of the people around him. After all, he was the one whose name was on the bumper sticker, and he won the election. What most observers failed to catch was that the Soviet Union watched the PATCO decision just like the rest of the country—but they were more impressed. They saw how the new American president matched rhetorical toughness with action, and how the outcome showed a side of Reagan others didn't see.

In those early months in Washington, the Reagans found themselves to be strangers to the established rituals and folkways of the city. Every administration was migratory of course, but Washington usually found ways to be welcoming in some circumstance. When John Kennedy was president, the country exulted in his drawl and good looks, while hostesses learned to serve clam chowder at parties. When Jimmy Carter arrived as a professed outsider, the city made his administration comfortable with grits and southern hospitality. No similar welcoming greeted the California Republicans.

The impression official Washington had of the new president in 1981 was inauspicious. Clark Clifford, the silver-haired Brahmin of the nation's political establishment, who had served presidents across half a century and prided himself on political access, pushed for a meeting in the first weeks after Reagan's inauguration. Michael Deaver reluctantly acquiesced to the request. That evening at the house of another Washington institution, Pamela Harriman, Clifford declared Reagan to be an "amiable dunce."[32] Nicholas von Hoffman of the *Washington Post* said it was "humiliating to think of this unlettered, self-assured bumpkin being our president."[33] Tip O'Neill, the venerable Massachusetts Democrat, opined, "He knows less than any president I've ever known." Anthony Lewis of the *New York Times* claimed he had only a seven-minute attention span.

What the insiders did not understand was that Ronald Reagan connected with the American people in a way few of them—regardless of their experience—could fathom. The president realized that the spirit of the nation was more important than any monthly statistics measuring economic progress, or poll results showing presidential popularity. Reagan's job was to inspire confidence in the future and reassure the country that things were going to work out. The optimism was not a trivial quality; instead, it was the essential approach to life that he carried from Dixon, Illinois to Hollywood, and to the governor's mansion and, finally, to the White House. With him as actor the country was one vast stage. He translated the complexities of a postindustrial economy and a dangerous world into phrases, jokes and stories that people could understand and believe.

Humor was a central part of who he was and how he related to others. One of his ways of dealing with criticism was not to get mad, but to undermine his critics by agreeing with them. Like older men, he preferred the comfort of a routine, arriving in the Oval Office at the same time, regular meetings and working through a schedule. "Faithfully, after dinner, he would read through to the last page of every colored folder (red for Classified, green for Action Items, gray for Speeches and Statements, blue for Information), checking what he approved and adding terse marginalia until duty was done and he could go to bed."[34] Yet, when the press said he was lazy, he didn't deny it. "I know hard work never killed anyone, but I figure why take a chance?"[35] The press was scandalized when Ed Meese chose not to wake the president in an early administration foreign policy crisis. Reagan's response: "I've laid down the law to my staff, to everyone from now on about anything that happens: No matter what time it is, wake me—even if it's in the middle of a cabinet meeting."[36]

There were stories he would tell on himself, and stories he would tell about others. Often the narratives, while compelling from a political standpoint, were pure fiction. Reagan confused scenes from movies with real events. The most serious of these gaffes was a story he used in both the 1976 and 1980 election campaigns. and repeated in 1983 at the annual convention of Medal of Honor winners. The setting was World War II Europe. During the course of a bombing raid over the continent a B-17 bomber was hit by antiaircraft fire. The ball-turret gunner was severely wounded, and the other crew members were unable to get him out of the turret. As the B-17 continued to lose altitude the commander ordered the men to bail out. "And as the men started to leave the plane . . . the boy knowing that he was left behind to go down with the plane, cried out in terror." The last man out was the commander, who took the boy's hand and said, "Never mind, son, we'll ride it down together." The Congressional Medal of Honor was posthumously awarded.

The story caused Lars-Erik Nelson of the *New York Daily News* to do some research. The reporter went through 434 citations of the Medal of Honor, and could find no such award. He wrote a column about the speech and Reagan's fictional storytelling. A reader responded that the story reminded him of a scene from the 1944 movie, *A Wing and a Prayer*. Another reader believed the story had appeared in an issue of *Reader's Digest*, and Nelson found the account there about a Flying Fortress base in England. Yet he could find no verification for the story. The best he could do was determine that the apocryphal incident, had become almost a legend around the base, but no one confirmed it had any basis in fact.[37]

It mattered little to Reagan if the stories he told were invented or real, what mattered was their effect on the audience. For an actor the effect of storytelling was measured in the response of the listeners, not the accuracy of the tale told. When informed of the Nelson article, Reagan justified the story by saying that he wanted to rebuild the military, and just as important as the hardware, was the military's morale. The president had an arsenal of emotional stories that he used with great effect. The press was constantly sniping at him for their accuracy, and official Washington made them the stuff of cocktail circuit conversation, but they missed the point. Hollywood was America's dream factory, and Reagan was a part of that manufactured culture. He incorporated fiction into political rhetoric to fit his own needs. It worked.

Humor was also Nancy Reagan's secret weapon, and one she used devastatingly well in the spring of 1982. After a year in office, the press was snipping at Nancy Reagan and she was feeling the pain. To the inside-the-beltway crowd, she was a frivolous socialite who hobnobbed with the idle rich and dressed in designer gowns with mink as an accessory. She set tongues wagging when the Reagans tapped private sources for $800,000 in fix-up expenses at the White House, and an additional $200,000 for new china. Nancy Reagan was said to be too much "Hollywood," enamored with the glitz and wealth of tinsel town.

First ladies always came in for some press scrutiny in Washington. Bess Truman and Mamie Eisenhower were criticized for their dowdy clothes, and while Jackie Kennedy was the epitome of glamour, she paid for her popularity with a lack of privacy. Betty Ford was treated well by the press, especially after her bout with breast cancer, but Rosalynn Carter was mocked for taking an interest in the policy issues that preoccupied her husband. In a 1981 poll by *Good Housekeeping*, Nancy Reagan did not even make the 10 "most admired" women on the list.[38]

The First Lady's Washington-wise secretary, Sheila Tate, suggested that she use the annual Gridiron Dinner in March 1982 as an opportunity to surprise the locals, and change her image. The event was a coveted ticket around town, a white-tie dinner held every spring for 600 invited guests. The program was always the same: members of the press performed clever and funny skits poking fun at both Democrats and Republicans. The skits were followed in turn by two speakers—one from each party. The evening ended with a brief toast to the president, followed by his response. Everything was off the record, but the evening could be memorable for barbs, laughs, and the way people handled criticism.

In 1982, the word was out that the press was going to do a skit poking fun at Mrs. Reagan's fashion tastes. Sheila Tate thought it would be good if Nancy Reagan appeared in her own skit, in a surprise role. But Nancy Reagan, a former MGM actress, had more than a bit part in mind. "Would you sing?" Tate asked. The former stage actress, turned first lady, said she would. "Would you dance?" Another nod of agreement followed the question. Someone suggested that Mrs. Reagan attack the press in her parody, but she knew show business better than the Washington insiders. "I'm not willing to attack the press. . . . If I'm going to do this at all; I think I should make fun of myself."[39]

A White House speechwriter put together a routine based on the old show tune "Second Hand Rose," and Mrs. Reagan rehearsed without telling the president. When the night arrived, and the Gridiron chorus did a version of "Secondhand Clothes," mocking the extravagance of Nancy Reagan, she stepped away from the head table for the ladies room. Some in the room thought her leaving was a sign that she was visibly upset at the parody, but the whole place was stunned a few minutes later to see her burst through a rack of clothes on stage wearing an aqua skirt, with red and yellow flowers held together by safety pins, a floppy hat and feathered boa.[40]

On stage, the old Fanny Brice hit from the 1920s got new lyrics:

Second-hand clothes.
I give my second hand clothes
To museum collectives and traveling shows
They were so happy that they got 'em
Won't notice that they were ragged at the bottom.
Goodbye, you old worn-out mess.

I never wear a frock more than once.
Calvin Klein, Adolfo, Ralph Lauren and Bill Blass.
Ronald Reagan's mama's going strictly First Class.
Rodeo Drive, I sure miss Rodeo Drive.
In frumpy Washington.

For a minute the act was greeted by thunderous silence, then the audience rose and yelled for an encore. Amid a standing ovation she repeated the routine. Ronald Reagan was just as enchanted as everyone else in the room. Gone was the image of a self-absorbed socialite, replaced by one of a politician's wife who cared what other people thought, and showed it.

Reagan enjoyed the time-consuming ceremonial part of the job. Anyone who standardly invited the president to an event might suddenly be shocked to find out that he accepted. In Washington, where socializing and access were part of the job, Ronnie Reagan was not one of the boys. In their first term, the Reagans threw 34 state dinners. He thought that parties and dinners were for fun, not work. In most social situations he preferred to tell stories, and when asked how he was bearing up under the strain of the office he would invariably tell a joke. He loved to hear the band play "Hail to the Chief," and Reagan grasped something Carter never did. Americans wanted their president to be a ruler. As Frank Reynolds, the *ABC News* correspondent said of the American electorate, "They *want* to look up to the president . . . [and] they don't like it when he goes on television wearing a sweater" (as Jimmy Carter had done).[41] Ronald Reagan never disappointed anyone when it came to respect for the office of the president.

Reagan's principal oddity, of course, was that he was a conservative ideologue in a city full of liberals, relativists, and compromisers. The last avowed conservative in town was Richard Nixon, and official Washington exposed him as a fraud and drove him from power. Denizens were suspicious of the new actor president, but he showed them in the years to come that he was tough, fair, and above the criticism. In the give and take of political compromise he could be resolute and unyielding. Reagan came to the office with a short to-do list: he had a clear idea of what he wanted to accomplish and he never wavered from it.

He liked the accouterments of power, but didn't need them because he had the real thing. Nancy Reagan said he never needed power like most men. He knew what he believed and he knew why, so did everyone else in town. He didn't want new programs; he didn't want to start anything. Reagan ran his administration as a show, and he loved to exercise authority. Larry Speakes, who took over as press secretary after James Brady was shot, recalled when the president and his top aides were discussing the need to keep the door open for the possibility of a future tax increase. First, Jim Baker said, "Mr. President, we really ought to leave ourselves an opening," and the president said no, and then Ed Meese went at it with the same answer. Finally, Speakes handed Reagan a written statement, which left some room for a tax increase. The president began to read and was no more than halfway through the statement before he reached into the front of a desk, where there was a stand with two pens in it. "He grabbed one of the pens with such force that the base of the stand flew across the room, and he wrote 'NO TAX INCREASE' across the piece of paper and said 'This is what I want to say!' "[42] Reagan paused to look into the faces of his startled audience, then said, "Strong message to follow," and everyone laughed.

In many ways Reagan was a throwback to Eisenhower and the confidence the country had after World War II. The major difference was this time the economy wasn't cooperating. White House operatives, who in 1981 envisioned a Republican congressional majority in the approaching elections, were wondering if the president would be reelected. At a campaign fundraiser in Minneapolis, Minnesota, before the midterm elections, Reagan emerged from his limousine to be greeted by a banner proclaiming, "Welcome President Hoover."[43] On Election Day in 1982, more than nine million Americans were out of work, and the jaunty optimism of the inaugural ceremony was beginning to fade.

The Republicans lost 26 seats to the Democrats in the midterm election, but the conservative boll weevil majority governing coalition survived. By the end of 1982 only 41 percent of Americans said they approved of Reagan's leadership, and in early 1983 that figure would drop to 35 percent. His was the lowest midterm figure for any president in 40 years.[44] "For the rest of 1982, news from both home and abroad was mostly depressing for the President, his Administration, and his party."[45] From this nadir he would surge to win reelection by a land-slide in 1984. How did he do it? Reagan's political triumph came from three things: first, an expanding economy that continued to grow into the next decade; second, his mastery of divided government and acceptance of budget deficits; and third, Soviet belligerence and hubris.

On the economic front, the problem was not that Reaganomics wasn't working; it was that it was having mixed results. Inflation fell dramatically in the first year the new president assumed office. Decreases in the costs of various goods, especially oil, helped stabilize an economy that had been in freefall. Gone were the gas lines that haunted his predecessor, replaced by a belief that the economic pie must be increased, not simply sliced differently. The conviction of growth was fundamental to supply-side, Reaganomic doctrine. The administration believers wanted an expanding economy, and by 1983 they were beginning to see signs that the indicators were turning up. But there was a down side as well; the costs of entitlement programs like Social Security, Medicare, and Medicaid soared. To cover the shortfall, government borrowing went to record levels.

Reagan campaigned in 1980 by rashly promising a balanced budget and huge reductions in federal spending as a cure for the nation's economic woes. But he also promised an increase in defense spending, and an economy in the doldrums meant decreased tax revenues. In 1981, Reagan sent to Congress a $695.3 billion budget for fiscal year 1982. At the time, he predicted that this would generate a $45 billion deficit. Congress approved a $695.5 billion budget, almost the exact amount requested by the White House. However, the real deficit ended up being $128 billion, nearly three times larger than predicted. Talk of a balanced budget disappeared. The difficulty of borrowing made businesses wary of new capital investment, despite the tax cuts. Foreign competition, especially from Japan, added to domestic uncertainty.

Every year he was in office, Reagan submitted budgets to Congress that were larger than the previous year, and every one contained sizeable budget deficits. Reagan's impressive victory in 1980, and his repeat in 1984, failed to crack Democratic hegemony in the U.S. House, though the Senate early went the way of the presidency. High budget deficits have occurred in times of divided government, when different parties control the executive and legislative branches of government. Economists generally accept that 3 percent or more of the GNP is a telltale sign of unacceptably high deficits. From World War II until 1980, the offensive deficits the country had occurred only during a time of divided government. Not surprisingly, in the years from 1981 to 1987, when Democrats controlled the House and Republicans the Senate and White House, deficits were the rule.[46]

This meant that Ronald Reagan, the champion of fiscal restraint, balanced budgets and conservative government, was driving the country into bankruptcy. Nowhere was the uneasiness more apparent than in the U.S. Senate, where majority leader Howard Baker had to deal with 13 GOP freshmen senators implacably opposed to budget deficits, government growth and raising the national debt ceiling. Before a crucial vote to allow more government borrowing, Baker rounded up the freshmen and put them around a conference table. Then he brought in Republican senator Strom Thurmond, the senior senator from South Carolina, who epitomized tight-fisted austerity and fierce independence. In his whole career, Thurmond had never voted to increase the debt limit. "But I've never had Ronald Reagan as president before," he told the assembled audience, "and I'm going to vote for the debt-limit increase . . . and so are you."[47] The incident captured the mood of the times; if the economy recovered, then no one would remember the deficits.

That is exactly what happened. Economic conditions improved markedly after the midterm elections. The Dow surged from its 1982 low of 776, to a high of 2,722 in August 1987, a gain of more than 250 percent. Federal programs affecting the general welfare were cut in the expectation that people would be working instead of applying for governmental assistance. The howl from what was known as the social pork barrel, those interest groups who lived off state subsidies, was shrill and unending. When Reagan was elected, programs for the poor made up about 10 percent of the federal budget. To shrink welfare spending, Congress passed Reagan's Reconciliation Act of 1981, which reduced the budgets of 212 federal programs. The cuts included 11 percent in food stamps, 28 percent in child nutrition programs, 13 percent in Aid to Families with Dependent Children (AFDC), 25 percent in student financial aid, and 28 percent in fuel assistance for the poor.[48]

When Ronald Reagan came into office he cut the Housing and Urban Development budget in fiscal 1981 from $34.2 billion to $16.6 billion. This was a cut in authorization, not outlays. Such an authorization was a spending limit, much like a Visa or MasterCard account sets a personal credit limit, but revealed nothing about the amount of money spent. The actual amount of HUD outlays went up in the Reagan years, but this fact was drowned in the tide of political fallout that came from the initial budget authorization cuts. The visible homeless on city streets were taken as the symbol of Reaganomics in action for administration critics. Activists declared in 1982 that some 2.2 million were homeless and that "the number of homeless people in the United States could reach 3 million or more during 1983." The *New York Times* echoed this sentiment in an editorial when it declared, "The problem is not going to go away."[49] A report to the HUD Secretary on the Homeless and Emergency Shelters (1984) concluded that the number of homeless was much less and probably ranged from 250,000 to 350,000 nationally. The emergency shelters, far from bursting at the seams, were only about two-thirds full.

No issue was more important to Ronald Reagan, or his administration, than his aversion to communism. It was a struggle that consumed him and touched the very center of his political and personal life. From the time he was president of the Screen Actors Guild, through his rise with General Electric to elected office, he was a devoted anticommunist. As a consequence, his foreign policy, just like his economic policy, was in defiance of the way Washington treated the Soviet bloc.[50]

The conventional wisdom was that communism would collapse because of the erroneous economic presumptions at its core, and that a meltdown was inevitable. The assumption was that people would not work under compulsion for others in defiance of their own self-interest, so communism was bound to fail. He campaigned in 1980 on the theme: "Peace through strength," and he meant it. The bipartisan foreign policy of containment, initiated in the Truman administration, declared that the United States would support peoples resisting subjugation by the USSR, but not intervene or directly confront the Soviets. The policy could be described as one of wait and watch; it allowed communism to collapse from its own weight.

In the meantime, the United States discouraged Soviet aggression by building up a large stockpile of nuclear weapons. The idea behind the policy was that present fears were less than horrible imaginings. If the Soviet Union knew a confrontation would end hopelessly with bombs and rockets hitting Moscow, then the chances for peace would be greater, or so the theory went. John Foster Dulles, the Secretary of State under Dwight Eisenhower, called the policy "massive retaliation." Later it would become "mutually assured destruction," with the more fitting acronym, MAD.

Ronald Reagan lived through World War II and the Cold War. He was opposed to this policy. American presidents dating back to 1969 were of the belief that if the United States waited and played its cards right, it could have security on the cheap without war or confrontation. This was called "détente." Reagan believed the USSR was in the last throes of life, and he despised the policy. He believed the Cold War wasn't permanent, and he wanted to end it in a way he once described as "we win, they lose." "It was a conviction that Reagan himself deeply believed was born not out of reality, but of political pathology at home: defeatism, pessimism and appeasement."[51]

The Reagan policy was more confident. The president enjoyed reading intelligence reports about life in the Soviet bloc after he was elected. The briefing books were detailed and based on better information than the newspaper clippings, special reports and verbal accounts he relied on in his prepresidential days. In his first year in office, Reagan chaired 51 meetings of the National Security Council. "He particularly enjoyed information about the economic troubles they [the Soviets] were experiencing," recalled David Wigg, the CIA liaison to the White House.[52] The president's plan was to expand the American economy, then increase American military spending, and squeeze the Kremlin. He believed Moscow could not grow their military budgets because their consumer economy was already on a starvation diet. The Russians could afford neither guns nor butter. Reagan reasoned that if the United States went forward with an arms race buildup, then the communist system would collapse. In short, the defense buildup was as much about economic warfare against the Soviets as it was about restoring American military power.

He wanted to challenge the communist ideology at its base and force the Soviets to roll back their expansionist plans. In one of the most significant speeches of his presidency, delivered to the National Association of Evangelicals in March 1983, Reagan described the Cold War as a "struggle between right and wrong, good and evil." He asked the audience to pray for those who lived in totalitarian darkness, and then he concluded about the governments that "they are the focus of evil in the modern world."[53] The "evil empire" phrase was a subject of scorn at the State Department and on college campuses, but Reagan kept using it in his speeches and it kept working on his audiences.

The speech captured Reagan's views, since he saw the conflict between East and West as fundamentally moral, and believed his first duty as president was to be the affirmation of values in the American political system. As president, he believed one system was basically good, and the other one was fundamentally evil. He repeatedly said the West did not have to fear communism, and Ronald Reagan did not fear it either.

Others did, and they attacked the administration without pause. Anthony Lewis of the *New York Times* had a hard time finding words to describe the policy: "sectarian," "terribly dangerous," "outrageous," and "primitive."[54] Historian Arthur Schlesinger returned from a trip to Moscow in 1982 and found "more goods in the shops and more food in the markets" than on any previous trip. He dismissed the Reagan policy of confrontation as misguided.[55] Lawrence I. Barrett in his book, *Gambling With History: Ronald Reagan in the White House*, argued that the president made a mistake in management, and "relied too heavily, too long on his subordinates . . . [who] were the general [managers] of national security affairs."[56] Massachusetts Institute of Technology economist Lester Thurow praised the Soviet economic achievements and declared it a mistake to think that the people of Eastern Europe were miserable.

The establishment thinking of the time was that the United States and the Soviet Union were both superpowers based on different systems; neither one nor the other was inherently superior. In this view, the United States should avoid saying or doing anything that Moscow might view as "provocative" or "destabilizing." Above all, it was foolish to try to roll back Soviet advances; instead, the West should try to moderate the designs of communism.

Almost alone, Ronald Reagan had an alternate view of the alleged power and virtue of the Soviet system. He knew that any state-planned economy that dictated individual decisions and regulated consumption was bound to fail. For him the Soviet Union was a sick bear, and the question was not *if* it would perish, but *when*. As he said to the graduates of his alma mater, Eureka College at their commencement in May 1982, "The Soviet Empire is faltering because rigid centralized control has destroyed incentives for innovation, efficiency and individual achievement."[57] What was out of the ordinary is that Reagan saw communism not just as incompetent, but as "evil." The blight of the idea and its effect on human beings was the focus of the president's ire.

The Italian philosopher Niccolo Machiavelli famously declared in his book, *The Prince*, that "fortune determines one half of our actions, but that, even so, she leaves us to control the other half."[58] In 1983, President Reagan was both the victim and the beneficiary of this maxim, with successes and failures in what he could control, and the recipient of fateful events he could not. On August 31, the Soviets shot down a Boeing 747 jumbo jet airliner, Korean Airlines Flight 007 over Sakholin Island, declaring that it had wandered into their airspace. The Reagan administration insisted from the beginning of the crisis that the Soviets knew they were firing on a civilian airline, and called the decision a "barbaric act" by a "ruthless, totalitarian state."[59] The public supported the president's hard stand.

When NATO deployed a new generation of Pershing and cruise missiles in Europe, more than two million people took to the streets to protest the event. The Western allies had agreed to station 108 Pershing II missiles and 464 Tomahawk cruise missiles to counter a Soviet buildup. The nuclear freeze in the United States, France and Germany arose to excoriate the United States for deploying the weapons and escalating the arms race. Jonathan Schell's best-selling book *The Fate of the Earth* (1982) declared that "we hold this entire terrestrial creation hostage to nuclear destruction, threatening to hurl it back into the inanimate darkness . . . the machinery of destruction is complete, poised on a hair trigger."[60] The question was who was right about the Soviet Union. Was it a growling bear or an aging, sick animal about to dies of its own diseases. In October 1983, the president, along with British Prime Minister Margaret Thatcher and West German Chancellor Helmut Kohl, led the West in seeing that the missiles were made operational. Across the United States, city councils, state legislatures, and even the Democratically controlled U.S. House of Representatives supported a nuclear freeze.

Reagan remained obdurate. He agreed to cut the U.S. program if the Russians would make corresponding reductions, but they refused. In the give and take at the bargaining table, Paul Nitze, the top negotiator for the United States, asked Reagan what he should say to the Soviets after the administration rejected a proposal. "Well, Paul," said the president in his best Hollywood humility, "you just tell them you're working for one tough son of a bitch."[61] He was, and the rest of the world, not just one country in opposition, was finding that out.

In a final gambit to win in the court of public opinion, the Soviet Union threatened to withdraw from all arms negotiations if the missiles were made operational. The peace movement ratcheted up the demonstrations, declaring that the opening scenes of the made for television movie *The Day After,* when East and West break off negotiations before a nuclear exchange, was coming true. The president directed U.S. negotiators to make no new concessions, and allow the Soviets to leave if they wanted to. Reagan knew that the Soviets needed the Americans as a foil to stay in power, and any withdrawal by them would only be temporary.

The struggle over missiles in Europe sent relations between the two superpowers to unplumbed depths. The constant confrontations with the USSR, and the resulting tension, led Reagan to embrace an alternative to the Mutual Assured Destruction (MAD) philosophy that had guided American policy throughout the Cold War. When he was governor of California, Reagan visited the facilities of Lawrence Livermore laboratory where Dr. Edward Teller, the father of the hydrogen bomb, showed him the work his students were doing on space-based lasers. Teller told the then-governor that the lasers could be used to destroy nuclear missiles fired at the United States. Not surprisingly, when the Joint Chiefs of Staff met privately with Reagan on a snowy day in December 1982 to discuss an alternative to MAD, they found him receptive. Robert McFarlane recalled that the president sat quietly and listened to the military proposals. "It was clear from his demeanor that he was convinced it could be done."[62]

Reagan had long been concerned that the United States had no defense against Soviet missiles. "We have spent all that money," he said to Martin Anderson after a briefing, "and have all that equipment and there is nothing we can do to prevent a nuclear missile from hitting us."[63] The president had confidence in American ingenuity dating back to his days as a spokesman for General Electric. Even though he had no fixed idea about what the system would look like, Reagan decided to announce the beginning of research and development of the program.

His enthusiasm became fixed on something known as the Strategic Defense Initiative (SDI), or "Star Wars," as it was called by the press. He proposed the program in a March speech as an antimissile protective shield of space satellites and rockets to shoot down incoming ICBM weapons. Critics said he had too much faith in technology, but Reagan had more confidence in himself and the country he led. Press and liberal antagonisms did not worry Ronald Reagan because he knew the public favored some shield, no matter how porous, as better than none. In a dangerous world of Russian missiles and communist incursions, the Reagan administration offered both confrontation and protection—not a bad political combination that.

The quarrel with communism became more than words in October 1983, when Eugenia Charles, the prime minister of Dominica, asked the United States to intervene in the neighboring island of Grenada. "We had already lost Cuba to Communism," Reagan wrote years later. "I was determined the Free World was not going to lose Central America or more of the Caribbean to the Communists."[64] The Marxist government of Bernard Coard invited Cuban soldiers into the country after seizing control in a bloody coup. Reagan saw Grenada as a timely opportunity to eliminate a communist government in the Caribbean and at the same time embarrass Fidel Castro. In two days, the United States sent in 5,000 troops and subdued the Cubans as they ousted Coard. The Grenada invasion was proof that the United States was willing to confront communism, and take decisive action.

That policy was put to the test in Lebanon during Reagan's first term in office. The Middle Eastern country was beset with factions: sympathizers with the Palestinians, the Israelis, the Syrians, Lebanese Christians, Muslims and other partisans. The mission of the U.S. Marines in 1983 was to be an interposition force in one of the most faction-ridden places on earth. The hope was that they would help stabilize the situation and allow for a strong government to return. Unfortunately, this wish was just another name for fear. At 6:22 A.M. on October 23, 1983,

The Reagans view victims of the bombing of the U.S. Embassy in Beirut, Lebanon, at Andrews Air Force Base, Maryland. (Courtesy Ronald Reagan Presidential Library.)

a young terrorist drove a yellow Mercedes truck loaded with explosives into the four-story concrete headquarters building where 350 members of the First Battalion, Eighth Marine regiment were sleeping. In the next six and a half hours, 234 bodies were recovered, and 7 more people would die in the next days, bringing the total to 241.[65]

The Grenada and Lebanon events happened at the same time, and both involved the military. Years later, Reagan would remember the time as the "saddest day of my presidency, perhaps the saddest day of my life."[66] It was the worst tragedy to befall the military since Vietnam. "I believed in—and still believe in—the policy and decisions that originally sent the Marines to Lebanon," wrote the president.[67] There was nothing else to do but declare publicly that the Marines would stay in Beirut. "Stay the course" was the motto of the time.

NOTES

1. Peggy Noonan, *When Character Was King* (New York: Viking, 2001), pp. 133–134.

2. Ronald Reagan, *An American Life* (New York: Simon and Schuster, 1990), pp. 225–226.

3. Nancy Reagan and William Novak, *My Turn* (New York: Random House, 1989), p. 233.

4. "Let Us Begin an Era of National Renewal," *New York Times*, January 21, 1981, p. B1.

5. Ibid.

6. "Notes on People," *New York Times*, January 28, 1981, p. C1.

7. *Statistical Abstract of the United States*, 1980.

8. http://stockcharts.com/freecharts/historical/nasdaq1978.html.

9. *Statistical Abstract of the United States*, 1980; *Time*, January 22, 1981.

10. "Let Us Begin."

11. J. David Woodard, *The America That Reagan Built* (Westport, CT: Praeger, 2006), p. 34.

12. James A. Baker III, *Work Hard, Study and Keep Out of Politics* (New York: G. P. Putnam's Sons, 2006), p. 177.

13. J. David Woodard, *The New Southern Politics* (Boulder, CO: Lynne Rienner Press, 2006), pp. 249–307.

14. Edmund Morris, *Dutch* (New York: Random House, 1999), p. 424.

15. Lou Cannon, *President Reagan: The Role of a Lifetime* (New York: Simon and Schuster, 1991), p. 114.

16. Philip Taubman, "Explosive Bullet Struck Reagan, F.B.I. Discovers," *New York Times*, April 3, 1981, p. A1.

17. Morris, *Dutch*, p. 428.

18. "Excerpts from Hospital about Victims," *New York Times*, April 1, 1981, p. A22.

19. Noonan, *When Character Was King*, p. 175.

20. Baker, *Work Hard*, p. 144.

21. Reagan and Novak, *My Turn*, p. 5.

22. Michael K. Deaver, *A Different Drummer: My 30 Years with Ronald Reagan* (New York: Perennial, 2003), p. 137.

23. Morris, *Dutch*, p. 431.

24. Woodard, *America That Reagan Built*, p. 37.

25. Morris, *Dutch*, p. 432.

26. John Ehrman, *The Eighties: America in the Age of Reagan* (New Haven, CT: Yale University Press, 2005), p. 55.

27. Dennis Farney, "President's Budget Wins House Vote on Rules Question," *Wall Street Journal*, June 26, 1981.

28. Bernard Weinraub, "Long Cutback Seen," *New York Times*, August 6, 1981, p. A1.

29. Howell Raines, "Tower Power," *New York Times*, August 7, 1981, p. A3.

30. Haynes Johnson, "Prickly, Unpretentious, Long-Batting American Beauty: Heroes," *Washington Post*, August 16, 1981, p. C1.

31. Gallup Poll, "Most Important Issue," October 1981.

32. Deaver, *A Different Drummer*, p. 113.

33. Peter Schweizer, *Reagan's War: The Epic Story of His Forty-Year Struggle and Final Triumph over Communism* (New York: Doubleday, 2004), p. 1.

34. Morris, *Dutch*, p. 426.

35. Noonan, *When Character Was King*, p. 229.

36. Ibid.

37. Lars Erik-Nelson, "Ronald Reagan's Medal of Honor Story," *New York Daily News*, December 13, 1983.

38. "Most Admired," *Newsweek*, December 21, 1981.

39. Reagan and Novak, *My Turn*, pp. 39–43.

40. Hedrick Smith, *The Power Game* (New York: Random House, 1988), pp. 393–397.

41. Haynes Johnson, *Sleepwalking through History* (New York: W. W. Norton, 1991), p. 94.

42. Larry Speakes, *Speaking Out: The Reagan Presidency from Inside the White House* (New York: Charles Scribner's Sons, 1988), p. 109.

43. Cannon, *President Reagan*, p. 233.

44. Gallup Poll, "Presidential Approval," January 28–31, 1983.

45. Morris, *Dutch*, p. 466.

46. Morris Fiorina, *Divided Government* (New York: Allyn and Bacon, 1996), pp. 91–95.

47. Smith, *Power Game*, pp. 459–460.

48. Paul Johnson, *A History of the American People* (New York: HarperCollins, 1997), pp. 924–925.

49. "The Homeless Won't Go Away," *New York Times*, August 23, 1982.

50. Schweizer, *Reagan's War*, p. xi.

51. Ibid., p. 15.

52. Ibid., p. 144.

53. Ronald Reagan Presidential Library, "Speeches," March 8, 1983.

54. Anthony Lewis, "What Reagan Wrought," *New York Times*, June 21, 1984, p. A23.

55. "Review: Familiar Barbarities," *New York Times*, September 25, 1983, p. A23.

56. Lawrence L. Barrett, *Gambling with History* (New York: Penguin Books, 1983), pp. 73–74.

57. Ronald Reagan Presidential Library, "Speeches," May 9, 1982.

58. Niccolo Machiavelli, *The Prince*, Chapter 25, in Michael Morgan, *Classics of Moral and Political Theory*, 4th ed. (Indianapolis, IN: Hackett, 2005), p. 523.

59. Woodard, *America That Reagan Built*, p. 54.

60. Jonathan Schell, *The Fate of the Earth* (Palo Alto, CA: Stanford University Press, 2000), p. vi.

61. Morris, *Dutch*, p. 466.

62. Schweizer, *Reagan's War*, pp. 147–148.

63. Cannon, *President Reagan*, p. 319.

64. Reagan, *An American Life*, p. 239.

65. "News Summary," *New York Times*, October 26, 1983.

66. Cannon, *President Reagan*, p. 516.

67. Reagan, *An American Life*, p. 461.

Chapter 9

MORNING

Democrats watched the calendar with a mounting sense of anticipation throughout the spring of 1984. For them the victories in the 1982 midterm elections, and each new development in the 1983–1984 political season, brought them closer to an end of what Richard Reeves called "the Reagan detour."[1] Their bright expectation was that the next presidential election would be the occasion for a rebirth of the ruling Democratic coalition in both the U.S. Senate and the White House, and an end to the former California governor who had cast them into outer political darkness. After all, they were destined to rule, and had done so with few interruptions since 1932.

The Republicans were counting the days to the election as well. "Nineteen-eighty-three and -four were Ronald Reagan's defining years as President . . . communism confronted, Western Europe fortified, the national economy thundering, and a general feeling of resurgent patriotism and optimism."[2] For them the improving economy and the personal popularity of their man in the White House was a harbinger of hoped for success in the fall. The president had an approval rating of 44 percent, and it was rising. The confidence Americans had in their government was increasing and for the first time in over 20 years respondents said they thought government cared about them.[3] The GOP had evidence that the supply-side solutions were working, and they expected a payoff in the voting booth. But they also knew that Republicans had a long history of being a minority party. Neither Eisenhower nor Nixon was able to translate a presidential victory into a governing majority for the GOP, and Reagan might prove no different.

Throughout his first term in office, President Reagan was aided by a legislative consensus and an executive staff that showed remarkable, if fragile, ideological and personal unity. The president got around the problem of an uncooperative Congress by winning over the country, which then put pressure on its elected representatives. The boll weevil Democrats and the Republicans united to barely pass the conservative economic program and affirm the growth in military spending. But the victories came at a partisan cost. The legislative order of battle "found 99 percent of the Republicans lined up against 89 percent of the Democrats."[4] The governing consensus was frail, and a GOP victory in the fall election was not going to be easy.

Republicans campaigned in 1980 on the slogan "Vote Republican— For a Change." That's because 37 percent of the electorate identified themselves as Democrats that year, as opposed to 27 percent claiming Republican affiliation, with some 30 percent claiming Independent loyalty.[5] The only way the GOP could win was to get Democrats and/or Independents to cross over on election day. By 1984, the persuasive president had skimmed some 4 to 5 percent of those voters in the country who claimed an alternate allegiance, but to win, the GOP still had to attract more attention from self-identified independents. These were voters who liked to say they voted "the man and not the party."[6] Despite economic and political problems in the midterm elections, the only question in the mind of party loyalists was whether the 73-year-old man in the White House would run again. If he did, and won, he would be the oldest president to be sworn into office.

Reagan didn't keep them waiting for long. On January 29 he formally announced that he would seek reelection with a five minute nationally televised speech. We have "'made new beginnings,' he said, but that work "'was not finished.'"[7] Polls at the time showed that a majority of Americans backed Reagan's policies, and the president was seen as a confident, decisive leader. Clearly, Reagan had a style that voters liked.

He enjoyed people and was unfailingly polite and courteous to them. Opponents did not find a confrontation with him personally uncomfortable, unless they were in the Soviet Union. Ambassador Dobrynin remarked that the president's extreme anticommunism might be a hindrance to his reelection. In response, Vice President George Bush replied, "Well, he's hard, very hard indeed."[8]

As the cherry trees thickened along the Mall, a packed Democratic field lined up to take on the incumbent. The favorites were Walter Mondale, Carter's vice president and an old Washington hand; John Glenn, who usually did well in hypothetical races against the president; and Colorado senator Gary Hart, whose movie actor good looks and idealism were reminiscent of the McGovern campaign that he managed in 1972. Five other candidates enlivened the race: Alan Cranston of California, George McGovern as a liberal nominee retread, and Jesse Jackson, who became the first African American given a serious chance of winning the nomination. The trailing two candidates were, Reubin Askew of Florida and Earnest "Fritz" Hollings from South Carolina.

Mondale was the clear favorite. He recognized the importance of interest groups in the Democratic Party and won the endorsement of the American Federation of Teachers, the National Organization of Women, the AFL-CIO and the National Federation of Labor. He also led in the contest for superdelegates, meaning Democratic senators and congressmen, as well as mayors and governors, given convention seats by the new party rules. In short, he was the establishment favorite, but in spite of these endorsements, polls repeatedly showed that Democrats were looking for a different face. Walter Mondale had all the things Democrats wanted in a candidate, but he touched their heads and not their hearts. In straw polls, John Glenn and Gary Hart often did better against Reagan than the front runner, even though they were not as well known.

At the center of the nomination process for the Democrats were the primaries and caucuses, all regulated by a new set of guidelines that led to front-loading the early contests, meaning the first primaries were most important in deciding the outcome. The Democrats had 34 primaries on the calendar, selecting 72 percent of their delegates to the national convention through the process.[9] The new rules resulted in a proportionate and bonus delegate selection system for the convention, and an expanding number of contests. Within the party itself, labor, black, and women's groups clamored for attention, and their demands joined the chorus of Hispanics, homosexuals, environmentalists, nuclear-freeze advocates, and Jews. Mondale appeared as the champion of them all, a fact that caused John Glenn to grouse, "Will we offer a party that can't say no to anyone with a letterhead and a mailing list?"[10]

Despite criticism, Mondale remained ahead in the weeks leading up to the Iowa caucuses. John Glenn opened a $2.5 million line of credit with four Ohio banks, but his prospects as a serious candidate faded, and Jesse Jackson was coming under increasing criticism for a series of anti-Semitic remarks and campaign blunders.[11] Mondale had been cultivating Iowa for two years from over the border in Minnesota. On television the Minnesota senator took the high ground, and praised his colleagues, refusing to indulge in petty political combat with anyone except Ronald Reagan. On election night his strategy was rewarded with 49 percent of the vote. In a national poll taken the following week, Mondale was the preferred candidate of 57 percent of the polled Democrats.

To all outward appearances, the former Minnesota senator and vice president seemed to be on his way; but even in victory problems were evident in his campaign, and the press was not reluctant to point them out. For one, Mondale was not popular with younger voters, and while he was well known, he was not especially well liked. In their search for a contest in an otherwise dull political year, the media focused on the "surprising" showing by Gary Hart in Iowa (16.5%) and the contrastingly poor performance of John Glenn (5%). Suddenly Hart was a serious challenger in New Hampshire, the only state where he had a serious grass roots organization.

With the media, and the candidate himself, suddenly exaggerating the results in Iowa, Democrats looking for an alternative to Walter Mondale fixed on Gary Hart. The low tax mentality of New Hampshire, and Hart's openness to free market solutions for the nation's economic woes, led him to a 37 percent to 28 percent victory over Mondale in the Granite State. Hart woke up to find himself on the cover of news magazines, television interviews and the label of "frontrunner." All this attention was attributable to a mere 12,000 votes in New Hampshire.[12]

The triumph was substantial enough to carry the Colorado senator to successive victories in the Maine and Wyoming caucuses, and in the nonbinding Vermont primary. Stories following the New Hampshire primary, which were once bereft of harsh criticism, suddenly changed in tone. The trailing candidates were neglected, and Askew, Cranston and Hollings withdrew. The focus shifted to the "Super Tuesday" primaries of March 13, when nine states would choose delegates. All of a sudden, the newly ordained Democratic leader, Gary Hart, had developed warts; and the once fawning press found inconsistencies in his record, ranging from issue positions to his last name and correct age.[13] Mondale rebounded smartly from his disappointment in New Hampshire to win the Alabama and Georgia primaries, opposite Hart's victories in the larger states of Massachusetts and Florida. A week later, Mondale defeated Hart and Jackson in Illinois. As Glenn and McGovern withdrew, a series of debates allowed voters to fill in the blanks for the contenders and Mondale inched ahead. Despite some later Hart victories, including upsets in Ohio and Indiana, as well as California; the Mondale victories in New York, Pennsylvania, and a host of smaller states, together with his substantial superdelegate convention numbers, worked to give Jimmy Carter's former vice president the nomination.[14]

Political conventions have long since ceased being deliberative political bodies; instead, they are media dramas designed to showcase the candidate before a national television audience. The problem for the Democrats in San Francisco for 1984 was that Mondale was overshadowed by two speakers, New York Governor Mario Cuomo and Reverend Jesse Jackson, who were spokesmen for traditional Democratic constituencies he was supposed to represent. Convention keynoter Mario Cuomo described the plight of "thousands of young people without jobs or an education giving their lives away to the drug dealers every day." His "Tale of Two Cities" theme was a contrast to Reagan's "City upon a Hill" optimism of 1980. The "Other America" Cuomo described was populated by millions who did not benefit from the Reagan recovery.[15]

Jackson's address was a primetime public apology confessing error and asking forgiveness for remarks made during the campaign. His stirring rhetoric to delegates, especially African Americans, declaring that "our time is come," drew a larger TV audience than Mondale's acceptance speech later in the week.[16] When Mondale came to the rostrum, he tailored his remarks to the groups in the hall, and offered the arm of the federal government in assistance. He tried a gambit that he thought would be bold because it illustrated his transparency as a candidate, but in the end it backfired.

"By the end of my first term," Mondale declared in his speech of July 19, 1984, "I will cut the deficit by two-thirds." "Let's tell the truth. Mr. Reagan will raise taxes, and so will I. He won't tell you. I just did."[17] The Reagan strategists could not believe their ears. Politicians do not win elections in America when people have to vote themselves a tax increase in the voting booth. Mondale left the convention behind in the polls, while the Reagan campaign took a public pledge the next week *not* to raise taxes.[18]

Democratic unity at the convention came more from a shared disdain for Ronald Reagan than any enthusiasm for their candidate, and this lack of loyalty showed up in the vice presidential nomination. Mondale undertook a very public process of interviewing candidates, more to placate interest group constituencies than to really choose someone he actually wanted as a running mate. In the end, party activists intruded and helped make his decision for him. Half the delegates to the convention were women, many of them committed feminists who threatened a floor fight if the nominee didn't put a female on the ticket. After a time, Mondale chose New York congresswoman Geraldine Ferraro, a decision that pleased his constituency, but added almost nothing to the national ticket.

Ronald Reagan's lack of an opponent allowed him to build a war chest and voter registration operation second to none. On June 6, 1984, he appeared in Normandy, France, for the fortieth anniversary of the D-Day invasion. Even though it was the end of the primary season for the Democrats, it was the Republican president who garnered the lion's share of television coverage for his trip.[19] Reagan read the letter of a daughter of one veteran who recalled her father's sacrifice before he died, and the camera panned an audience as tears filled many eyes. "These are the men who took the cliffs. These are the champions who helped free a continent. These are the heroes who helped end a war."[20]

The D-Day commemoration recalled one of America's greatest triumphs, and Reagan's moving speech was later excerpted as a commercial for the campaign. In his book, *Our Country*, political historian Michael Barone says that Reagan's reelection was assured after just this one appearance because the president was able to reach the electorate better than any of his Democratic rivals.[21] Clearly Reagan had advantages beyond incumbency; he was an exceptional speaker who could reach the hearts, as well as the minds, of his audience.

The fall election matched two candidates from opposite ends of the ideological spectrum. Not since Lyndon Johnson trounced Barry Goldwater in 1964 were voters presented choices that differed as markedly as those of incumbent president Ronald Reagan and former vice president Walter Mondale. Unlike 1964, this time the rout was on the conservative side. Reagan's "Morning in America" campaign theme tapped into a powerful need many Americans had to forget the struggles of the past, and redefine what had happened in a way that pleased a nation grown weary of its own conflicts.

The paid advertising for the campaign was destined for immortality. This was the election when Walter Mondale mimicked a Burger King commercial to ask Gary Hart, "Where's the beef?" about the content and credibility of his ideas. But the lasting legacy was Reagan's own, his message that "everything is okay again" was embodied in the theme: Morning in America. Two commercials remain as vivid and effective today, nearly three decades after they were aired, as when they were used in 1984.[22]

The first commercial was titled "Ronald Reagan: Prepared for Peace." It featured Reagan's voice over 13 separate images: like a guard holding up a large picture of the Ayatollah Khomeini, tanks rolling down rural, dirt, jungle road, and a burning American flag. It ended with a shot of President Reagan delivering a speech:

This was America in 1980, held in contempt by foreign nations. Across the world, people were losing their freedoms. So many countries thought America had seen its day, but we knew better. So we stopped complaining together and started working together. Today America is strong again. We are looking to the future with confidence and pride. America's best days, and democracy's best days, lie ahead.

Another commercial in the campaign was titled "President Reagan: Leadership That's Working." This spot, just like the other one, featured a narrative over a montage of images, but this time the speaker was not President Reagan. The spoken narrative conveyed the theme:

> It's morning again in America. Today more men and women will go to work than ever before in our country's history. . . . This afternoon 6,500 young men and women will be married, and with inflation at less than half of what it was just four years ago. . . . It's morning again in America, and under the leadership of President Reagan, our country is prouder and stronger and better.

The advertisement presented an idealized view of a successful middle class life in America. As the newspaper delivery boy rode out of the picture, a man got in a car just as the speaker said: "work than ever before in our country's history." The economic recovery guided the visuals in the commercial. The images dissolved into a shot of the U.S. Capitol as the underlying music rose to a brief crescendo, and the next few images were of flags being raised. The montage ended with a prolonged shot of the American flag and the question: "Why would we ever want to return to where we were less than four short years ago?"

The country wasn't going back. The images associated with the "Morning Again in America," theme implied, and in some cases stated, that Ronald Reagan was the reason why things were better, and that he was responsible for turning the nation around and bringing it out of darkness into light. The viewer had an emotional connection between the positive images of America, with the flags, workers, weddings, and Ronald Reagan. The president was comfortable with this approach; after all it was what Hollywood did every day. His critics were less charitable, they found the ads misleading and vacuous in content. The irony of the whole media campaign was that Reagan's approval ratings were so strong that no special paid advertising was really necessary. The "Morning Again in America" theme successfully encapsulated the mood of the country in a way no other presidential campaign had, or would again.

Reagan also benefited from the Olympic Games being in Los Angeles, in the golden California sunshine. The Russians boycotted the events that year, in reprisal for America's refusal to go to the Moscow games in 1980. The televised events produced a harvest of gold medals for the USA that contributed to the exuberant mood and feeling that the United States was a better and happier place than at any time in the recent past.

The euphoria carried over into the fall campaign, but it came to an abrupt end on October 7, when the two candidates debated in Louisville, Kentucky. The president fumbled and repeated himself, his recall of statistics was unclear, and at one point he said he was "confused" by the format. "I was just awful," Reagan confessed after it was over.[23] Suddenly the campaign became a pitched battle. Internal polls in the Reagan campaign showed the president dropped 13 points, and while still comfortably ahead nationally, the gap closed in major states like New York, Pennsylvania and California. Reagan's top advisors changed tactics. They went over the schedule and concluded that their candidate was overprepared, so the campaign team focused on restoring his confidence. Almost everything, from the number of debate preparations to his stump speech, was changed.

At the next debate in Kansas City, the president was more relaxed and confident. Henry Trewhitt of the Baltimore *Sun* asked if Reagan, the oldest president in U.S. history, was up to the job. Trewhitt continued, "Is there any doubt in your mind that you would be able to function in such circumstances?" Reagan remained calm, glancing down at the podium in his best straight man style, "Not at all, Mr. Trewhitt, and I want you to know that I will not make age an issue in this campaign. I am not going to exploit, for political purposes, my opponent's youth and inexperience."[24] Everyone laughed, including Mondale, and the quip surged the president back into a comfortable lead.

It is impossible to find a turning point in an election that led to a 49 state landslide. Michael Barone might be right; maybe the election was over in June. What Reagan understood was that the American people craved something bigger in their history and national memory than Gerald Ford's evacuation of Saigon or Jimmy Carter's malaise speech. When the 56 Americans were held for ransom by Khomeini's Iran, the press said it was "America held hostage." By contrast, the

D-Day story was about America as ferocious liberators, not backroom barterers. Reagan was a rescuer.

Almost half the voters had made their decision at the beginning of the election year, and only one-fourth waited for the televised debates to decide.[25] Reagan gained 59 percent of the popular vote, a record 525 electoral votes, losing only Minnesota and the District of Columbia. The previous record for a landslide in American politics was 523 for Franklin Roosevelt in 1936, and 520 for Richard Nixon in 1972. The victory was all the more remarkable given that Reagan was mired in very low approval numbers just two years earlier.[26] In winning, he garnered more votes for his Republican presidency than had ever been cast for a U.S. politician, and again took 24 of the top 30 media markets. But that enthusiasm did not extend to the Congress, where Republicans lost two seats from their majority in the Senate, and made only a modest gain of 14 in the House. The fragile governing coalition would continue.

The first inaugural for Ronald Reagan was the warmest on record, the second was the coldest. The day dawned sunny, but bitterly cold. The estimated noontime swearing-in temperature was seven degrees Fahrenheit, with wind chills from the -10 to -20 degree range. Because January 20, 1985, fell on a Sunday, the public Inauguration ceremony was scheduled for Monday, January 21. No outside swearing in was possible. A private ceremony was held in the White House at the bottom of the Grand Staircase. The swearing in was witnessed by about 84 people, mostly family and Cabinet officials. The public Inauguration was moved indoors to the Rotunda, and became a semiprivate ceremony. In his abbreviated inaugural address, Reagan said the nation was "poised for greatness" in his second term. "Let history say of us, 'These were golden years—when the American Revolution was reborn, when freedom gained new life, when America reached for her best.'"[27]

Over the years, official Washington had become used to Cabinet changes in the second term of a president. In fact, changes had been the rule rather than the exception. But the city had never seen anything like what happened in January 1985. Chief of Staff James Baker swapped jobs with Treasury Secretary Donald Regan. Edwin Meese became attorney general, and Chief of Staff Michael Deaver resigned to go into private business. The swaps set off a chain of Cabinet-level changes.[28] The history of second terms for American presidents is that they are usually not as successful as first terms because the Cabinet and staff are less enthusiastic, more prone to mistakes and not as loyal as the initial appointees. The most glaring example, of course, was the Watergate scandal in Richard Nixon's second term. But Sherman Adams, Dwight Eisenhower's chief of staff, was also caught up in a gift-giving scandal in the second term. All the maladies of past presidents would return to haunt Ronald Reagan, when extreme measures were taken in pursuit of personal goals, or with good intentions, but without an understanding of the consequences.

The first crisis began as part of a well-intentioned plan to observe the fortieth anniversary of V-E Day, May 8, 1945. Reagan was scheduled to attend an economic summit in Bonn that week in 1985, and West German Chancellor Helmut Kohl saw an opportunity to demonstrate the strength of the friendship that existed between the two men and the nations they led. Kohl appealed to Reagan in November 1984, in a visit to Washington, to join him in appearing at a German military cemetery to symbolize the reconciliation between the former foes. Reagan agreed. As he later told an aide, he felt he owed Helmut Kohl, who despite considerable public and political opposition, had stood with the president on the deployment of Pershing missiles in West Germany a few years earlier.

In February 1985, White House deputy chief of staff Michael Deaver made an advance trip to plan the visit to Kolmeshohe Cemetery in Bitburg, a quaint little town in the Eifel hills where nearly 11,000 Americans attached to a nearby airbase lived in harmony with about the same number of Germans. Deaver was suffering from alcoholism, and was not the public relations maestro he had been in two political campaigns, and as an aide to Reagan since his gubernatorial days. He failed to discover that 49 Nazi soldiers were buried at Kolmeshohe, and West German officials did not mention this fact either. When asked later, the White House said both German and American soldiers were buried in the cemetery, but reporters found out that all U.S. soldiers had long since been removed from German soil. The White House began to backpedal. To add to the embarrassment about the incident, the interred soldiers were a combat branch of the Third Reich's elite guard, created to serve as Hitler's personal protectors. They committed numerous atrocities and massacres throughout Europe during World War II.[29]

The itinerary immediately created a firestorm of controversy. Jewish leaders like Elie Wiesel, chairman of the U.S. Holocaust Memorial Council, asked, "May I implore you to do something else, to find another way, another site." Nancy Reagan agreed, but Director of White House Communications, Pat Buchanan, argued that the president should resist the pressure from the Jewish lobby and the liberal media and go to Bitburg. White House staffers hoped that Chancellor Kohl would retract his invitation, but they were confronted by a surprise obstacle: the president himself. "There is no way I'll back down and run for cover," he wrote in his diary.[30] Reagan had a powerful ally, Helmut Kohl, who called to urge the president to keep his commitment. A poll in West Germany found that 72 percent of West Germans thought the visit should go forward as planned despite the controversy.[31]

Suddenly Reagan's visit, made almost as an afterthought, assumed vast moral significance. The White House was quick to point out that the president had scheduled a ceremony at the site of the Bergen–Belsen concentration camp on the same visit. No matter. The International Network of Children of Jewish Holocaust Survivors, the American Legion, the Union of American Hebrew Congregations, decorated World War II American veterans, 53 senators and 257 U.S. Representatives all urged the president to cancel the trip. Polls at the time showed that a majority of Americans, both Democrats and Republicans opposed the scheduled trip.[32]

Reagan would not budge, and neither would Kohl. The president had a stubborn character trait that once something was in the script, it stayed put. "His beliefs were as inerasable as the grooves of an LP . . . the only reliable way to recognize the approach [was] to listen for signal phrases: 'As I've said many times.'" White House aide Robert McFarlane would say after the controversy, "Once Reagan learned that Kohl would really be badly damaged by a withdrawal, [Reagan said], 'We can't do that, I owe him.'"[33]

President Reagan spent only eight minutes at the Bitburg Cemetery, along with Kohl, 90-year-old General Matthew Ridgway, who commanded the 82nd Airborne in World War II, and Luftwaffe ace General Johannes Steinhoff. There were almost no protestors at the site, and the rally at the nearby American airbase was spectacularly successful. Reagan told his deputy chief of staff, "History will prove I'm right. . . . If we can't reconcile after forty years, we are never going to be able to do it."[34]

Lost in the flames of the controversy was the moving speech Reagan gave at Bergen–Belsen before going to Bitburg. Summoning his exceptional rhetorical skills, the president said, "All these children of God under bleak and lifeless mounds . . . here they lie, never to hope, never to pray, never to live, never to heal, never to laugh, never to cry . . . beyond the anguish, the pain and suffering, and for all time, we can and must pledge: Never Again." One reporter who covered the trip said, "It was a striking example, of which there have been many in Reagan's life, when he was rescued from poor judgment by a successful performance."[35] In the weeks after the event, the president showed another habit; he forgot what happened and never looked back.

The Bitburg fiasco had lingering consequences, but it was more important for what it showed about the way things were being done in the White House, than for any immediate political fallout. It would take another incident, a far more serious one, before the problems would surface again. There was a word for the more extreme measures being used by individuals in pursuit of their private agendas in the administration: scandal. It was about to acquire a synonym: Iran-Contra.

The stage for the most disastrous of calamities to strike the Reagan presidency was set by an awful terrorist act. On June 14, 1985, TWA Flight 847, from Athens to Rome, was hijacked with 153 passengers and crew aboard, including 135 Americans. The pilot was forced to fly from Beirut to Algiers, and then back to Beirut where the hijackers brutally beat and then shot to death a U.S. Navy diver. After refueling, the plane was flown back to Algiers and again to Beirut, where most of the passengers were released. In the final terror-filled odyssey, 39 American passengers and crew members were herded off TWA 847 and held captive in Lebanon. Ultimately they were released through diplomatic pressure and the intervention of Syrian president Hafez Assad, but the hijacking itself made a mockery of Reagan's tough talk about swift and effective retribution against terrorism. What is more, hostage taking became a means of foreign policy in the region.

A month later, in July 1985, a delegation of visitors from Israel met with National Security Advisor Bud McFarlane with a proposal to help free hostages in the region. They proposed to act as an intermediary by shipping American-made TOW antitank missiles and HAWK anti-aircraft missiles to Iran in exchange for American hostages being held by Iranian sympathizers. Once the exchange was made, the United States would ship replacement missiles to Israel.[36] On first hearing the proposal, it did not sound like an effective way to defeat terrorism or rescue its victims, but the pressure to do something about hostages was unrelenting.

Ronald Reagan understood problems best when they were personalized, and when he met the families of the hostages he wanted to do something. His staff found a way to help him. After five years in office, Reagan was not curious about the legality of recommendations from his staff, and he wanted plausible deniability if anything went wrong. The less he knew, he better off he was.

Back in 1979, when 56 Americans were being held at the U.S. Embassy in Tehran, one of Jimmy Carter's first reactions was to impose an embargo on arms shipments to Iran. Reagan won the election of 1980 with a promise to be tougher on the Iranians than his predecessor. He could not be the forceful president he wanted to be, and not free the hostages. The Israeli proposal was in violation of American law, policy and proclaimed rhetoric. Even so, it had an appeal that went beyond principle.

The hostages provided an emotional motive to open secret negotiations, and the opportunity of building a relationship with moderates operating within the Khomeini government in Iran. "On balance my interests are to see our larger interest in establishing an entrée to someone in Iran," wrote Robert McFarlane.[37] Reagan was recuperating from surgery to remove a malignant tumor from his intestine, and did not hear of the plan for a month. When he was told, he found Secretary of Defense Weinberger and Secretary of State Schultz in rare agreement that the proposal was outrageous. But the president was cheered by the prospect of getting hostages out of Lebanon, and he approved it in principle. The transfer of arms took place over the next two months.

In retrospect, the outcome of the first round of negotiations with the hostage takers was not good for the United States, and did not justify the risk, but the promise was that these first steps would lead to a breakthrough. The Israelis informed McFarlane that they could not deliver all the hostages, but only one. It was up to McFarlane to decide which one. After some delay, the Muslims released Benjamin Weir, a

Presbyterian missionary who had been held 16 months. To some in the administration, his freedom was tangible proof that the policy, no matter how conspiratorial, had some beneficial effects.

The captive whose fate most concerned the administration in Washington was William Buckley, who had been the CIA station chief in Beirut. Because of the sensitive nature of his mission, Buckley was especially vulnerable, and intelligence reports indicated he had been cruelly tortured by his Muslim captors.[38] He was the prize captive in the administrative strategy, and the main one they wanted back. The Israelis were vague about Buckley's status; in reality he had been brutally murdered and was not even available for a hostage exchange. Concern over the captives led to another round of negotiations, even though there was no evidence that earlier efforts had been effective. This time the Israelis proposed to ship additional missiles in exchange for the release of all remaining American hostages. During this second round of negotiations, McFarlane was working to prepare Reagan for a summit meeting with Mikhail Gorbachev, so he entrusted the details of the assignment to his deputy, Oliver North. North was a Vietnam veteran with a Bronze Star, a Silver Star, two Purple Hearts, and a Navy Commendation Medal. He was zealous to succeed in his covert mission, even though he admitted later that he was largely unfamiliar with what was being done.

While Israel and the United States worked in the same direction on Iran, officials from both countries had long since joined paths in Central America. As early as May 1983, Washington and Tel Aviv developed an arrangement for the Defense Department to buy Soviet bloc weapons captured from the Palestine Liberation Organization (PLO) in Lebanon. The arms were transferred to the "Contras," from the Spanish word *contrarrevolucionario*, the CIA backed rebels battling the Cuban-backed Sandinista regime in Nicaragua. The new proposal in 1985 allowed an American intermediary, rather than Israel, to sell arms to Iran in exchange for the release of the hostages, with profits funneled to the Contras. The proceeds from the arms sales were diverted by Colonel Oliver North, still working in the White House but now as an aide to U.S. national security advisor John Poindexter.

The whole Iran-Contra scandal is complicated, but it is easier to understand if one begins with Reagan's inviolate hatred of communism. The president's determination to eradicate communism worldwide fo-

cused on the Sandinistas in Nicaragua, who were backed by the Soviet Union and Cuba. The Sandinistas also supported left-wing rebels
against the government in El Salvador, which had received substantial
U.S. support and was the scene of a destructive civil war throughout
the 1980s. The president saw the whole of Central America as under a
communist threat. Even though Congress voted in 1982 to halt aid to
the Contras, Reagan was determined to help. In 1985, the Sandinista
movement won in elections validated by some international observers
as fair and free, but rejected by the Reagan administration as fraudulent.
A determined and unyielding Reagan told National Security Advisor
Robert McFarlane about the situation in Nicaragua, "I want you to do
whatever it takes to help these people keep body and soul together."[39]

They had three options: raising money from private donors like Ross
Perot, working in concert with other nations and using proceeds from
one covert operation to support another convert operation. Probably
Reagan's aides took his general plea as a carte blanche to do everything
necessary to achieve that end. The president had become frustrated at
his inability to secure the release of the American hostages being held
by Iranian terrorists in Lebanon, and Congress had already passed a law
to tie his hands on giving military aid to the Contras. The hatred Ronald Reagan had for communism led him into temptation. "He was the
guy that knew the Iranians had rubbed Jimmy Carter's nose in it. . . .
Now all of a sudden he's got the same situation, and he's responsible for
it. . . . Ronald Reagan eats his heart out over this."[40]

In January 1986, Reagan allegedly approved a plan whereby arms
would be sold to Iran in exchange for the release of the hostages, with
profits funneled to the Contras. With the marked up income of the
exchange being some $10 million in the administration's pocket, the
Contras could be supplied without asking Congress for more money.
Meanwhile, in the Middle East, the Iranians captured new hostages as
soon as they released the old ones. This was the end of the arms-for-
hostages deals, but the United States continued to ship weapons and
spare parts to Iran from May to November.

With, or without, the president's knowledge, the diversion plan continued, and Oliver North was at the controls. The Marine would later
testify: "I don't think it was wrong. I think it was a neat idea."[41] He
opened negotiations for a third round of arms sales to the Iranians,

even though the released hostages were merely being replaced in what Secretary of State George Shultz would later call "a hostage bazaar." The problem on the one end was that the Americans were being swindled by the Iranians, and on the other the U.S. supported rebels were floundering on the battlefields of Nicaragua. All the while, the public posture of the administration was that the United States did not negotiate with terrorists and was resolute in its determination to rid the world of the international evil.

In the midst of this charade, the Reagan administration had a public opportunity to act against, instead of just denounce, the terrorists. The most blatant public face of terrorism in the world was Colonel Muammar el-Quaddafi, the ruler of Libya. Quaddafi was an outlandish personality who allegedly had a private fetish for wearing women's clothing and makeup. But behind the façade, Libya was an active state sponsor of terrorism. Early in April 1986, terrorists blew up a discotheque in West Berlin that was a hangout for U.S. servicemen. Two Americans and a Turkish woman were killed, and 230 others were injured. Evidence pointed to Libya as the culprit. Reagan would later declare that the United States had proof of a direct Libyan role, and that a raid on that country would cause Quaddafi to "alter his criminal behavior." At last, the administration had an opportunity for Reagan to back up his thundering rhetoric with military action.

On April 14, U.S. Air Force bombers based in England and Navy fighters on carriers in the Gulf of Sidra dropped 90 2,000 pound bombs on the Quaddafi compounds in Tripoli and Benghazi. The bombs killed Quaddafi's adopted two-year-old daughter, and wounded two of his sons.[42] Quaddafi escaped injury because he was sleeping outside the compound, but scores of civilians were killed. In the wake of the raid, Secretary of State Schultz declared that the raid was the beginning of a more militant policy by the Reagan administration toward terrorism. The public face of the policy was affirmed, but no one knew about what was going on behind the scenes.

The secrecy was beginning to take its toll. Robert McFarlane resigned his position in the White House, leaving John Poindexter and Oliver North at their posts. Then on October 5, 1986, an antiquated cargo plane was shot down over Nicaragua by a surface-to-air missile. The lone survivor, Eugene Hasenfaus of Marinette, Wisconsin, was captured and his haggard photo was soon on the television and the front page of every newspaper.[43] Half a world away, Lieutenant Colonel Oliver North was in negotiations with Iranian government representatives for yet another hostage exchange. The next month, the first public allegations of the weapons-for-hostages deal surfaced on November 3, when the Lebanese magazine *Ash-Shiraz* reported the United States had been selling weapons to Iran in secret to secure the release of American hostages in Lebanon.

For most Americans, the two events were unconnected, and played out at opposite ends of the globe. But back in Washington, Oliver North and his secretary, Fawn Hall, began shredding documents implicating them and others in the arms-for-hostages arrangements. On November 25, President Reagan and Attorney General Edwin Meese shocked the country by disclosing that the two operations were in fact intertwined. When Attorney General Meese found a so-called diversion memo, which North wrote in the spring of 1986, detailing the scheme to skim money from arms sales to the Contras, he went directly to the president. "He [Reagan] decided that we should immediately make a complete disclosure of our findings, and this resulted in a full-scale press conference the following day at noon."[44] For this offense, North was fired and his superior, National Security Advisor John Poindexter, who knew and approved the plans, was allowed to resign.[45]

The subsequent press conference did little to relieve the pressure on the administration, but the political effects were dramatic. "When the scandal broke in late 1986 . . . it had a devastating impact [on] Reagan's approval ratings [which] dropped precipitously from nearly 70 percent to around 35 percent."[46] The public outrage over the Iran-Contra revelations were partly to blame for GOP reverses in the 1986 midterm elections, where Democrats picked up five seats in the U.S. House, and more significantly, gained eight in the U.S. Senate to take control. The fragile governing majority was at an end. It was Nancy Reagan who intervened with her husband to make changes in the White House staff and be more forthcoming with the press. The timing of the shakeup could not have been worse, but it was necessary. The word *impeachment* was being used on Capitol Hill, and a weeping Nancy Reagan demanded that her husband fire Donald Regan. Secretary of State George Shultz threatened to resign in protest to both the Iran Initiative and the Contra Diversion. Ultimately, documents and testimony produced during subsequent investigations showed that North and Poindexter were part of a much larger group within the administration circumventing the law and misleading Congress. These machinations involved many foreign governments, including Israel, Saudi Arabia, South Africa, China, Taiwan, Panama, Costa Rica, Guatemala, El Salvador, and Honduras.

Faced with mounting pressure, Reagan appointed a Special Review Board headed by Senator John Tower to look into the scandal. The president claimed he had not been informed of the operation despite an entry in his own diary stating otherwise. The Review Board implicated North, Poindexter and Weinberger, but could not conclusively determine the degree of Reagan's involvement. In the final Tower Commission report, Reagan was rebuked for not having a firm control on his national security staff.[47] The day after the report was released, Don Regan resigned as chief of staff. President Reagan went on national television to explain his actions. "My heart tells me we did not take arms for hostages, facts tell a different story."[48] His poll numbers rose immediately.

A partial explanation for presidential mismanagement came to rest with his wife. After the attempted assassination of her husband, Nancy Reagan began regular consultations with an astrologer, Joan Quigley, whose charts helped set the president's schedule.[49] Ronald Reagan was casual in his superstitions, but Nancy Reagan became convinced that Quigley's advice had protected her husband from repeated assassination attempts. Real, and imagined, dangers led the White House staff to defer final acceptance for any event until Mrs. Reagan had approved. Much of the Bitburg fiasco was attributable to Nancy Reagan's superstitions, and the world will never know how much of the Iran-Contra mismanagement was a consequence of her and her astrologer.

Despite the Iran-Contra fiasco, the image of Nancy Reagan remained strong because of her "Just Say No!" to drugs campaign. In 1982, Mrs. Reagan adopted the campaign slogan after visiting Longfellow Elementary School in Oakland, California and hearing a little girl say she would "Just Say No" if offered drugs. Mrs. Reagan traveled throughout the United States as the campaign spokesperson, visiting drug rehabilitation centers and abuse programs. She appeared as herself in popular sit-com television programs to garner public support. In 1985, she expanded the campaign internationally, and even addressed the United Nations.

Research later showed that the campaign was a success, and drug use declined as the decade aged. Mrs. Reagan said in an interview that her reasons for initiating the program came from calls from lifelong friends who had lost children and loved ones to drug abuse.[50] Her reputation was as a loyalist to her husband in any contest, but she was also influential with the press and his advisors. But even she could not stem the increasing effects of the Iran-Contra fallout.

Congressional hearings into the Iran-Contra Affair, and the criminal trial of North and others, were inconclusive. After months of speculation, the highlight came on July 7, 1987, when ramrod straight Marine Lieutenant Colonel North appeared in the Caucus Room of the Russell Senate Office Building to testify before the committee. The comparisons with Watergate by the press were inevitable, but Oliver North was no conspirator and he would be no scapegoat. "I had faith and belief in the goodness of my country and what democracy and freedom meant. . . . I thought, if I could convey those feelings, then the American people would understand. . . . I didn't think it was wrong, I thought it was a neat idea."[51] North's candid testimony, laced with throat-clutching patriotism, gradually turned the national audience to his side. He did what he did not for money or power, but out of loyalty to his president and the country.

Speculation about the involvement of President Reagan, Vice President Bush—who would face questions about Iran-Contra as he ran for president—and other administration officials continued for the next eight years. Fourteen people were charged with crimes. In the end, North's conviction was overturned on a technicality and President Bush issued six pardons, including one for Robert McFarlane, who had already been convicted, and one to Caspar Weinberger before he stood trial.

In 1988, a report by the Senate Subcommittee on Narcotics, Terrorism and International Operations concluded that various people in the Contra movement were involved in drug trafficking. The World Court ruled in favor of the Nicaraguan Sandinistas and charged the United States to pay restitution fines to the government, which it refused to do.

The United Nations General Assembly passed a similar resolution, which the United States similarly ignored. Finally, the Sandinistas lost power in fresh elections in February 1990, following a decade of U.S. economic and military pressure.

One year after taking the presidential oath for a second time, the president was called to the role of counselor and comforter, this time for the most dramatic failure in U.S. space science history. NASA's Shuttle program began in the 1970s to create reusable craft for transporting cargo into space. By the 1980s, four shuttles were in the fleet. The launch of space shuttle *Challenger*, set for January 1986 would be the 25th mission for the program. *Challenger* had flown nine successful times and the only thing unusual about this mission was that Sharon Christa McAuliffe, a New Hampshire high school teacher, would be the first educator in space.

Earlier in the year, space agency officials worked feverishly to prepare the space shuttle *Columbia* for launch only to encounter weeks of frustration and a record seven postponements. The *Columbia* astronauts were 25 days late going up, and its return landing was postponed twice because of bad weather. At the same time, insurance companies began to shy away from the space program because since 1968, insurers had paid out $500 million in claims for failed or lost communication satellites. All in all, the glint was off the NASA rose.

From the beginning, the *Challenger* mission was plagued with problems, it had been rescheduled five times. The launch was the first one from a new pad, this one closer to the viewing public and many in the audience said later that it was the loudest and most stunning liftoff ever. *Challenger* left the launching pad at 11:38 Eastern Standard Time. That morning the countdown went smoothly, despite freezing temperatures. The flight administrators later said that "there was absolutely no pressure to get this particular launch off."[52] A subsequent investigation showed that substantial pressure was brought by NASA on dissenting engineers to approve the launch in the face of questions they had about the weather.

A great spurting spout of yellow-white flame erupted from the three engines as the cameras showed the shuttle held on the launch pad for four incredible seconds. About one minute 13 seconds after launch, as students across the country watched on live television feeds, the shuttle exploded killing all seven crew members. Apparent in the pictures of the accident was evidence that the shuttle was a potential bomb that carried 385,000 gallons of liquid oxygen at liftoff, and any leak was like a blasting cap.

The *Challenger* disaster sparked national mourning on a scale not seen since the assassination of President John F. Kennedy. "If there was any moment when Ronald Reagan could be said to have arrived at the climax of power and popularity," said his biographer, it was in the months after he addressed the national in the wake of the *Challenger* explosion.[53] President Reagan watched the explosion on television at the White House in "stunned silence." At 4:00 P.M., he addressed the nation.[54]

> The crew of the space shuttle *Challenger* honored us by the manner in which they lived their lives. We will never forget them, nor the last time we saw them, this morning, as they prepared for the journey and waved goodbye and "slipped the surly bonds of earth" to "touch the face of God."

Throughout his presidency, Reagan had ample opportunities to comfort the country. Among them were the shooting down of the Korean airliner, the Beirut hostage victims, the war in Lebanon, the invasion of Grenada, the murder of the American ambassador to Pakistan, the terrorist bombing in Beirut, airline hijack victims and the *Challenger* explosion. He was excellent each time. Reagan's age and life experience all made him able to fill the role of all-knowing, wise father figure to the country. Even the crusty Tip O'Neill, Democratic Speaker of the House and inveterate White House opponent, dabbed his eyes after the president's remarks on the *Challenger* disaster and said, "He may not be much of a debater, but with a prepared text he's the best public speaker I've ever seen."[55]

In the end, it was not Reagan's rhetoric, but his convictions, that defined him and his presidency. Nowhere was this more apparent that in his support for the Strategic Defense Initiative (SDI). He often declared, "It was my idea to begin with," and he was right. The beginnings of his convictions are traceable back to 1957 when he talked to scientists at Livermore Research Laboratory in California. The frightening fact was that the total number of nuclear weapons in the world had surpassed 60,000, enough for a million Hiroshimas. SDI was a defensive shield for the people in a dangerous world.

It was a formidable technological undertaking, but the president had full confidence in American know-how, after all he saw at General Electric. What Reagan lacked in technical expertise he made up for in concept enthusiasm. Domestic critics scoffed at SDI, but the Soviets took it seriously. Since 1983, when Reagan first addressed the concept, he believed the issue was at base moral, not technological. British Prime Minister Margaret Thatcher, who was at first skeptical of the idea, later wrote, "It is now clear to me that Ronald Reagan's original decision on SDI was the single most important of his presidency."[56]

The great turning point in the Cold War tension between East and West coincided with Ronald Reagan's second term and the first four years of Mikhail Gorbachev's leadership of the USSR. The prelude was set by the deaths of Soviet leaders, Leonid Brezhnev in 1982, Yuri Andropov in 1983, and Konstantin Cherneko in 1984. These three leaders were old men who adhered to the Marxist–Leninist ideology in spite of the suffocating effect it had on their own nation, and the rest of the world. At home and abroad the Soviet system was regarded with increasing cynicism, contempt, and ridicule.

Ronald Reagan was chief among the accusers. He specialized in collecting jokes about the inefficiency and cruelty of the Russian system, but beneath the humor was an abiding belief that communism was fatally flawed and on the verge of collapse. The Soviets recognized the president's disdain, and during the 1984 presidential election attacks from them, and the American left, regularly stressed that Reagan's foreign and defense policies were pushing the world to the verge of nuclear war. Averill Harriman, a former ambassador to the Soviet Union and an advisor to five presidents, wrote of Reagan's policies, "If permitted to continue, we could face not the risk but the reality of nuclear war."[57]

The nuclear prospect constantly haunted Reagan, who was awed by the biblical prophecy of Armageddon, which he imagined as a nuclear hell spoken of in the book of Revelation. The opportunity for change came in September 1984, when Soviet Foreign Minister Andrei Gromyko met with Reagan. Nicknamed "Grim Grom" in the White House because of his inflexible and hard-line manner, Gromyko had become Ambassador to the United States in 1943, and was a familiar mouthpiece of bad news for American administrations. The president sensed from Gromyko's complaints that instead of pushing the world to the brink of war, his defense expenditures were really exposing an inherent weakness in the Soviet economy. Just as Reagan prophesied, the USSR was unable to simultaneously maintain a rapid growth in defense spending and at the same time satisfy demands for consumer goods and services. If the United States engaged in a military buildup, the president believed Moscow would not be able to keep up.

Economists at the U.S. Treasury provided Reagan with an estimate that a $5 drop in the price of a barrel of oil on the world market increased the gross national product of the country by 1.4 percent.[58] The friendship between the United States and Saudi Arabia was an economic weapon that Reagan exploited to force the Soviets into a defensive posture. Lower oil prices also reduced the U.S. trade deficit. In the summer of 1985, the Saudis opened the oil spigots and the domestic economy boomed.

That expansion spelled trouble for the Soviet Union, with its Afghanistan incursion and multiplying problems at home. The new leader, Mikhail Gorbachev came from a family of peasants who suffered under Stalin's ruthless effort to drive farmers off their private land onto collectivized farms. He was not a deep believer in communism. As an agricultural minister he knew the limits of a command economy, and at age 54 he was no dyed-in-the-wool cold warrior either. Instead, Gorbachev was an idealist in a sea of guardians, a change agent in a room full of bureaucrats. He had a magnetic personality and almost limitless confidence. Once at the top of the Soviet hierarchy, Gorbachev declared, "We have to awaken society from its lethargy and indifference as quickly as possible and involve the people in the process of change."[59]

Reagan immediately dispatched Secretary of State George Schultz and Vice President George Bush with a letter to the Soviet premier inviting him to a summit. The date was set for mid-November in Geneva. Between them, Gorbachev and Reagan would have four historic summits (Geneva, Reykjavik, Washington, and Moscow), and exchange more than a dozen personal letters between visits. In the end they would ratify the Intermediate Nuclear Forces (INF) Treaty, which banned all intermediate nuclear missiles, and conclude the outline of the Strategic Arms Reduction Treaty (START), that dramatically reduced long-range nuclear forces. In short, they changed the world and brought about the ultimate end of the Cold War.

Before 1985, U.S.–Soviet relations were at an all-time low. The downing of KAL-007 and the deployment of missiles in Europe, resulted in the Soviet Union walking out of arms control talks. From the beginning, the new Soviet premier had two problems: the first was the need for military disarmament, and the second was the Afghanistan invasion. Gorbachev needed disarmament to revive the Russian economy, and an honorable way out of the war. Reagan was not about to give Gorbachev either one. The president fervently defended the SDI and signed a security order that sent Kalashnikov-pattern (AK-47) rifles, Soviet heavy machine guns, 10,000 Soviet-made rocket-propelled grenades, and eventually more than 1,000 Stinger American-made shoulder-fired antiaircraft missiles to the rebels in Afghanistan. Of the weapons supplied, it was the Stinger missiles that turned the tide in the conflict.

Amid this tension, Gorbachev arrived at the Geneva summit unable to conceal the failures of the communist experience from the Soviet people. He hoped to open up Soviet society (glasnost) and restructure its economy (perestroika). The summit took place from November 19 to November 20, where the two men engaged in three private meetings and four plenary meetings. Prior to the meeting, Gorbachev initiated a moratorium on nuclear testing, and proposed a 50 percent reduction in previously installed long-range strategic missiles.

Reagan felt up for the summit after months of preparation, much as actors do before a big performance. As he stepped out of Chateau Fleur d'Eau and into the icy air blowing off nearby Lake Geneva, the president wore no coat, hat or scarf. Gorbachev stepped out of a limousine dressed in a charcoal-gray hat, matching scarf and wrapped in a heavy overcoat. A surprised Gorbachev shook Reagan's hand and asked, "Where is your coat?" "It's inside," said Reagan leading the visitor in by the elbow.[60]

Reagan and Gorbachev understood that all the problems between the United States and the Soviet Union could not be resolved in two days; what they both seemed to believe was that a frank exchange would allow them to establish a foundation for a permanent peace later on. The talks were blunt, and little progress was made at first, in part this was because of contention over the SDI. At one point the two leaders met at a pool house near the shore of Lake Geneva before a roaring fire, one that would give the meeting its name: "the fireside summit." After rambling through several topics, Reagan looked into Gorbachev's eyes and told him: "I do hope for the sake of our children that we can find some way to avert this terrible, escalating arms race." Then he paused, and Gorbachev, thinking Reagan was finished, opened his mouth to speak, but the president was not through, "because if we can't America will not lose it, I assure you."[61] Reagan continued staring into Gorbachev's eyes while the Russian interpreter translated his words.

Moscow was receptive to a gradual reduction in arms, but believed that "arms reductions must be viewed through the interrelationship to space weapons." In short, Gorbachev demanded reductions be linked to a ban on the Strategic Defense "Star Wars" Initiative (SDI). It was on the way back from the pool house that Reagan proposed the most substantive accomplishment from the first summit, that being the agreement to hold future summits. The Soviet offer to cut nuclear weapons was historic, and remained on the table, but to Reagan SDI was no bargaining chip. The president believed SDI could make nuclear weapons obsolete, rendering the Kremlin's most powerful asset, their missile technology, obsolete. The Geneva summit ended without substantial progress, but both sides showed flexibility, and—something unheard of between the two countries—trust.

Five months after the first summit, a catastrophe transformed world attitudes about Soviet intentions and heightened nuclear fears worldwide. On April 25, 1986, the worst nuclear power accident in history occurred at Chernobyl, a nuclear power plant located about 80 miles north of Kiev. The plant had four reactors, and one exploded at 1:23 A.M. creating a fireball that blew off the reactor's heavy steel concrete roof. The accident killed more than 30 people and resulted in high radiation and the immediate evacuation of 135,000 people.[62]

Reagan was convinced that the Chernobyl explosion damaged Gorbachev's leadership at home, and made him more receptive to the need for arms reduction. When Gorbachev proposed a preparatory meeting with Reagan in a private letter before the second summit, the presi-

dent quickly accepted. The formal agenda was unclear, saying it was
just to discuss "unresolved issues." So on October 11 and 12, 1986, at
Reykjavik, Iceland, Gorbachev and Reagan met a second time. While
the leaders labeled it a "presummit," the session very nearly produced
a radical agreement and set the stage for ultimate bilateral superpower
disarmament.

From their earliest discussion, it was clear to Reagan that Gorbachev
was under tremendous pressure at home and abroad, and was anxious
to deal with the West. The president proposed the elimination of all
offensive ballistic missiles within 10 years, and Gorbachev recipro-
cated by proposing to eliminate the even larger category of *all* strategic
weapons—period. The sticking point was Gorbachev's insistence that
Reagan confine SDI to the laboratory, and not move to test and deploy
it in space. Again, Reagan said he would not go back on his promise
to make the system operational in fact, and not just in theory. When
the Soviet leader refused to continue talking until SDI disappeared,
Reagan closed his briefing book and stood up, effectively ending the
summit. "The meeting is over," he said. "Let's go, George (Shultz),

*President Reagan says goodbye to Soviet General Secretary Gorbachev after the
last meeting at Hofdi House, Reykjavik, Iceland, in October 1986. (Courtesy
Ronald Reagan Presidential Library.)*

we're leaving."[63] Gorbachev was stunned, and the Reykjavik meetings, which were supposed to last another day, collapsed.

The world expressed grave disappointment at the outcome. Their remorse matched that of Secretary of State Shultz and Ambassador Gromyko. The diplomats backpedaled before the cameras, and the criticism was that Reagan went to the presummit unprepared. Nevertheless, a *New York Times/CBS* poll showed an 11-point jump to 72 percent of Americans who thought the president was successfully handling relations with the Soviet Union. The legacy of Reykjavik was hope, and it came as much from Gorbachev as from Reagan. "We have reached agreements on many things," said the Soviet general secretary. "We have traveled a long road."[64]

The spirit of disarmament continued after the summit in various meetings with representatives of both sides, but Reagan was mired in the Iran-Contra revelations and on the political defensive through much of the spring and summer of 1987. Like presidents before him, Reagan sought solace by traveling abroad, even though at his age trips were a strain. In June, he made a 10-day tour of Europe, capped by a visit to West Berlin. There, before a worldwide audience, he challenged the Soviet Union to make good on its proposals for world peace. "If you seek liberation: Come here to the gate! Mr. Gorbachev, open this gate! Mr. Gorbachev, tear down this wall!"[65] The speech was the most impressive since John Kennedy confronted the Soviet Union at the same place, but this time the United States stood poised to abolish its adversary.

Reagan seemed to have the momentum in negotiations as well as rhetoric, but in the Washington summit that December, it was Gorbachev who was the media star. After meeting with Khrushchev in Vienna, former president John F. Kennedy described him as "rude and savage," with a "vicious and sneering manner."[66] That was the stereotype of Russian leaders until Gorbachev came to Washington. The Soviet leader campaigned like a candidate running for elective office, driving the Secret Service and the KGB mad by stopping his limousine on Connecticut Avenue in the city so he could get out and shake hands with well wishers. In staid Washington they called it "Gorby fever."

The epidemic produced results; both sides signed the Intermediate Nuclear Force (INF) treaty that would lead to the immediate destruction of 859 U.S. nuclear missiles and 1,836 Soviet nuclear missiles with a range between 300 and 3,400 miles. This was the first treaty of any kind between the United States and the Soviet Union to provide for on-site verification of arms destruction. Asked by the press if he resented the attention given Gorbachev in Washington, Reagan replied, "I don't resent his popularity. Good Lord, I co-starred with Errol Flynn once."[67]

Before the final summit, Gorbachev improved his popularity in the United States by withdrawing Soviet forces from Afghanistan. The U.S. policy of helping the rebels proved successful. At a summit discussion in Washington, Reagan interrupted to tell Gorbachev, "What you are doing in Afghanistan is burning villages and killing children. It's genocide and you are the one to stop it." By the time the two leaders came to Moscow in the spring of 1988, Reagan was less interested in securing diplomatic agreements, than in pushing for human rights. On May 29 he found himself the recipient of popular attention when crowds lined the street to welcome him. Reagan met with Jewish refusniks, Pentecostals imprisoned for their faith, human rights activists and he even visited a monastery that was a spiritual oasis for the faithful in Moscow. The next day he spoke on free markets beneath a gigantic white bust of Lenin at Moscow State University. When he finished, the president was greeted with wild applause. "It was not the Reagan we expected," said one of the students. "There was nothing old fashioned or stale about him. He seemed so lively, active and thinking."[68]

If there is one aspect of the national character that the Reagan years showed, it was that the present was a final restoration of an unreconstructed past. After two decades of instability and self-examination, the country wanted a father figure for comfort, and Ronald Reagan filled the bill. On the campaign trail in 1980, he promised he would cut the inflation rate, which was running at 12.8 percent then and had reached a high of 14.8 percent earlier. After the tax cuts and the recession, inflation was at less than 4 percent. He said he would cut taxes. The day he walked into the Oval Office, the top rate for individuals was 78 percent, the day he left office it was down to 35 percent. The Dow Jones was less than 800 when he took office, it was at 2,400 at the end of his second administration. Unemployment went from a high of 7.4 percent when he came into office, to 5.4 percent when he left.

He decentralized oil prices, reduced regulations and cut the federal budget. Reagan supported freedom movements worldwide, rebuilt the armed forces and encouraged capitalism.

Every presidential term opens or closes the doors of change in American society. Reagan's presidency signaled a major shift from Democratic to Republican Party dominance in political life. From the 1930s through the 1960s, the Democrats were preeminent, controlling the principal elective institutions in Washington and the states for most of these years. In the 1970s, Democratic hegemony came in for scrutiny. By 1980, the Democrat's seemingly command posture began to unravel. Reagan won two elections, the GOP captured control of the Senate, and the conservative message began to trickle down to the state level.[69]

In his last address to the American people, Ronald Reagan asked a rhetorical question about the "shining city" that was the American political experiment. "And how stands the city on this wintry night? More prosperous, more secure and happier than it was eight years ago?" Ronald Reagan changed not only the country but the world. He showed in his rhetoric and character that the century-old ideas of the founders of the American republic were as relevant as anytime in the past.

As *Newsweek* put it, Reagan embodied "America as it imagined itself to be—the bearer of traditional Main Street values of family and neighborhood, of thrift, industry and charity instead of government intervention."[70] The nation could neither repeat its past, nor leave it behind. After intervening in foreign conflicts, the country turned inward, seeking comfort from middle-American values with a dash of California cool. "So we beat on against the current," wrote F. Scott Fitzgerald at the end of his novel about another age in America, "borne back ceaselessly into the past."[71]

NOTES

1. Richard Reeves, *The Reagan Detour* (New York: Simon and Schuster, 1985).

2. Edmund Morris, *Dutch* (New York: Random House, 1999), p. 469.

3. Harold W. Stanley and Richard G. Niemi, *Vital Statistics in American Politics* (Washington, DC: Congressional Quarterly Press, 2010), Table 3.8, "Individual Confidence in Government: 1952–2008."

4. Gerald M. Pomper, *The Election of 1984* (New York: Chatham House, 1985).

5. Stanley and Niemi, *Vital Statistics*, Figure 3.1, "Partisan Identification, American National Election Studies, 1952–2005."

6. William H. Flanigan and Nancy H. Zingle, *Political Behavior of the American Electorate*, 8th ed. (Washington, DC: Congressional Quarterly Press, 1994), p. 64.

7. Hedrick Smith, "One Campaign Issue Dominates: The Leadership of Ronald Reagan," *New York Times*, January 30, 1984, p. A1.

8. Morris, *Dutch*, p. 480.

9. Stanley and Niemi, *Vital Statistics*, Table 1.23, "Presidential Primaries, 1912–2008."

10. Pomper, *Election of 1984*, p. 16.

11. Fay S. Joyce, "Jackson Denies Using Term Offensive to Jews," *New York Times*, February 20, 1984, p. A10.

12. Hedrick Smith, "The Campaign Reshaped," *New York Times*, February 29, 1984, p. A1.

13. Phil Gailey, "Democrats Focus on the South as Hart Answers Criticism," *New York Times*, March 13, 1984, p. A1.

14. Howell Raines, "Big Delegate Lead," *New York Times*, April 11, 1984, p. A1.

15. James Reston, "Cuomo's Theme," *New York Times*, July 17, 1984, p. A23.

16. Peter W. Kaplan, "Networks at Odds over Coverage," *New York Times*, July 20, 1984, p. C24.

17. "Transcript of the Mondale Address," *New York Times*, July 20, 1984, p. A12.

18. Francis X. Cline, "President Denies Plan to Increase Tax in Next Year," *New York Times*, July 25, 1984, p. A1.

19. "D-Day Anniversary," *ABC News*, June 6, 1984, *CBS News*, June 6, 1984, *NBC News*, June 6, 1984.

20. Lou Cannon, *President Reagan: The Role of a Lifetime* (New York: Simon and Schuster, 1991), p. 484.

21. Michael Barone, *Our Country* (New York: Free Press, 1990), p. 640.

22. Kathleen Hall Jamison, *Packaging the Presidency*, 3rd ed. (New York: Oxford University Press, 1996).

23. Bob Schieffer and Gary Paul Gates, *The Acting President* (New York: E. P. Dutton, 1989), p. 185.

24. William Safire, "Reagan Comes Back," *New York Times*, October 22, 1984, p. A21.

25. Pomper, *Election of 1984*, p. 70.

26. "Presidential Elections, 1789–2008," www.infoplease.com/ipa/A0781450.html.

27. Bernard Weinraub, "President Sees U.S. at 'Turning Point' as 2D Term Begins," *New York Times*, January 22, 1985, p. A1.

28. Peter T. Kilborn, "Baker Supported for Treasury Job: Confirmation Expected," *New York Times*, January 23, 1985, p. A1.

29. Michael Deaver, *A Different Drummer: My 30 Years with Ronald Reagan* (New York: Perennial, 2003), pp. 200–202.

30. Morris, *Dutch*, p. 522.

31. Jason Manning, "Bitburg," http://www.eightiesclub.tripod.com bitburg/id342.htm.

32. Gallup Poll, June 9, 1985.

33. Morris, *Dutch*, pp. 414–415.

34. Manning, "Bitburg."

35. Cannon, *President Reagan*, p. 587.

36. Theodore Draper, *A Very Thin Line* (New York: Touchstone Books, 1991).

37. "Firewall: The Iran-Contra Conspiracy and Cover-Up," in *The Lanahan Cases in Leadership, Ethics and Decision Making*, ed. Douglas M. Brattebo and Eloise F. Malone (Baltimore: Lanahan Publishers, 2002), p. 142.

38. Theodore Draper, *A Very Thin Line*, p. 157.

39. Ibid., p. 33.

40. Cannon, *President Reagan*, p. 611.

41. "Day 2: The President's Knowledge and the Ayatollah's Money," *New York Times*, July 9, 1987, p. A10.

42. Edward Schumacher, "In the Skies over Libya's Capitol," *New York Times*, April 15, 1985, p. A1.

43. "Nicaragua Says It Downed Plane with 4 U.S. Crewmen, Killing 3," *New York Times*, October 7, 1986, p. 1A.

44. Edwin Meese, *With Reagan* (Washington, DC: Regnery Gateway, 1992), p. 245.

45. Gerald M. Boyd, "Reagan Weighed Granting Pardon to 2 Former Aides," *New York Times*, December 23, 1986, p. A1.

46. Dinesh D'Souza, *Ronald Reagan* (New York: Touchstone, 1997), p. 247.

47. Gerald M. Boyd, "Panel Said to Find Reagan Was Told of Iran Dealings," *New York Times*, February 27, 1987, p. A1.

48. "Transcript of Reagan's Speech," *New York Times*, March 5, 1987, p. A18.

49. Morris, *Dutch*, p. 577.

50. Interview with Judy Woodruff, "Nancy Reagan: The Role of a Lifetime," February 6, 2011.

51. Peter Jennings and Todd Brewster, *The Century* (New York: Doubleday, 1998), p. 500.

52. Diane Vaughn, *The Challenger Launch Decision* (Chicago: University of Chicago Press, 1996), p. 23.

53. Morris, *Dutch*, p. 576.

54. http://teachingamericanhistory.org/library/index.asp?docu print=147.

55. Morris, *Dutch*, p. 577.

56. Margaret Thatcher, *The Downing Street Years* (New York: HarperCollins, 1993), p. 463.

57. Theodore H. White, "New Power, New Politics," *New York Times*, February 5, 1984, p. SM22.

58. Schweizer, *Reagan's War*, p. 239.

59. Ibid., pp. 256–257.

60. R. W. Apple Jr., "Reagan Confers with Gorbachev in Geneva Parley," *New York Times*, November 20, 1985, p. A1.

61. Schweizer, *Reagan's War*, p. 252.

62. Ibid., p. 257.

63. Cannon, *President Reagan*, p. 769.

64. Ibid., p. 770.

65. http://www.historyplace.com/speeches/reagan-tear-down.htm.

66. William Manchester, *The Glory and the Dream* (New York: Little, Brown, 1973), p. 910.

67. D'Souza, *Ronald Reagan*, p. 192.

68. Schweizer, *Reagan's War*, p. 276.

69. Ronald Reagan Presidential Library, "Speeches," January 11, 1989.

70. *Newsweek*, December 18, 1988.

71. F. Scott Fitzgerald, *The Great Gatsby* (New York: Scribner, 1999), p. 178.

Chapter 10

SUNSET

Transitions of power in the presidency of the American political system can be uncomfortable events. In 1933, Republican Herbert Hoover was so exhausted and bitter at the end of his term that he canceled the traditional inauguration eve dinner with Democratic president elect Franklin Roosevelt. In response to a return invitation for tea, Hoover strode across the room and towered over the next occupant of the Oval Office menacingly, "Mr. Roosevelt, when you have been in Washington as long as I have, you will learn that the President of the United States calls on nobody!"[1] FDR was furious. Anytime the occupants of the mansion are from the opposite party, tensions are likely to be high. Jacqueline Kennedy was appalled at the housekeeping routines of Mamie Eisenhower and the condition of the family quarters in the White House when she moved there in 1961. She redecorated not only them but the Red, Green, and Blue rooms downstairs as well.[2] Then there was the snub the Carters gave the Reagans on their first day in Washington.

The contrast in 1989 was stark. In the last senior staff meeting before leaving office, president elect George H. W. Bush said it well: "I came by to say thank you for the last eight years. Believe me, I wouldn't be President if it hadn't been for my, uh, teacher here." For his part, Reagan nodded and smiled. He often joked with aides that in eight years on the job, "George never once checked my pulse." It must have been a relief and a privilege to leave office to a running mate. While 14 vice presidents became president, most opted for the job because of the death of a predecessor. Only five men became president immediately after serving as vice president.[3] After eight years together, Ronald Reagan genuinely liked George Bush and supported him by getting out of the way. The former president was about to undertake the role of remaining in the background while his legacy was defined by others.

After the inauguration, Ronald and Nancy Reagan took their last helicopter ride to Andrews Air Force base for the trip back to California. They purchased a home in Bel Air, an exclusive suburb of Los Angeles, in addition to the Reagan Ranch in Santa Barbara. The couple lived mostly in Bel Air, and it was from there that they witnessed the collapse of the Soviet Union. After years of bellicose rhetoric and bad press, the "Evil Empire" was imploding, just like Reagan said it would.

The undoing began six months after the Reagans moved into their new home. It started with Lech Walesa and "Solidarity," the Polish trade union, bringing down the government in June. The end of East and West Germany was next. Chancellor Helmut Kohl declared in November, with the Berlin Wall in tatters, that "without the U.S. this day would not have been possible."[4] Czechoslovakia's Velvet Revolution began the same month, with a general strike that proved fatal for the regime as it collapsed without major bloodshed. Finally, before Christmas, the people of Romania threw off the rule of Nicolae Ceausescu with chants of "Down with Communism" and "God Is with Us." Even China, with the world's most dictatorial regime, underwent changes in Tiananmen Square that were broadcast around the world.

The mainstream press, which was never sympathetic with Mr. Reagan, concluded that communism was spent, it had run its course, and no president was responsible for the collapse. Or rather, all of the presidents were collectively responsible. It was fashionable to downplay Reagan's role in the drama, declaring that he just happened to be in office at the end when the contradictions of communism surfaced. The American people knew better. Ronald Reagan's rhetoric at Berlin, "Mr. Gorbachev, tear down this wall," and his unfailing belief in himself and the values of American exceptionalism made history. All the press venom about the Bitburg visit, the Strategic Defense Initiative being a "Star Wars" fantasy, and his pushing the world close to nuclear holocaust was forgotten in the euphoria of the communist collapse. It was Reagan, and Reagan alone, who had the vision and the commitment to principle that brought about the Soviet demise. In Bel Air, Reagan gave a rare response to a letter from Peggy Noonan, "I never thought of myself as a great man, just a man committed to great ideas. I've always believed that individuals should take priority over the state. . . . This is what sets America apart."[5]

In retirement Reagan finished his memoirs, was handsomely paid for speaking engagements and kept reminding audiences of his unfinished agenda. The former president favored a line item veto for his successors, a constitutional amendment for a balanced budget, and repeal of the 22nd amendment that limited presidents to two terms in office. Reagan followed Dwight D. Eisenhower's lead in saying that the amendment eroded a second-term president's power and influence. He also formed the Ronald Reagan presidential foundation, and spent time at his ranch.

It was the place where he went for peace, physical movement and thoughtfulness, what he called an "open cathedral." He put a wooden sign hanging from a fence rail that read: RANCHO DEL CIELO, RONALD REAGAN. The ranch was high above sea level, in green, lush mountains that overlooked a beautiful valley with the ocean on the other side and the Channel Islands just beyond.

What Americans did not know was that the house on the property was "humble, basic, simple [and] unpretentious . . . like him."[6] The building was a small one story stucco building with adobe walls, and a red tile roof. Its appearance must have shocked Queen Elizabeth II on her visit there in 1983, but he showed it to her at her Highness's request. The place would have astounded all the liberal pundits who decried Reagan's millionaire status and alleged sybaritic lifestyle. The ranch house was about 1,500 square feet, with a kitchen that looked like a house in suburban Indiana, circa 1950.

In November 1991, the Ronald Reagan Presidential Library opened in lavish dedication ceremonies. All presidential libraries are special, but this one was unusual because it housed a retired Air Force One, as well as Reagan's papers. At the dedication ceremonies, five presidents were in attendance, as well as six first ladies, making it the first time such a congregation had appeared in one place in public in the nation's history. Of all the speeches, Reagan's words were the ones people remembered. "Today is the latest chapter in a story that began a quarter of a century ago when the people of California entrusted me with the stewardship of their dreams . . . the last, was ten years [ago] after we summoned America to a new beginning, we are beginning still."[7]

The next year Reagan addressed the Republican National Convention. George Bush was in the fight of his life for reelection, and Reagan summoned all his rhetorical skills to inspire allegiance to the party regulars. "My dream is that you will travel the road ahead with Liberty's lamp guiding your steps and Opportunity's arm steadying your way. My fondest hope for each of you—and especially for young people—is that you will love your country, not for her power or wealth, but for her selflessness and her idealism."[8] When he came to mentioning the next generation, young delegates in the hall began to chant "Reagan, Reagan" so loud that he had to pause. Four years out of office, Ronald Reagan was doing what he always did, appealing to the best in his audience. He made two more public appearances that year, one a public speech at a tribute for him in Washington, D.C., and his last public appearance was at Richard Nixon's funeral on April 27, 1994.

In August 1994, at age 83, Ronald Reagan was diagnosed with Alzheimer's disease. The illness is incurable; it gradually destroys brain cells and ultimately causes death. In his own hand, Ronald Reagan wrote his final farewell to the American people.

> I have recently been told that I am one of the millions of Americans who will be afflicted with Alzheimer's Disease. . . . At the moment I feel fine. I intend to live the remainder of the years God gives me on this earth doing the things I have always done . . . I now begin the journey that will lead me into the sunset of my life. I know that for America there will always be a bright dawn ahead. Thank you, my friends, May God always bless you.[9]

Although the course of Alzheimer's is different for every individual, its effects on the former president were never disclosed to the American public. It was a long goodbye for Nancy Reagan: ten years. In her own words she said, "I didn't want anyone to see him like that."[10] When the announcement was made of his medical condition, a host of reporters and critics chimed in to analyze his presidency from the perspective of the disease. Every misstatement and repeated sentence was parsed, even though his physicians at the time he was in the White House denied that the former president had "any signs of dementia or Alzheimer's." The critics were unrelenting in their reanalysis. Lesley Stahl, who covered the White House for CBS *News* in the Reagan years, said that she recalled Reagan having had a "vacant stare," and others talked about his forgetfulness.

The disease destroyed Regan's mental capacity. Edmund Morris, his official biographer, relates an incident of the type that is typical of this tragic disease. Morris recalled a day when Nancy Reagan was with the president in California, when he came into the room clutching something in his hand with his sleeve wet to the elbow. Nancy asked what he was holding, and prized his fingers apart to find a miniature replica of the White House in his grasp. The plastic model was in his aquarium, and Ronald Reagan looked at his wife to implore: "It has something to do with me."[11]

A lifetime of outdoor activities and exercise kept him healthy while the disease ravaged his mind. He took walks, played golf and kept out of the public eye. In 2001, Reagan suffered a fall at his house in Bel Air and broke his hip. The fracture was repaired and he underwent physical therapy. In the late stages of the disease, Mrs. Reagan became an advocate for federally funded stem cell research in defiance of the GOP political position on the issue. She believed that such research could lead to a cure, or at least a minimizing, of the suffering for both the patient and the caregiver.

Ronald Reagan died at his home on June 5, 2004. Nancy Reagan made the announcement, and tributes poured in from around the world. President George W. Bush declared June 11 a National Day of Mourning. Reagan's body was taken first to Santa Monica, California, where thousands of well-wishers stood beside the road in tribute, and then he lay in repose at the presidential library, until his casket was removed to Washington. Reagan was the tenth president to lie in state under the rotunda of the U.S. Capitol guarded by members of the armed forces. While there, more than 100,000 people filed past to pay their last respects.

The state funeral was held in the Washington National Cathedral. President George W. Bush said in his eulogy, "Ronald Reagan belongs to the ages now, but we preferred when he belonged to us." Eulogies were delivered by former British prime minister Margaret Thatcher, former Canadian prime minister Brian Mulroney, and both presidents Bush.

After the ceremony, the Reagan entourage was flown back to the Ronald Reagan Presidential Library in California, where he was interred. The words on Reagan's granite headstone could sum up his presidency, and his life. "I know in my heart that man is good. That what is right will always eventually triumph, and there's a purpose and worth to each and every life."

NOTES

1. William Manchester, *The Glory and the Dream* (Boston: Little, Brown, 1974), p. 75.

2. Theodore C. Sorensen, *Kennedy* (New York: Harper and Row, 1965), pp. 431–432.

3. Fourteen vice presidents have become president, eight because of the death of a president. The eight so-called accidental presidents were John Tyler, Millard Fillmore, Andrew Johnson, Chester A. Arthur, Theodore Roosevelt, Calvin Coolidge, Harry S. Truman, and Lyndon B. Johnson. The other vice presidents were John Adams, Thomas Jefferson, Martin Van Buren, Richard M. Nixon, Gerald R. Ford, and George H. W. Bush. Of these six, all but Nixon became president immediately after serving as vice president. Gerald Ford was the only vice president to assume the office because of a president's resignation.

4. *Newsweek*, November 9, 1989.

5. Peggy Noonan, *When Character Was King* (New York: Viking, 2001), p. 317.

6. Ibid., p. 109.

7. Ronald Reagan, "Ronald Reagan Library Opening Ceremonies," November 4, 1991.

8. Ronald Reagan, "Speech to 1992 GOP Convention," August 18, 1992.

9. Ronald Reagan, "Alzheimer's Letter," http://www.doctorzebra.com/prez/z_x40alz_letter_g.htm.

10. Nancy Reagan, "The Role of a Lifetime," interview with Judy Woodruff, January 2011.

11. Eugene Jarecki, *Reagan*, aired February 6, 2011 (New York: HBO, 2011).

Chapter 11

EPILOGUE

The centennial of Ronald Reagan's birth, on February 6, 2011, was an occasion for an outpouring of affection for the former president. The magazine *National Review* put 100 of its favorite pictures of him on its website, and the *Weekly Standard* had a lead article titled "The Future of Reaganism."[1] Such tributes from the conservative press were expected; what was surprising was that *Time* magazine had a similar accolade and a cover story titled "Why Obama Loves Reagan."[2]

All the mythmaking about his legacy would not have interested Ronald Reagan as much as a fair-minded assessment of his public career. As he told former speechwriter Peggy Noonan in a letter after he left office, he was more interested in great ideas than in being remembered as a great person. A major reason for the lack of any balance where Reagan is concerned is that academics as a group treat the conservative movement, and Reagan as its greatest champion, as an irregularity in American politics. The presumptive right of liberals and liberalism to rule the country is an understood assumption by them, and has been since the New Deal of Franklin Roosevelt. The criticism Ohio senator Robert A. Taft had of New Deal spending, and Senator Barry Goldwater had of the envisioned "Great Society" of Lyndon Johnson, as well as Ronald Reagan's disagreements with the resulting welfare state, are presented as aberrant ideas. Take, for example, a typical account written immediately after Reagan left office. Titled *The Acting President,* the book's subtitle shows this orientation: *Ronald Reagan and the Supporting Players Who Helped Create the Illusion That Held America Spellbound.* The premise of the book is that Reagan fooled people into thinking he was a great leader when in fact he was merely mediocre.

The accomplishments of the Reagan presidency, in both foreign and domestic policy, were not illusory. The collapse of the Soviet Union after his challenge and the economic recovery, along with the largest political election landslide in American history, are tangible accomplishments. None were more important than the restoration of confidence in American ideals and the office of the presidency. Certainly the times helped make Reagan. From John Kennedy's election in 1960 to Jimmy Carter's politics of "malaise," the country endured drift and disappointment in the presidential office. The notion was gaining credence at the time that the position itself was inherently flawed for the complex modern world.

Many political scientists thought wholesale reform was necessary, with a six-year term and some kind of legislative union like a parliamentary system to overcome the gridlock of checks and balances. James McGregor Burns, who authored a biography of Franklin Roosevelt, argued for a repeal of the 22nd Amendment limiting the president to two terms, "to compel second-term Presidents to face the fact that they *might* want another term, and hence be compelled to maintain their standing with the electorate."[3] Similarly, presidential scholar Richard M. Pious asked in the opening of his 1979 book if the presidential power was "poison," declaring that recent presidents were faring far worse than their predecessors.[4]

Criticism went beyond the political office itself to the men who occupied the office. Presidents Johnson, Nixon, Ford, and Carter were reckoned to be failures to one degree or another. Conservatism, especially after Barry Goldwater's disastrous defeat in 1964, was considered the providence of the uninformed, the uneducated, the unaware, the un-Harvard, the un-Yale, the un-*New Republic,* the un-East Coast, and the un-West Coast. When conservatives did elect one of their number, as with Richard Nixon in 1968, he turned out to be worse than the liberal alternative. "Watch what we do, not what we say," said Nixon secretary of health, education, and welfare Robert Finch to the press in 1969.[5] What followed was the birth of new regulatory agencies, government spending at unprecedented levels, and a federally mandated minimum guaranteed household income: the very essence of socialism. Nixon's relationship with conservatives went from qualified support to outright hostility.

Richard Nixon joined the establishment liberalism reigning in Washington that influenced politics and policy for those who happened to occupy the presidential office. The pattern was for candidates to campaign on conservative themes and then adopt liberal policies once in power. Teddy Roosevelt came from a conservative background, but once in office, he embraced reform politics. Woodrow Wilson followed a similar path, becoming convinced that the nation needed a permanent ruling class of public bureaucrats, with him at the top. Lyndon Johnson kept the Kennedy appointees, the "Harvard types," as he called them, and fell into disappointment. An outsider like Jimmy Carter adopted fashionable liberal politics when he settled into office.

Ronald Reagan was different. He remained the first, and arguably the only, outsider president in the post–World War II era to keep his conservative convictions in office. He embraced tiny Eureka College in Illinois and credited in his speeches the thousands of employees of General Electric plants who gave him "a postgraduate education in political science." He was blatantly, and even proudly, conservative in his politics and convictions.

Reagan did not have the devious, all-consuming ambition of so many politicians such as Lyndon Johnson and Richard Nixon before him and Bill Clinton after him. Maybe it was his age or his accomplishments in Hollywood, but whatever it was, he seemed more secure in himself than his immediate predecessors or successors. "Reagan knew himself better than most presidents and he kept his identity separate from politics."[6] He was the same person off camera as on.

His self-confidence came from his life experiences. His nearsightedness left him with an early acute auditory ability, diminished by hearing loss when he was in office but evident in the attention he gave people when he met them for the first time. His good looks and winsome personality opened doors that were closed to others. After all, what is more impressive: being one of a handful of movie stars in Hollywood or winning elective office? After you've fallen off the mountain with a public divorce and faced down gossip columnists, how threatening can the White House press corps be? The greatest shock about Reagan was that he believed what he said, and he didn't change when he got into office. He commanded the establishment in Washington by disagreeing with it. Political scientist Aaron Wildavsky was one who believed that such behavior in office, rooted in Reagan's conservative ideology, was the very essence of leadership. No one in the Reagan administration ever wondered what the president believed or what he thought about issues. As a result, he was able to command allegiance that few other presidents could.

He was a nice man, easygoing and self-deprecating in his humor. George H. W. Bush recalled in an interview that Reagan was "a kind man. He wasn't mean. He didn't carry grudges and didn't want to get even."[7] Yet Edmund Morris, his own biographer, said that the president was the most ordinary of men when alone with his staff. The problem with such comments is that they are often betrayed by the facts. Peggy Noonan, to take just one example, recalled in her first meeting with Reagan that he took her hand, and she understood that "it is not possible to be nervous in his presence."[8] Such abilities are not commonplace among American politicians.

Ronald Reagan was the epitome of sincerity in a time when it was out of fashion, especially among intellectuals. He really believed in American exceptionalism, optimism, the power of markets, and individuals. What's more, he had a remarkable ability to communicate his beliefs to others, to voters, to people he met, and to those who heard his voice on radio or saw him on television. Part of his popularity came from the policies and values of those who occupied the office after him. When President George H. W. Bush broke his "no new taxes" pledge in office, he lost the core conservatives of the Reagan revolution. Even the victory in Iraq could not restore allegiance to the former vice president. Bill Clinton's sexual escapades with women demeaned the presidential office and stimulated a host of remembered comments from Reagan staffers about how their boss would not remove his suit coat when working in the Oval Office out of respect for the job he had. George W. Bush favored big government conservatism over the smaller, less intrusive model advocated by Reagan. Barack Obama's deficit spending, along with his mandated health care plan, was the very embodiment of the welfare state liberalism opposed by the former president in office.

By the centennial of Ronald Reagan's birth, the country was uncomfortably close to the economic despair and foreign terrorist humiliations of the Carter years. Unemployment was higher in 2011 than in 1980, and national self-confidence was again in decline. The worst recession since World War II left the nation doubting its future, and this time, there was no candidate to talk about "starting the world all over again."

If what Reagan said in his biography had happened, and he really had gotten that job at Montgomery Ward after college, it is doubtful that biographers, historians, political scientists, and the general public would have had a lot of interest in him. The reason why the Reagan Library is the most popular of all those of the former presidents, why more than 11,000 books have been published about the 40th president, and why people long for him today is rooted in his convictions and his accomplishments and the way he made people feel about themselves and their country.

Almost no detail about Ronald Reagan, and his presidency, escapes scrutiny, especially the scandals of his second term. Critics decry Iran-Contra as a perversion of presidential authority and an example of reckless policy making in the White House by subordinates. Reagan's hands-off management style, not to mention his forgetfulness, left him vulnerable. The mismanagement left him vulnerable to attack, especially after the Democrats took back the Senate in 1986. The consolation for this neglectful behavior came in 1989, when communism collapsed and, to a certain extent, his sins were venial.

The sum of Reagan's actions in domestic and foreign policy is their own testimony as to his effectiveness and is central to an assessment of his dual-term presidency. Most scholars agree that Ronald Reagan was an above average president, but with the passage of time, he has risen in most people's estimation as a near great, or great, president. History and posterity will decide, but Reagan's abiding popularity seems to confirm that he will only improve with age. Without demeaning any of the men who held the presidency within a quarter of a century before or after him, he was peerless by comparison. Even the focus on his Alzheimer's only shows that his mind was free, focused, and rooted in conviction at the time. That was the key to his success, and it remains the best way to understand his greatness.

NOTES

1. Jeffrey Bell, "The Future of Reaganism," *The Weekly Standard,* February 7, 2011.

2. *Time,* February 7, 2011.

3. James McGregor Burns, *The Power to Lead* (New York: Simon and Schuster, 1984), p. 182.

4. Richard M. Pious, *The American Presidency* (New York: Basic Books, 1979), p. 6.

5. "Schools Make News," *Newsweek,* February 17, 1969, pp. 260–273.

6. Steven Hayward, *The Age of Reagan: The Conservative Counter-revolution, 1980–1989* (New York: Crown Forum, 2009), p. xxi.

7. Judy Keen, "Elder Bush Recalls Reagan's 'kindness,' 'Earthly Humor,'" *USA Today,* January 24, 2011, p. 1A.

8. Peggy Noonan, *What I Saw at the Revolution* (New York: Ivy Books, 1990), p. 67.

BIBLIOGRAPHY

Apple, R. W., Jr. "Reagan Confers with Gorbachev in Geneva Parley." *New York Times*, November 20, 1985, p. A1.

Baker, James A., III. *Work Hard, Study and Keep Out of Politics.* New York: G. P. Putnam's Sons, 2006.

Barone, Michael. *Our Country.* New York: Free Press, 1990.

Barrett, Lawrence L. *Gambling with History.* New York: Penguin Books, 1983.

Bell, Jeffrey. "The Future of Reaganism." *The Weekly Standard*, February 7, 2011.

Black, Conrad. *Richard M. Nixon: A Life in Full.* New York: PublicAffairs, 2007.

Boyd, Gerald M. "Panel Said to Find Reagan Was Told of Iran Dealings." *New York Times*, February 27, 1987, p. A1.

Boyd, Gerald M. "Reagan Weighed Granting Pardon to 2 Former Aides." *New York Times*, December 23, 1986, p. A1.

Buckley, William F. *The Reagan I Knew.* New York: Basic Books, 2008.

Burns, James McGregor. *The Power to Lead.* New York: Simon and Schuster, 1984.

Cannon, Lou. *Governor Reagan: His Rise to Power*. New York: PublicAffairs, 2003.

Cannon, Lou. *President Reagan: The Role of a Lifetime*. New York: Simon and Schuster, 1991.

Clarke, Sally C. "Advance Report on Final Divorce Statistics, 1989 and 1990." *Monthly Vital Statistics Report* 43, no. 9 (March 22, 1995): 1–20.

Cline, Francis X. "President Denies Plan to Increase Tax in Next Year." *New York Times*, July 25, 1984, p. A1.

Crouse, Timothy. *The Boys on the Bus*. New York: Free Press, 1972.

Davis, Patti. *The Long Goodbye*. New York: Plume Press, 2004.

Deaver, Michael K. *A Different Drummer: My 30 Years with Ronald Reagan*. New York: Perennial, 2003.

Draper, Theodore. *A Very Thin Line*. New York: Touchstone Books, 1991.

D'Souza, Dinesh. *Ronald Reagan*. New York: Touchstone, 1997.

Edwards, Anne. *Early Reagan*. New York: William Morrow, 1987.

Edwards, Lee. *The Conservative Revolution*. New York: Free Press, 1999.

Ehrman, John. *The Eighties: America in the Age of Reagan*. New Haven, CT: Yale University Press, 2005.

Elliot, Marc. *Reagan: The Hollywood Years*. New York: Harmony Books, 2008.

Erik-Nelson, Lars. "Ronald Reagan's Medal of Honor Story." *New York Daily News*, December 13, 1983.

Evans, Thomas W. *The Education of Ronald Reagan*. New York: Columbia University Press, 2006.

Farney, Dennis. "President's Budget Wins House Vote on Rules Question." *Wall Street Journal*, June 26, 1981.

Fiorina, Morris. *Divided Government*. New York: Allyn and Bacon, 1996.

Fitzgerald, F. Scott. *The Great Gatsby*. New York: Scribner, 1999.

Flanigan, William H., and Nancy H. Zingle. *Political Behavior of the American Electorate*. 8th ed. Washington, DC: Congressional Quarterly Press, 1994.

Frum, David. *How We Got Here*. New York: Basic Books, 2000.

Gailey, Phil. "Democrats Focus on the South as Hart Answers Criticism." *New York Times*, March 13, 1984, p. A1.

Goff, Tom. "Legacy for State." *Los Angeles Times*, September 29, 1974.

Halberstam, David. *The Powers That Be*. 4th ed. New York: Random House, 2000.

Hayward, Stephen F. *The Age of Reagan: The Conservative Counterrevolution, 1980–1989*. New York: Crown Forum, 2009.

Hess, Stephen, and David Broder. *The Republican Establishment*. New York: Harper and Row, 1967.

Jamison, Kathleen Hall. *Packaging the Presidency*. 3rd ed. New York: Oxford University Press, 1996.

Jennings, Peter, and Todd Brewster. *The Century*. New York: Doubleday, 1998.

Johnson, Haynes. "Prickly, Unpretentious, Long-Batting American Beauty: Heroes." *Washington Post*, August 16, 1981, p. C1.

Johnson, Haynes. *Sleepwalking through History*. New York: W. W. Norton, 1991.

Johnson, Paul. *A History of the American People*. New York: HarperCollins, 1997.

Joyce, Fay S. "Jackson Denies Using Term Offensive to Jews." *New York Times*, February 20, 1984, p. A10.

Kaplan, Peter W. "Networks at Odds over Coverage." *New York Times*, July 20, 1984, p. C24.

Keen, Judy. "Elder Bush Recalls Reagan's 'Kindness,' 'Earthly Humor.'" *USA Today*, January 23, 2011, p. B4.

Kengor, Paul. *God and Ronald Reagan: A Spiritual Life*. New York: HarperCollins, 2004.

Kilborn, Peter T. "Baker Supported for Treasury Job: Confirmation Expected." *New York Times*, January 23, 1985, p. A1.

Lasch, Christopher. *The Culture of Narcissism*. New York: W. W. Norton, 1978.

Lewis, Anthony. "What Reagan Wrought." *New York Times*, June 21, 1984, p. A23.

Manchester, William. *The Glory and the Dream*. Boston: Little, Brown, 1974.

Meese, Edwin. *With Reagan*. Washington, DC: Regnery Gateway, 1992.

Morgan, Michael. *Classics of Moral and Political Theory*. 4th ed. Indianapolis, IN: Hackett, 2005.

Morris, Edmund. *Dutch*. New York: Random House, 1999.

Newsweek. "Most Admired." December 21, 1981.

Newsweek. "Schools Make News." February 17, 1969, pp. 260–273.

New York Times. "Day 2: The President's Knowledge and the Ayatollah's Money." July 9, 1987, p. A10.

New York Times. "Excerpts from Hospital about Victims." April 1, 1981, p. A22.

New York Times. "The Homeless Won't Go Away." August 23, 1982.

New York Times. "Let Us Begin an Era of National Renewal." January 21, 1981, p. B1.

New York Times. "Nicaragua Says It Downed Plane with 4 U.S. Crewmen, Killing 3." October 7, 1986, p. A1.

New York Times. "Notes on People." January 28, 1981, p. C1.

New York Times. "Review: Familiar Barbarities." September 25, 1983, p. A23.

New York Times. "Transcript of Reagan's Speech." March 5, 1987, p. A18.

New York Times. "Transcript of the Mondale Address." July 20, 1984, p. A12.

Noonan, Peggy. *What I Saw at the Revolution*. New York: Ivy Books, 1990.

Noonan, Peggy. *When Character Was King*. New York: Viking, 2001.

Nordheimer, Jon. "Reagan Blames 'Machine States,' Says Foes Used 'Pressure' to Defeat Him, Plans to Become Commentator." *New York Times*, August 20, 1976.

Nordheimer, Jon. "Reagan Says That Texas Shows He Is the Best Candidate." *New York Times*, May 3, 1976.

Pemberton, William E. *Exit with Honor*. New York: M. E. Sharpe, 1998.

Pious, Richard M. *The American Presidency*. New York: Basic Books, 1979.

Pomper, Gerald M. *The Election of 1984*. New York: Chatham House, 1985.

Prindle, Donald F. *The Politics of Glamour*. Madison: University of Wisconsin Press, 1988.

Raines, Howell. "Big Delegate Lead." *New York Times*, April 11, 1984, p. A1.

Raines, Howell. "Tower Power." *New York Times*, August 7, 1981, p. A3.

Reagan, Nancy, and William Novak. *My Turn*. New York: Random House, 1989.

Reagan, Ron. *My Father at 100*. New York: Viking, 2010.

Reagan, Ronald. *Abortion and the Conscience of a Nation*. Nashville, TN: Thomas Nelson, 1983.

Reagan, Ronald. "Acceptance Speech." Republican National Convention, August 23, 1984.

Reagan, Ronald. *An American Life*. New York: Simon and Schuster, 1990.

Reagan, Ronald. "A Time for Choosing." *Human Events*, November 28, 1964, pp. 8–9.

Reagan, Ronald. *Where's the Rest of Me?* New York: Karz, 1981.

Reagan, Ronald. "The Republican Party." *National Review*, December 1, 1964, p. 105.

Reeves, Richard. *The Reagan Detour*. New York: Simon and Schuster, 1985.

Regan, Donald T. *For the Record: From Wall Street to Washington*. New York: Harcourt, 1988.

Reston, James. "Cuomo's Theme." *New York Times*, July 17, 1984, p. A23.

Robinson, Peter. *How Ronald Reagan Changed My Life*. New York: Regan Books, 2003.

Safire, William. *Before the Fall*. New York: Doubleday, 1975.

Safire, William. "Reagan Comes Back." *New York Times*, October 22, 1984, p. A21.

Sandburg, Carl. "One Parting." in *Honey and Salt*. New York: Harcourt Brace Jovanovich, 1953, p. 70.

Schell, Jonathan. *The Fate of the Earth*. Palo Alto, CA: Stanford University Press, 2000.

Schieffer, Bob, and Gary Paul Gates. *The Acting President*. New York: E. P. Dutton, 1989.

Schumacher, Edward. "In the Skies over Libya's Capitol." *New York Times*, April 15, 1985, p. A1.

Schweizer, Peter. *Reagan's War: The Epic Story of His Forty-Year Struggle and Final Triumph over Communism*. New York: Doubleday, 2004.

Shirley, Craig. *Reagan's Revolution*. Nashville, TN: Nelson Current, 2005.

Shirley, Craig. *Rendezvous with Destiny*. Wilmington, DE: ISI Books, 2009.

Skinner, Kiron K., Annelise Anderson, and Martin Anderson, eds. *Reagan: A Life in Letters*. New York: Free Press, 2003.

Skinner, Kiron K., Annelise Anderson, and Martin Anderson, eds. *Reagan: In His Own Hand*. New York: Free Press, 2001.

Smith, Hedrick. "The Campaign Reshaped." *New York Times*, February 29, 1984, p. A1.

Smith, Hedrick. "One Campaign Issue Dominates: The Leadership of Ronald Reagan." *New York Times*, January 30, 1984, p. A1.

Smith, Hedrick. *The Power Game*. New York: Random House, 1988.

Sorensen, Theodore C. *Kennedy*. New York: Harper and Row, 1965.

Speakes, Larry. *Speaking Out: The Reagan Presidency from Inside the White House*. New York: Charles Scribner's Sons, 1988.

Sperling, Cass Warner, and Cork Millner. *The Brothers Warner*. Lexington: University Press of Kentucky, 1994.

Stanley, Harold W., and Richard G. Niemi. *Vital Statistics in American Politics*. Washington, DC: Congressional Quarterly Press, 1988.

Stanley, Harold W., and Richard G. Niemi. *Vital Statistics in American Politics*. Washington, DC: Congressional Quarterly Press, 2010.

Stockman, David. *The Triumph of Politics*. New York: Harper and Row, 1986.

Susman, Barry, and Paul Ferber. "Economic Prospects Give Carter Edge." *Washington Post*, September 14, 1980.

Taubman, Philip. "Explosive Bullet Struck Reagan, F.B.I. Discovers." *New York Times*, April 3, 1981, p. A1.

Diane Vaughn. *The Challenger Launch Decision*. Chicago: University of Chicago Press, 1996.

Weinraub, Bernard. "Long Cutback Seen." *New York Times*, August 6, 1981, p. A1.

Weinraub, Bernard. "President Sees U.S. at 'Turning Point' as 2D Term Begins." *New York Times*, January 22, 1985, p. A1.

White, Theodore H. *The Making of the President, 1960*. New York: Atheneum House, 1961.

White, Theodore H. "New Power, New Politics." *New York Times*, February 5, 1984, p. SM22.

Wilson, James Q. "Reagan Country: The Political Culture of Southern California." *Commentary*, May 1967.

Woodard, J. David. *The America That Reagan Built*. Westport, CT: Praeger, 2006.

Woodard, J. David. *The New Southern Politics*. Boulder, CO: Lynne Rienner Press, 2006.

INDEX

About the Author

J. DAVID WOODARD is professor of political science at Clemson University in Clemson, South Carolina. He is the author of *The New Southern Politics*, *The Politics of Morality*, and *The America That Reagan Made* and is a consultant for Republican political candidates.